The Early Warning Syst
Principle of Subsidiarit

This book offers a comprehensive systematic analysis of the European Union's Early Warning System (EWS) for subsidiarity, which was introduced by the Treaty of Lisbon. The book includes both a detailed theoretical analysis of the EWS as well as an assessment of how national parliaments have responded to EU legislative proposals under the system. Philipp Kiiver explores whether the EWS could function as a mechanism of legal accountability offering a partial remedy to the European Union's much-discussed accountability deficit. The Early Warning System for the Principle of Subsidiarity provides an overview of the historical developments of national parliamentary involvement in the EU and also considers the broader implications of the EWS, including its relationship to democracy and legitimacy.

The book will be of particular interest to academics and students of EU Law, Constitutional Law and Political Science.

Philipp Kiiver is an associate professor of European and comparative constitutional law at Maastricht University. He obtained his law degree (2003) and his PhD (2005) from Maastricht, and specializes in international parliamentary studies. He is the co-author of an introduction to comparative constitutional law and has published several books and articles on the role of national parliaments in the European Union.

Routledge Research in EU Law

Available titles in this series include:

Centralized Enforcement, Legitimacy and Good Governance in the EU
Melanie Smith

EU External Relations and Systems of Governance
The CFSP, Euro-Mediterranean Partnership and migration
Paul James Cardwell

The European Constitution, Welfare States and Democracy
The Four Freedoms vs. National Administrative Discretion
Christoffer C. Eriksen

EU External Relations Law and the European Neighbourhood Policy
A Paradigm for Coherence
Bart Van Vooren

The Evolving EU Counter-terrorism Legal Framework
Maria O'Neill

The Early Warning System for the Principle of Subsidiarity
Constitutional Theory and Empirical Reality
Philipp Kiiver

Forthcoming titles in this series include:

New Governance and the European Strategy for Employment
Samantha Velluti

Human Rights and Minority Rights in the European Union
Kirsten Shoraka

Local Government in Europe
The 'Fourth Level' in the EU Multi-Layered System of Governance
Carlo Panara and Michael R. Varney

Criminal Law and Policy in the European Union
Samuli Miettinen

The Early Warning System for the Principle of Subsidiarity

Constitutional theory and empirical reality

Philipp Kiiver

Routledge
Taylor & Francis Group

LONDON AND NEW YORK

First published 2012
by Routledge
2 Park Square, Milton Park, Abingdon, Oxfordshire OX14 4RN

Simultaneously published in the USA and Canada
by Routledge
711 Third Avenue, New York, NY 10017

Routledge is an imprint of the Taylor & Francis Group, an informa business

First issued in paperback 2013

© 2012 Philipp Kiiver

British Library Cataloguing in Publication Data
A catalogue record for this book is available from the British Library

Library of Congress Cataloging in Publication Data
Kiiver, Philipp.
The early warning system for the principle of subsidiarity:
constitutional theory and empirical reality / Philipp Kiiver.
    p. cm.
ISBN 978–0–415–68522–1 (hardback) — ISBN 978-0-203-
12700-1 (e-book)   1. Central–local government relations—
European Union countries.   2. Federal government—European
Union countries.   3. Subsidiarity.   I. Title.
KJE5094.K55 2012
342.24'042--dc23   2011034947

ISBN: 978–0–415–68522–1 (hbk)
ISBN: 978–0–415–73050-1 (pbk)
ISBN: 978–0–203–12700–1 (ebk)

Typeset in Garamond
by RefineCatch Limited, Bungay, Suffolk

Contents

Preface   vii

1 **Introduction**   1

2 **National parliaments in the European Union**   5
   2.1   *The European role of national parliaments 5*
   2.2   *Analytical studies of national parliaments 11*
   2.3   *National parliaments and constitutional theory 13*
   2.4   *Towards a new realism 16*

3 **The institutional and procedural logic of the early
   warning system**   18
   3.1   *Introduction 18*
   3.2   *The inception of the EWS 19*
   3.3   *The form and scope of review 20*
   3.4   *Reasoned opinions: voting thresholds 26*
   3.5   *Timeframe 34*
   3.6   *The EWS and regional parliaments 40*
   3.7   *The EWS and the judiciary 42*
   3.8   *On the definition of national parliaments 48*
   3.9   *The logic of the distribution of votes 62*
   3.10 *Conclusion 67*

4 **The material scope of the early warning system: subsidiarity and
   other criteria**   69
   4.1   *Introduction 69*
   4.2   *Subsidiarity: a legal analysis 69*
   4.3   *The difficulties of applying subsidiarity in practice 71*
   4.4   *The quality of the justification 74*
   4.5   *The empirical reality of the subsidiarity principle 76*

4.6   *Analytical assessment of subsidiarity in action 91*
4.7   *Defining subsidiarity: a bottom-up approach 96*
4.8   *Conclusion 101*

5 **The early warning system as an accountability mechanism   103**
5.1   *Introduction 103*
5.2   *The EWS as an accountability relationship 106*
5.3   *The direction of accountability: vertical, diagonal and horizontal 110*
5.4   *The plurality of forums: networks and redundancies 113*
5.5   *The purpose of accountability: democratic or otherwise 117*
5.6   *The EWS as a legal accountability mechanism 117*
5.7   *Conclusion 124*

6 **The early warning system as legal review: national parliaments as councils of state   126**
6.1   *Introduction 126*
6.2   *National parliaments as councils of state 127*
6.3   *Implications for the EWS 130*
6.4   *Conclusion 132*

7 **National parliaments in the constitutional reality of the early warning system   134**
7.1   *Introduction 134*
7.2   *The legal setting of the EWS: greater complexity than meets the eye 134*
7.3   *A new typology of national parliaments 136*
7.4   *The impact of reasoned opinions: observations and hypotheses 140*
7.5   *The constitutional context of the EWS: democracy, accountability, transparency 145*
7.6   *Strengthening the EWS 146*
7.7   *Conclusion 148*

Notes   149
Bibliography   165
Index   174
Index of Treaty Provisions   176

Preface

This book is the result of a research project funded with a Veni grant by the Netherlands Organization for Scientific Research (NWO). The project had originally started as a study into different accountability mechanisms in national parliaments, but it eventually developed into an in-depth analysis of the European Union's early warning system for subsidiarity with, it is hoped, many gems for both academics and practitioners. I am grateful to NWO which has funded this research, and to my colleagues at the Montesquieu Institute Maastricht and within the growing international community of lawyers and political scientists who deal with national parliaments in the EU. I appreciated the opportunity to discuss my papers and draft chapters with them. Thanks to Thomson Reuters for the kind permission to reprint part of an earlier article in the *European Law Review* and incorporate it in Chapter 6 of this book. Special thanks go to Professors Aalt Willem Heringa and Luc Verhey who both, as always, gave me much freedom to pursue various endeavours which included, but were not limited to, writing this book.

Maastricht, June 2011

1 Introduction

The Treaty of Lisbon introduced several innovations to the European Union's institutional architecture. One of the most prominent of them was the inclusion of a so-called early warning system for the principle of subsidiarity.[1] Under this system, national parliaments of the EU Member States are entrusted with the task of reviewing EU legislative proposals and of issuing, if they find that a proposal breaches the principle of subsidiarity, a written complaint called reasoned opinion. Incoming reasoned opinions are counted and weighed as votes: each parliament has two votes, chambers in bicameral parliaments have one vote each. If the number of votes reaches certain thresholds then the initiator of the proposal, typically the European Commission, may withdraw, amend or maintain its proposal but must, in that case, justify its decision. The entry into force of the early warning system marks a culmination of a sequence of Treaty reforms that addressed the principle of subsidiarity and the involvement of national parliaments in EU lawmaking. It was the Maastricht Treaty of 1992 that featured a subsidiarity clause in its text[2] and two Final Act declarations in its annex dealing, respectively, with the role of national parliaments in the EU and with the cooperation between national parliaments among themselves and collectively with the European Parliament.[3] The Treaty of Amsterdam included Protocols on both the details of the application of the subsidiarity principle and on the role of national parliaments in the EU.[4] And now the Constitutional Treaty and, after it failed to enter into force, its successor instrument, the Lisbon Treaty, included an early warning system based on both Treaty provisions and Protocols.[5] In fact this system addresses national parliaments and subsidiarity together, by allowing the former to enforce the latter.

Yet while the early warning system (EWS) has been presented as a major selling-point in the ratification process for both the Constitutional Treaty and the Treaty of Lisbon, we should note that it was also met with rather mixed feelings. Political declarations of course stressed what a positive breakthrough this system supposedly was. But a cynic might dismiss the entire EWS as pure window-dressing, and indeed there are several highly critical academic commentaries on it already from the period when the EWS was originally inserted into the Draft Constitutional Treaty drawn up by the European

Convention.[6] Most academic criticism was, and is, based on the observation that the EWS is a non-binding mechanism and does not amount to a 'red card'. The Commission is at no point obliged to amend, let alone withdraw, any of its proposals irrespective of the number of reasoned opinions issued by national parliaments. The basic feature is a 'yellow card'. The addition by the Lisbon Treaty of a supplementary mechanism called 'orange card', whereby the European Parliament or the Council may reject proposals if more than half the national parliaments' votes had constituted objections,[7] still leaves the discretion with the EU institutions and does not amount to a national parliamentary veto power either. A very fundamental observation can therefore be made that essentially the EWS did not grant the national parliaments any rights they did not already have.[8] The absence of a genuine veto right for national parliaments, while it was widely acknowledged, was not universally criticised, though. Several authors approved of the system as an appropriately 'soft constitutional solution',[9] in that it did not infringe too much upon the Commission's independence[10] and did not excessively distort or block the smooth running of European decision-making in general.[11]

On a practical note, it is pointed out by both scholars and practitioners that the time periods for subsidiarity review are prohibitively short and thresholds seem unattainably high so that the EWS may in fact never be triggered. Under the Lisbon regime, national parliaments have eight weeks for their review although in practice this may well be both longer than that and, through an urgency clause that is usually overlooked, significantly shorter than that.[12] Regarding thresholds, to trigger the initiator's obligation to withdraw, amend or re-justify proposals the EWS prescribes one-quarter of total votes to constitute objections for proposals regarding the area of freedom, security and justice, and one-third for all other proposals.[13] In an EU with 27 Member States this means 14 and 18 out of 54 votes, respectively. As an illustration, to generate the standard 18 votes one would need negative reasoned opinions originating, for example, in five unicameral parliaments (two votes each), four lower chambers and four upper chambers (one vote each).[14] However, much depends on what one counts as a reasoned opinion, and it shall be argued later on that a broad understanding of the scope of the EWS is in order.[15]

Finally, it is pointed out that breaches of subsidiarity do not seem to be a problem in real life. As Raunio notes:[16]

> The image of Commission and other EU institutions, constantly stretching and overstepping the limits of their powers, is also somewhat outdated. There appears to be a broad consensus, also among national MPs, that the overwhelming majority of the Commission's legislative proposals have not been problematic in terms of the subsidiarity principle.

The Finnish parliament had reported already in 2004 that it had reviewed all its EU dossiers since Finland's EU accession in 1995 and that it had not discovered a single case where it might have established a breach of subsidiarity, although possibly of proportionality.[17] Proportionality is however not formally included as a review standard for reasoned opinions under the EWS, in spite of the fact that EU legislative proposals must be justified in the light of both subsidiarity and proportionality.[18] Still, a case can and shall be made that the scope of the subsidiarity principle can and should be interpreted sufficiently broadly.[19]

Either way, notwithstanding all these highly critical considerations, there are good reasons to have a closer look at the EWS and to view it in a much more positive light.[20] For the truth is that the EWS did not just come into existence on 1 December 2009 when the Lisbon Treaty entered into force. Already in late 2004, when the EU was still anticipating the ratification of the Constitutional Treaty, COSAC, the half-yearly conference of the European affairs committees of the national parliaments and a delegation from the European Parliament, had decided to start experimenting with the EWS as if it was in force.[21] Furthermore, after the ratification of the Constitutional Treaty had failed, the Barroso initiative committed the Commission to observing the EWS procedure nevertheless.[22] This means that when the EWS came into force officially in 2009, already several years' worth of practical experience as well as correspondence between national parliaments and the Commission had accumulated.[23] This in turn allows us to subject the EWS not only to a theoretical analysis from a legal and political science point of view, but also to an empirical analysis. This empirical analysis first of all reveals that EWS practice in reality does not entirely match the black-letter law. It also allows us to see the EWS in a new light as far as its added value is concerned, and to develop much more robust theories regarding its actual and potential impact on national parliamentary involvement in the EU.

The present volume thus represents an in-depth study of the EWS that includes both a theoretical and an empirical analysis. It first provides an overview of the historical developments of, and the legal and political science literature on, national parliamentary involvement in the EU (Chapter 2). It then thoroughly discusses virtually each and every procedural aspect of the EWS, including implications that are not evident and that are therefore usually overlooked (Chapter 3). The book continues with an empirical analysis of how national parliaments seem to define the principle of subsidiarity based on the wording of their reasoned opinions (Chapter 4). After all, it is known that subsidiarity is hard to define in practice, and this book offers a bottom-up approach based on how parliaments *themselves* use it on the ground. For that purpose, as well as for the purpose of the other chapters, the book systematically incorporates the body of material that has resulted from the correspondence between national parliaments and the European Commission thus far: again, not just since the entry into force of the Treaty of Lisbon in 2009 but since the start of COSAC's informal pilot projects in 2004.

The book then goes on to offer two innovative, even unorthodox analytical theories of the EWS. One discusses the EWS as an accountability mechanism

(Chapter 5), specifically as an instance of legal accountability. It should be noted that the existing literature does not usually treat the EWS as an accountability regime and, furthermore, tends to associate legal accountability with courts rather than with parliaments. As such, the EWS might turn out to play a role in the EU's much-discussed accountability deficit. The other theory offered here draws an analogy between the role of national parliaments under the EWS and the domestic consultative role of a council of state as it exists in France as well as in southern European countries and the Benelux countries (Chapter 6). Many national parliaments are still struggling to find a proper role in the EU, and the role of a council of state offers, it is argued, a workable and recognisable role model. The final analytical section (Chapter 7) discusses some broader implications of the EWS, including its relation with democracy and legitimacy as well as the typology of national parliaments as it results from the empirical analysis of EWS practice.

The main argument of this study is that we should not be quick to dismiss the EWS as meaningless, for two reasons. The first is that a national parliament's participation in the EWS might raise European awareness among parliamentarians, which might in turn translate into greater attention to the political aspects of proposed EU legislation and the government's opinion on it. Without conferring any significant powers on national parliaments, the EWS might thus become a catalyst for the exercise of those powers that national parliaments already have.[24] The second reason is that it is sensible to appreciate the value of the EWS in its own right, not just as a catalyst but also as an actual involvement mechanism, even though it might amount to little more than a minimum standard of participation. The precondition for such an appreciation is that we make sure that our expectations are realistic. This concerns the scope, purpose and effect of the EWS as well as the nature of national parliaments and their interest and capacity to use it. As a start we should, for example, stop assuming that the EWS is primarily about the right to *veto* EU legislation: such assumption is bound to lead to disappointment. Instead, based on both the constitutional theory and the empirical reality of the EWS, we should accept that it is much more about the duty to *justify* legislation. Thus, with realistic expectations and an open mind, we should be able to embrace the EWS for what it is: not a panacea, not even a major institutional rupture, but definitely more than mere window-dressing.

2   National parliaments in the European Union

The involvement of national parliaments in the EU legislative process had been one of the most prominent features of the Treaty establishing a Constitution for Europe, its Draft version as presented by the Convention and its successor, the Treaty of Lisbon. However, attention for this issue had already been growing throughout the 1990s in both politics and the literature.

2.1 The European role of national parliaments

In the 1960s the parliaments of the then six Member States of the European Economic Community confined their involvement mostly to the consideration of an annual government report on the progress of European integration.[1] A somewhat greater activity was noticed in 1973 when – along with Ireland – the United Kingdom and Denmark joined the Community. These newcomers were both more sceptical about the merits of ever-closer union and had more robust parliamentary traditions.[2] The UK Parliament became famous for adopting a scrutiny reserve resolution barring British ministers in principle from agreeing to Council measures pending scrutiny in the national parliament; the Danish Folketing gained notoriety for issuing negotiating mandates to Brussels-bound ministers, although it may be questioned whether the Danish system is truly convincing or, due to the national idiosyncrasies, suitable as a role model for other Member States.[3] Still, with progressive integration and thus with the conferral of more competences to European institutions, especially after the adoption of the Single European Act and the Maastricht Treaty, parliamentary scrutiny of governments' EU policy gained importance in other Member States as well.[4] The phenomenon national parliamentarians saw themselves confronted with was that legislative powers were delegated to the EU institutions, notably the Council, and therefore to what is domestically the executive. Whereas in a parliamentary system the government is accountable to the national parliament, this is much more difficult to enforce in the context of EU decision-making. Here, after all, the agenda is set externally, transparency is traditionally poor, complexity is high, compromise-building is crucial, and the possibility that individual governments are simply outvoted in the Council makes it hard to allocate responsibility for a certain policy decision with any one participant. Besides, we should not forget that policy preferences or a political culture of benevolent consensus for EU integration, of non-competition with the European Parliament, and of deference to the government in foreign affairs, as well as an absence of salience and of voter interest, are all factors that contribute to a low willingness on the part of parliamentarians to invest time, energy and political capital in European affairs in the first place.

Still, the traditional and, according to empirical findings, the most commonly used mechanism for national parliamentary involvement in the EU is the calling to account of ministers and, possibly, the consultation with them before they attend the Council of Ministers in Brussels.[5] The Treaty of Amsterdam sought to accommodate national parliaments somewhat as its Protocol on the role of national parliaments granted them a six-week period before Commission proposals would be put on the Council agenda so that a minimum time window for scrutiny could be observed.[6] The Constitutional Treaty affirmed the Amsterdam Protocol and added, as far as the legislative process is concerned, a number of additional involvement facilities for national parliaments, including the subsidiarity early warning system (EWS); this the Treaty of Lisbon took over, and it expanded the minimum scrutiny delay from six to eight weeks. Furthermore, additional rights including veto rights have been added by the Constitutional Treaty and the Treaty of Lisbon. As a result, national parliaments now enjoy a catalogue of rights, privileges, facilities or explicit mentions as a matter of EU law, most though by no means all of which are summarised in Article 12 TEU.

It should be noted that Article 12 TEU is a rather odd provision. It starts out by stating that:

> National Parliaments contribute actively to the good functioning of the Union:

whereby the colon implies that parliaments' contributions to the good functioning of the Union are effected only through those means that are expressly listed in the remainder of the Article. This cannot be right, though. A host of provisions are not restated in Article 12 whereas there is no reason to assume that in those cases national parliaments somehow do *not* contribute to the Union's good functioning, or to any lesser extent than under those provisions that are included. Nor is it the case that Article 12 only refers to other TEU provisions and not to TFEU provisions: it refers to relevant Articles in both Treaties, it simply does not mention all of them. In all likelihood, Article 12 TEU is an attempt to upgrade the visibility of national parliaments in a prominent part of the EU Treaty, only one that has been made too hastily and thus a tad sloppily. For practical purposes, it would therefore be pragmatic to treat this first sentence of Article 12 TEU as a declaratory stand-alone provision, ignore the colon and pretend that it ends with a full stop. The remainder is then a non-exhaustive list of examples of national parliamentary contributions pursuant to EU Treaty law. In order to provide a better overview, listed below are all explicit instances of national parliamentary involvement pursuant to EU Treaty and Protocol provisions. The list roughly distinguishes between such instances depending on whether national parliaments are addressed in a passive or active capacity.

2.1.1 *Information rights*

- The national parliaments' right to receive directly the Commission's consultative documents, the annual legislative programme as well as any other instrument of legislative planning or policy (Article 12 (a) TEU and Article 1 Protocol No. 1 TEU/TFEU);
- the right to receive directly EU draft legislative acts: from the Commission if it concerns Commission proposals, from the European Parliament if it concerns initiatives of the European Parliament, and from the Council if it concerns proposals from a group of Member States or requests or recommendations from the Court of Justice, the European Central Bank or the European Investment Bank (Article 12 (a) TEU and Article 2 Protocol No. 1 as well as Article 4 Protocol No. 2 TEU/TFEU);
- the right to receive amended drafts and legislative resolutions of the European Parliament and positions of the Council on draft legislative acts (Article 4 Protocol No. 2 TEU/TFEU);
- the right to receive directly the agendas for and the outcome of meetings of the Council (Article 5 Protocol No. 1 TEU/TFEU);
- the right to have special attention drawn to planned applications of the flexibility clause (Article 352 TFEU) in the context of the regular subsidiarity enforcement procedure of Protocol No. 2 TEU/TFEU;
- the right to be notified of planned applications of the ordinary Treaty revision procedure (Article 12 (d) and Article 48 (2) TEU);
- the right to be notified of planned applications of the general passerelle within the simplified Treaty revision procedure (Article 12 (d), Article 48 (7) TEU and Article 6 Protocol No. 1 TEU/TFEU);
- the right to be notified of planned applications of the special passerelle in the area of family law (Article 81 (3) TFEU);
- the right to be notified of the receipt of EU membership applications (Article 12 (e) TEU and Article 49 TEU);
- the right to receive an annual report from the Commission on the application of Article 5 TEU on the principles of conferral, subsidiarity and proportionality (Article 9 Protocol No. 2 TEU/TFEU); and
- the right to receive the annual report of the Court of Auditors (Article 7 Protocol No. 1 TEU/TFEU).

2.1.2 *Provisions envisaging or implying an evaluation by national parliaments*

- The national parliaments' right to be informed of the content and results of evaluations of policies in the area of freedom, security and justice (Article 12 (c) TEU and Article 70 TFEU);
- involvement in the evaluations of the activities of Eurojust (Article 12 (c) TEU and Article 85 (1) TFEU) pursuant to regulations to be adopted on Eurojust's structure, operation, field of action and tasks;
- involvement in the political monitoring or scrutiny of Europol (Article 12 (c) TEU and Article 88 (2) TFEU) pursuant to regulations to be adopted on Europol's structure, operation, field of action and tasks; and
- the right to be informed of the proceedings of the Council's standing committee on the operational cooperation on internal security (Article 71 TFEU).

2.1.3 *Provisions envisaging or implying active input from national parliaments*

- The respect by the EU institutions of an eight-week period between the transmission of a draft legislative act and its placing on the Council's provisional agenda, during which no agreement may be reached; the respect of a ten-day period between the draft act's placing on the provisional agenda and the adoption of a position; and the duty for the Council in each case to justify exceptions in cases of urgency (Article 4 Protocol No. 1 TEU/TFEU). In the light of the first two recitals of the Preamble of Protocol No. 1, this minimum delay rule is meant as an opportunity for domestic parliamentary scrutiny and the expression of opinions on EU draft legislative acts;
- the enforcement of the principle of subsidiarity (Article 12 (b) TEU as well as Article 5 (3) TEU, and again Article 69 TFEU specifically for the area of freedom, security and justice, all referring to Protocol No. 2 TEU/TFEU). The Protocol in turn includes:
  - ○ the EWS for the submission of reasoned opinions which in turn triggers certain consequences when certain thresholds are reached (Article 3 Protocol No. 1 and Articles 6 and 7 of Protocol No. 2 TEU/TFEU); and
  - ○ the jurisdiction of the Court of Justice to hear annulment actions for alleged breaches of subsidiarity notified by Member States on behalf of national parliaments (Article 8 Protocol No. 2 TEU/TFEU);
- the participation of representatives of national parliaments in Treaty amendment Conventions within ordinary Treaty revision (Article 12 (d) and Article 48 (3) TEU);

- the right for each parliament to veto the application of the general passerelle within simplified Treaty revision (Article 12 (d) and Article 48 (7) TEU);
- the right for each parliament to veto the application of the special passerelle in the area of family law (Article 81 (3) TFEU); and
- inter-parliamentary cooperation in accordance with Protocol No. 1 TEU/TFEU (Article 12 (f) TEU). Protocol No. 1 TEU/TFEU in turn includes:
  - the right for COSAC to issue contributions, without however binding national parliaments or prejudging their positions (Article 10 Protocol No. 1 TEU/TFEU); and
  - the task for COSAC to promote the exchange of information and best practice between national parliaments and the European Parliament (Article 10 Protocol No. 1 TEU/TFEU).

It is evident that the above list is significantly longer than the list contained in Article 12 TEU. Article 12 includes relatively banal rights, such as the right to be notified of EU membership applications, but it at the same time omits rather significant facilities like the binding veto right of each national parliament in the family law passerelle. Be that as it may, apart from these instances inside and outside of Article 12 TEU there is a general declaratory provision contained in the second clause of Article 10 (2) TEU, stating that:

> Member States are represented in the European Council by their Heads of State or Government and in the Council by their governments, themselves democratically accountable either to their national Parliaments, or to their citizens.

The extent to which this statement is actually true depends on domestic constitutional law and practice, it cannot have any constitutive value in that it neither prescribes nor codifies any particular accountability arrangements in parliamentary, presidential or semi-presidential systems. Indeed, in spite of all the cited facilities and in some cases actual rights reserved for national parliaments, primary EU law maintains that it does not seek to prescribe how parliaments control their own governments when the latter act in a European capacity. The Preamble of Protocol No. 1 TEU/TFEU on the role of national parliaments in the EU, already in its original Amsterdam version, continues to stress in the very first recital that:

> the way in which national Parliaments scrutinise their governments in relation to the activities of the Union is a matter for the particular constitutional organisation and practice of each Member State.

And indeed, the effect or effectiveness of much if not all of the EU rights and facilities essentially depends on what parliaments or chambers themselves are willing to make of it. In fact, the UK House of Lords was already worried that the EU might compel national parliaments to engage in European decision-making as a matter of duty. Article 12 TEU now starts out by stating, as noted, that 'National Parliaments contribute actively to the good functioning of the Union'. Yet in an earlier draft the provision stipulated that national parliaments 'shall contribute', and the pointed question was whether a parliament could be sued for not being active.[7] Now that the 'shall' has been dropped, Article 12 TEU can be safely described as a somewhat messy and incomplete, competence-neutral summary of provisions found elsewhere in the Treaties and Protocols. As Barrett noted, 'it adds precisely nothing in terms of substantive content' to the rights already provided under either the predecessor Constitutional Treaty or under the actual Lisbon Treaty that included it.[8] Its first sentence is a purely declaratory clause.

Crucially, it should be noted that all the cited instances of national parliamentary involvement are only instances pursuant to EU law itself. Domestic constitutional law typically provides for European involvement of national parliaments as well. Among the most important are, first, information rights that are independent from, and that go beyond, EU law requirements, including the obligation for the government to provide explanatory memoranda and a political assessment of proposals on its own and to keep the parliament informed about the EU legislative process also after initiation. Such arrangements may be laid down in constitutional provisions, statutory law and/or parliamentary resolutions.

Second, the transposition of EU law into domestic law may require national parliamentary action to the extent that transposition must occur by legislation and the national parliament is competent to adopt such legislation. We should recall that Article 288 TFEU does not say, and its predecessors never said, that directives are to be implemented by national parliaments: instead, a reference is made to 'national authorities' which may in turn be national parliaments but which just as well may be regional parliaments or quite simply the executive.

Third, where domestic constitutional law so provides, parliaments are the authority to ratify new Treaties or Treaty amendments. This is true for the 'ordinary procedure' (Convention plus IGC),[9] the semi-simplified ordinary procedure (only IGC, no Convention)[10] as well as the so-called 'simplified procedure' for competence-neutral changes to Part III of the TFEU (unanimous European Council decision, no IGC and no Convention).[11] The national parliamentary veto for the general passerelle version of simplified Treaty revision under Article 48 (7) TEU (unanimous European Council decision to introduce more instances of co-decision and qualified majority voting) and for the area of family law under Article 81 (3) TFEU is not strictly speaking a ratification of a Treaty amendment but a veto right *against* a Treaty amendment. But where ratification must take place, such national parliamentary involvement does not follow from Article 48 TEU itself, which in all cases merely speaks of ratification (in the ordinary procedure) or approval (in the simplified procedure) by the Member States 'in accordance with their respective constitutional requirements.' Apart from the fact that there is no actual difference between ratification and approval in this context, 'respective constitutional requirements' may demand different and possibly elevated voting thresholds for ratification and may also prescribe, or allow for, a referendum instead of a parliamentary vote. The same of course holds true for the ratification of Accession Treaties[12] and of other international agreements if they require domestic ratification in the Member States.

Fourth, prior parliamentary approval of the government's agreement to measures in the Council or European Council may be required as a matter of domestic arrangements. This may be a political or conventional rule, as in the case of the UK or Denmark, where a general scrutiny reserve and a mandating procedure, respectively, applies to ministers acting in the Council. It may also be a matter of domestic statutory law, as in the case of the Netherlands whose parliament has retained a prior approval right for certain former Third Pillar matters, and whose parliament may furthermore declare any proposed EU decision politically sensitive thus requiring enhanced information by the government.[13] And it may even be a matter of constitutional constraints, as in the case of Germany whose Federal Constitutional Court had ruled in 2009 that German consent to a range of EU decisions that actually or potentially imply a Treaty amendment, including among others the general passerelle but also the application of the flexibility clause, without prior domestic legislative approval would violate the Basic Law.[14]

Fifth, wherever a parliamentary or at least semi-parliamentary system of government applies, which is everywhere in the EU except Cyprus – a presidential system – governments rely on parliamentary confidence or at least tolerance to stay in office and are therefore subject to parliamentary accountability for what they do. This way, any government decision with EU relevance is, in theory, subject to national parliamentary oversight and accountability, not just the negotiation and voting on regulations and directives in the Council, but also decisions such as whether or not to launch an annulment action before the Court of Justice, or whom to nominate as the national candidate for the European Commission. Here we return to the core of parliamentary scrutiny in EU affairs, including the various factors that make such activity so difficult even where there is political will to actually engage in it, which, again, is not always the case.

2.2 Analytical studies of national parliaments

From the mid-1990s onwards, political science was the first academic discipline to take a systematic interest in the study of national parliamentary involvement in the EU. Efforts were directed, first of all, at taking stock, mostly through edited volumes, of how various national parliaments had adapted their internal institutions and procedures, such as their committee structure, to the challenge of ensuring oversight in EU affairs.[15] In addition, attempts were made to explain variations in the patterns of adaptation by identifying factors contributing to the form and intensity that European scrutiny eventually takes. Most of the relative intensity of scrutiny seems to be explained by the degree to which political parties and the public are Eurosceptic and by the pre-existing shape of government–parliament relations in domestic policy areas.[16] However, a number of complementary factors have been put forward as well, such as the timing of EU membership (the later the entry the sharper the scrutiny), political culture regarding deference to the executive especially in foreign policy, the presence in a Member State of federal sub-units guarding their competences, the question whether a cabinet is a minority cabinet or not and whether parliament had secured oversight powers at crucial junctures such as Treaty ratifications.[17]

Related efforts were made to rank parliaments, in one way or another, along scales of strong, moderate and weak, or to classify them based on other categorisations. Norton distinguished three types of parliaments: strong policymakers, who can amend government policies and substitute them with their own; moderate policy-influencers, who can reject or amend government policies but not substitute them; and parliaments with little or no policy effect.[18] Another pioneer attempt to rank national parliaments in EU affairs as strong, moderate or weak has been made by Bergman,[19] based on the degree to which national parliamentary opinions were binding upon the government but also based on the parliaments' internal organisation. Maurer and Wessels adopted a matrix rather than a ranking of parliamentary performance in EU matters, defining parliaments as players on the national and the European arena.[20] Fraga proposed to focus on the *method* of scrutiny rather than on any comparative strength indicators, and differentiated between 'mandate-givers', which put the procedural emphasis on briefing the competent minister immediately prior to a Council meeting, 'systematic scrutinisers' which carry out a sifting of all incoming EU documents while reserving the right to pass resolutions where appropriate, and 'informal influencers' which raise opinions only incidentally and more or less informally.[21] I myself proposed to integrate several approaches and to distinguish parliamentary scrutiny mechanisms in EU matters in general along five dimensions: the time at which scrutiny sets in (ex ante or ex post scrutiny); the relative centralisation of scrutiny (European affairs committees or sectoral committees); the methods of government influencing (mandating system, systematic sifting of documents, incidental resolutions, scrutiny reserves); the legal basis for scrutiny (constitutional, statutory or conventional); and the relative 'strength' of national parliaments at European scrutiny (strong, moderate, weak).[22]

Now that this stock-taking and systematisation has taken place, two current trends can be identified in the academic community working in this field. One is to pay less attention to the generalist European affairs committees and instead to study the European interest and involvement of sectoral committees where specialist policy expertise tends to be clustered. The second is to seek to move more deeply into empirics in order to analyse parliamentarians' actual behaviour in EU context rather than the institutional setup of the chambers of which they are members. The present study may actually be seen as a contribution to this next step of the research agenda, whereby the actual use of – in this case – subsidiarity control by national parliaments is analysed empirically.

2.3 National parliaments and constitutional theory

While a lively branch of empirical, political science-driven scholarship has been trying to identify and explain the role of national parliaments in the EU, another branch of literature, mainly driven by constitutional law, has been developing thoughts about how, as a matter of principle and perhaps at a more abstract level, national parliaments should define their role in the Union's institutional landscape. Here the starting point is often the alleged or real democratic deficit of the European Union. Much of this deficit can, after all, be brought down to an alleged or real *parliamentary* deficit: national parliaments are said to be insufficiently involved in EU decision-making, presumably compared with domestic decision-making, while the European Parliament at EU level insufficiently compensates for what is lost at the domestic level.[23] In that immediate context, profound arguments have been exchanged about the underlying relationships between sovereignty, nationhood, democracy, citizenship and statehood in a transnational context. One of the central themes in the literature is whether the values that are cherished in a nation-state setting can or need to be adapted, or preserved, if the constitutional environment changes through progressive European integration or if key elements of those values are absent. Hence the perennial questions, for example, whether democracy can exist without a demos, whether a sense of citizenship can transcend ethnicity or the belonging to a particular nation or state, whether a transnational constitutional order requires a *pouvoir constituant* or a constitutional moment or both, or whether politics can take shape without there being a polity and vice versa.[24]

At a somewhat lower level of abstractness, attempts are made to translate constitutional concepts into actual implications and normative assumptions for the role of national parliaments in the EU. In a traditional Euro-federalist narrative, national parliaments would not play a prominent role.[25] In fact they may even come to be perceived as a nuisance. One should only recall, in the context of the implementation of EU law, the distrust Mancini has of national legislatures which in his view are merely a liability likely to slow down smooth implementation.[26] Instead, implementation should be left with the governments which were, after all, the very same players who had negotiated the EU legislation in the first place and which should therefore be in a better position than parliaments to finalise the process. To address the democratic deficit, efforts should in his view be directed at the European Parliament,[27] a view shared in fact by many national parliamentarians.[28] Other authors suggest a presidentialisation of the Commission through direct elections,[29] which equally identifies a democratic deficit at the EU level and presumes that solutions should be sought there as well.

Somewhat more conciliatory notes are struck by those who argue that both national and European loci of representation matter for the democratic legitimacy of the European Union. This thought is in fact reflected in the wording of Article 10 (2) TEU, introduced by the Lisbon Treaty but featuring already in the Constitutional Treaty, which states that citizens are directly represented at Union level in the European Parliament while the Member State representatives in the European Council and the Council of Ministers are democratically accountable to their national parliaments or to their citizens. In other words, the Union in that view rests on a double legitimacy, one democratic and one federal whereby even the federal one, manifested in the intergovernmental bodies, is democratically legitimised.

This basic acceptance of more than just one linear track of conveying democratic legitimacy can be taken further, to a pluralist conceptualisation of the EU constitutional order as a whole. This would mean that 'European constitutional law' is not just the institutional part of European Union law proper.[30] Nor would it be placed in a hierarchical relationship with otherwise autonomous Member State constitutions in any traditional sense.[31] Instead, European constitutional law would refer to a set of norms of both European and national origin that are together underpinning a pluralist, contrapunctual,[32] multi-layered, multi-level or composite constitution.[33] The perception of the European constitution as a composite, and above all polycentric rather than hierarchical order, for example, would imply that national parliaments should not feel constrained by the boundaries of their 'level' of government to interacting only with other domestic institutions, such as their own ministers, but that they should feel free to reach out to engage in direct dialogues and demand accountability for, say, actions of the Council as a whole.[34] This would then not detract from the legitimacy of e.g. the European Parliament in its own right.

Still, even if one finds both European and national parliamentary legitimacy important, there are plenty of variations in how to put this notion into effect. Assuming that the European Parliament, certainly after the Treaty of Lisbon, does not really suffer from a lack of power, or rather that a lack of power is not its main problem, attention would naturally turn to the national parliaments. The conclusion that national parliaments play a marginal role in the EU is quickly made, as is the conclusion that this is not an accident but a structural phenomenon in a system of executive federalism.[35] The German Constitutional Court, in its *Maastricht* and its *Lisbon* rulings, also acknowledged both the European Parliament and national parliaments as sources of democratic legitimacy in the EU but clearly declared the former to be supplementary at best and the latter to be decisive and in need of strengthening. But how would one strengthen these national parliaments?

Van Gerven, for instance, sees national parliamentary involvement as vital in order to hold the Council to account. However he rather puts the emphasis on the national parliaments' collective involvement, rather than on sharper scrutiny of individual governments, as the solution that is most compatible with his conception of an EU modelled largely after a traditional federal state.[36] Majone, by contrast, in his critique of functionalist European 'integration by stealth' and of federal blueprints for the Union, as well as Harlow in her exposal of several accountability gaps in the EU, take the view that it is in fact essential to pay closer attention to the preferences of the individual constituent parts in what should be a *con*federal Union.[37] Weber-Panariello points out that the involvement of parliaments in EU policy can be abused by governments in order to instrumentalise their parliaments, in the sense of co-opting them into the decision-making process. The key is therefore, in his view, to extend information facilities for parliaments, allowing the opposition to articulate its opinion.[38] At the same time, one could wonder whether too much oversight would be compatible with the view that at least the intergovernmental aspects of EU decision-making follow the logic of consociational democracy, a point made by Weiler.[39] Consociationalism implies that the elites of the insulated segments of a society – in this case Member States in the EU – engage in consensus-seeking while their constituents follow along. Such models would arguably require a certain degree of permissive consensus to executive action on the part of national parliaments. And yet, as Saalfeld argues, there is a difference between permissiveness and a downright abdication of power.[40] Where parliaments ratify European Treaties but do not follow up on the resulting delegation of power with mechanisms to verify whether the exercise of delegated powers takes place in accordance with their preferences, or even within the boundaries of the powers actually delegated, abdication might indeed be a term that is more apt than delegation.

All of this should not make us forget, though, that if national parliaments become active, they are bound to formulate opinions in the light of the interest of their own respective Member State. In a constitutional sense, that is because they have a representative task with respect to *their* people, not with respect to *foreign* peoples. In a political science sense, that is because extensions of parliamentarians' tenure in office depend on re-election by *their* electorate, not by voters abroad. This prospect will surely make some observers feel more uncomfortable than others, and it is not objectionable in itself, it is just a reality we should face. As Curtin put it:[41]

> Even if we view the national legislature (connected to the voters) as delegating power upwards via the national governments to the EU supranational actors (in particular the Commission, much less so the Council of Ministers), it is difficult to link that same authorization by the national legislature with the output of the EU actors. Moreover the national legislatures may be connected to the national voters but the elections are on purely national matters not on the output of the supranational actors.

And while we weigh the pros and cons of parliamentary involvement, we must always take care that we do not expect national parliamentarians to solve something that they cannot solve even with maximum involvement. A very fundamental feature of the EU remains that, apart from its institutional complexity, there is no plausible way for voters at elections to vote the rascals or scoundrels out of office. There is no single EU government to throw out, allocating blame with individual Council members let alone civil servants is near-illusory, and swapping political parties in the European Parliament will by itself not change the overall agenda – a fact that the German Constitutional Court observed as well in its *Lisbon* judgment. In other words the institutional reality of the European Union must be taken into account. Certainly, Harlow has argued that as long as the Union's structural democratic problems are not solved, it should not be assigned too much power.[42] At the same time Menon and Weatherill aptly retort that in a transnational market, purely domestic action can impose costs on those who are not represented in that nation, that supranational decision-making is therefore needed, and that calls for the EU to simply restrain itself would be anachronistic.[43] Effects from enhanced national parliamentary involvement that takes place within that institutional reality of the Union will thus likely be gradual and subtle rather than radical.

Furthermore, we should refrain from expecting national parliamentarians to do something in EU context which they are not even doing in domestic context. It often appears as though national parliaments' European performance is perceived as disappointing because as European policy-makers they are not passionate enough; however parliaments in general simply are not policy-makers to begin with.[44] It is far more typical of them to critically assess government proposals – the opposition being evidently more critical than the governing parties – to ask sharp questions as to why the proposal is justified, and ultimately to legitimise the outcome through their consent. Any proposal to enhance the EU involvement of national parliaments must take these considerations into account lest they create expectations that simply cannot be met. And as far as the potential for national parliamentary mobilisation is concerned, constitutional theory and political philosophy can take us only that far. An interdisciplinary link with political science is crucial to appreciate why certain realities exist and where the limitations of parliamentary behaviour, which is human behaviour, lie.

2.4 Towards a new realism

Constitutional theory is in a good position to conceptualise and to advocate a certain role for national parliaments in the European Union, but without a firm grounding in empirics such thoughts risk being unrealistic. A claim that parliaments should play a stronger role, for example, is easily made based on a contemplation of available sources of democratic legitimacy in a policy process. However, such a claim could easily overlook the fact that parliaments of different Member States, and chambers of parliament within one and the same Member State, are very diverse. It would also easily overlook that parliamentarians have very concrete reasons and incentives for doing what they are doing, starting with the fact that they are either in government or in opposition, and that they are usually interested in getting re-elected before much else. Thus, when reviewing the merits of the EWS, as we do here, we should not make the mistake of simply cheering parliamentarians on and of expecting of them, and of the EWS itself for that matter, something that neither parliamentarians nor the EWS can deliver. However, with a realistic outlook that is grounded in both constitutional theory and empirical reality, we can recommend ways of how parliamentarians can make the most out of the EWS in a way that suits their needs while it acknowledges the legal and practical limitations of such activity. In the following chapters, we shall dissect the EWS and its procedural setup, propose a way of how to use the system based on the practical preferences of national parliaments, look at the EWS as an accountability mechanism and as a legislative advice procedure, and place it in the context of democracy and legitimacy in Europe. The book's main thesis is that the EWS is not about national parliaments' power to veto European directives, but about the duty of Brussels to explain and justify its legislative initiatives. The EWS will not perform any miracles, national parliamentarians will not turn into superhumans, the Union will not transform into the foremost democratic home for the citizens of Europe. But an added measure of transparency, accountability and a fostered dialogue across levels of government are not unworthy goals, and they will, if they materialise, in themselves suffice to justify the inception and entry into force of the EWS.

3 The institutional and procedural logic of the early warning system

3.1 Introduction

The following paragraphs shall dissect the European Union's early warning system (EWS) for the principle of subsidiarity into small pieces and subject them to analytical scrutiny regarding their meaning and practical implementation. The statement that national parliaments have eight weeks to send a reasoned opinion if they think an EU legislative proposal violates the principle of subsidiarity, that reasoned opinions count as votes, and that proposals must be justified again (yellow card) or can be rejected by the European Parliament or the Council if enough national parliaments have voted against them (orange card) cannot be anything more than a very crude summary. A whole world of details, twists and practical problems lies beneath it.

Thus, we shall consider the exact scope of the EWS (par. 3.3): the system's applicability to various legislative procedures, the documents that are covered by subsidiarity review and those that are not, the standards of review and the distinction between subsidiarity and other criteria, as well as the 'political dialogue' which the Commission has offered in parallel to the EWS. We shall furthermore consider the details of the voting thresholds (par. 3.4) under the yellow and orange card, the question whether these procedures are alternative or cumulative, and the effects of total and partial breaches by a draft legislative act of the subsidiarity principle and the effects of reasoned opinions which challenge an act for diverging reasons. We shall discuss the ins and outs of the timeframe of the EWS (par. 3.5), in particular when exactly the review period starts and when exactly it ends, how a parliament can gain extra time and how it should deal with the month of August when it usually is in summer recess. We shall devote attention to the role of regional parliaments (par. 3.6) and of the national and European judiciary (par. 3.7) in the context of the EWS. We shall go on to discuss some of the constitutional choices that have been made during the system's inception: the definition of the very term 'national parliament' which is less straightforward than it seems (par. 3.8), and the distribution of EWS votes between parliaments and between chambers of the same parliament (par. 3.9). The already mentioned question of how we should actually define the principle of subsidiarity for the purposes of the EWS, e.g.

whether a breach can be objectively established and where to draw the border with other principles like proportionality, is so extensive and crucial that it shall be dealt with in even greater depth in a separate chapter.[1] We shall start our discussion with a brief look at the history of the inception of the EWS itself.

3.2 The inception of the EWS

The idea that national parliaments and subsidiarity might be strengthened by letting the former enforce the latter had been put forward at EU summits throughout the 1990s. The thought gained momentum as the European Council adopted the Laeken Declaration on the Future of the European Union to assemble a Convention of representatives of the Commission and of the European Parliament, of national governments and of national parliaments from both existing Member States and candidate countries, to draft a new Treaty proposal that would take these issues into account, along with others. The European Convention, which came to be chaired by Valery Giscard d'Estaing, included two Working Groups principally responsible for the design of the EWS, namely Working Group I on subsidiarity and Working Group IV on the role of national parliaments. These two Working Groups did hold joint meetings in the course of the Convention process.[2] The result was not very surprising, though, since the main expectations had already been more or less pre-formulated, in the form of a question, in the Laeken Declaration:

> Should [the national parliaments] focus on the division of competence between Union and Member States, for example through preliminary checking of compliance with the principle of subsidiarity?

The upshot is that here the preferences of the various stakeholders converged on a system that would be visible but not too intrusive. Thus, the basic principle of the EWS is that the subsidiarity compliance of proposals gets checked ex ante, by existing national parliaments rather than by a new EU institution, and without any binding veto effect of negative national parliamentary opinions.

As regards a European senate bringing together national parliamentarians, this idea had been mooted by Giscard early on in the Convention process but had been firmly rejected. As Raunio notes, the 'deliberations and outcome of the Convention also confirmed that politicians throughout the EU display hardly any support for the establishment of a collective organ of national MPs or for changing the consultative role of COSAC'.[3] Regarding the binding effect of the EWS, it suffices to consult those proposed amendments that would have upgraded the system but which were not adopted by the Convention. Poul Schlüter had suggested not only a more detailed and restrictive definition of subsidiarity, but also a lower EWS threshold (one-quarter instead of one-third generally), and a red card to be triggered by more than half of parliaments,[4] although in fact an even higher threshold (two-thirds) had been proposed as well, for fear that otherwise the legislative process might be paralysed.[5]

The Convention's Draft Treaty establishing a Constitution for Europe was presented to an IGC which, after inserting some modifications, went on to adopt the (definitive) Treaty establishing a Constitution for Europe. As the ratification process for the Treaty was abandoned in 2005 due to negative referendum outcomes in two Member States, the Treaty of Lisbon was adopted in 2007 and ratified by the last Member States in 2010. Along the way, i.e. between the Convention Draft and the Lisbon Treaty, the basic idea of the EWS remained unchanged but the relevant Protocol No. 2 did undergo a number of modifications. Apart from minor editorial changes, these were:

Changes between the Convention's Draft and the final Constitutional Treaty:

• Instead of mentioning only unicameral and bicameral systems, the EWS now envisages unicameral and multicameral systems including bicameral systems.[6]

Changes between the Constitutional Treaty and the Lisbon Treaty:

• It is specified that the eight-week EWS period starts with the transmission of draft legislative acts *in the Union's official languages*;[7]
• an 'orange card' is added to the 'yellow card' procedure.[8]

3.3 The form and scope of review

Subsidiarity is defined as a rule that, 'in areas which do not fall within its exclusive competence, the Union shall act only if and in so far as the objectives of the proposed action cannot be sufficiently achieved by the Member States, either at central level or at regional and local level, but can rather, by reason of the scale or effects of the proposed action, be better achieved at Union level'.[9] Already in the 1990s, it had been noted that subsidiarity might be an interesting subject for national parliaments to address,[10] assuming that domestic legislatures should have an interest in retaining competences at the domestic level and might thereby act as a decentralising corrective vis-à-vis Brussels. The Laeken Declaration of 15 December 2001, the original mandate for the Convention that went on to draft the Constitutional Treaty, also explicitly referred to subsidiarity review as a possible task for national parliaments.

3.3.1 *Types of legislative procedures*

The EWS applies to all draft legislative acts within the meaning of Article 3 of Protocol No. 2 TEU/TFEU, namely:

proposals from the Commission, initiatives from a group of Member States, initiatives from the European Parliament, requests from the Court of Justice, recommendations from the European Central Bank and requests from the European Investment Bank, for the adoption of a legislative act.

Article 6 of that Protocol provides for reasoned opinions on any draft legislative act. This means that the EWS as such is not restricted to the ordinary legislative procedure formerly known as co-decision but applies to all legislative procedures. The only element of the EWS that is restricted to the ordinary legislative procedure is the so-called orange card mechanism. This mechanism explicitly refers to the Commission as the initiator, which may maintain its proposal even if a majority of total EWS votes from national parliaments represent objections, and to the European Parliament and the Council as the legislator of the Union which may decide to reject the proposal on subsidiarity grounds.[11]

3.3.2 *The objects of review: draft legislative acts*

While the term 'draft legislative act' is broader than just 'Commission proposal', we should nevertheless be clear about which types of drafts fall within the EWS and which types do not. As noted, draft legislative acts are defined as proposals from the Commission, which evidently attract most attention, but they also include, in accordance with Article 3 of Protocol No. 2 TEU/TFEU, initiatives from a group of Member States, initiatives from the European Parliament, requests from the Court of Justice, recommendations from the European Central Bank and requests from the European Investment Bank for the adoption of a legislative act in the meaning of Article 289 (4) TFEU.

Pennera pointed out that the EWS also covers draft legislative acts which purely pertain to the internal organisation of EU institutions and their staff and where subsidiarity cannot possibly be an issue.[12] However, as long as the Treaties do not differentiate between internal and external legislation for EWS purposes, there is no reason to accept any limitation, especially since the eight-week scrutiny delay from Article 4 of Protocol No. 1 TEU/TFEU applies anyway, even if no EWS review takes place during that period.

What is surely more pertinent is what the term 'draft legislative act' does *not* include. It does not, for example, cover the Commission's consultation documents within the meaning of Article 1 of Protocol No. 1 TEU/TFEU, i.e. 'green and white papers and communications'. This is important as some parliaments, notably the Nordic ones, focus exclusively on these types of documents in their correspondence with the Commission while some other parliaments, while also responding to draft legislative acts proper, occasionally respond to consultation documents as well.[13] Strictly speaking, these responses are therefore not reasoned opinions within the meaning of the EWS, but letters for the purpose of the so-called political dialogue between national parliaments and the Commission.[14]

The other important type of document that is not covered by the EWS are 'amended drafts' within the meaning of Article 4 of Protocol No. 2 TEU/ TFEU, as well as legislative resolutions of the European Parliament and common positions of the Council in accordance with that provision. These documents also have to be forwarded to national parliaments like draft legislative acts, however the duty to 'consult widely' does not apply to them,[15] nor does the eight-week time freeze,[16] the duty to justify under subsidiarity[17] and the duty to re-justify under the EWS.[18] This means, above all, that if the initiator amends the proposal after or as a result of the EWS, the amended version is not subject to a second round of EWS review. A perhaps unintended side-effect, though, is that another important type of amended draft is excluded from the scope of Protocols No. 1 and 2, namely altered proposals introduced by the Commission under Article 293 (2) TFEU before the Council has adopted a position.[19]

The French National Assembly clearly realised this when it stated, as it reviewed the 2008 proposal for an equal treatment directive,[20] that its positive opinion on subsidiarity compliance was contingent upon the preservation, without amendment, of a crucial provision in the proposal regarding the status of secular state and religious institutions, and that any change to that provision in the course of the legislative process would be likely to affect the chamber's opinion. The EWS would by then be over, however, so any national parliamentary opinions from that moment onwards, as well as attempts to verify whether amendments triggered by the EWS are sufficient, would have to be directed at the legislative institutions themselves: at the European Parliament (for example via fellow members of domestic political party groups), the Council (most probably via one's own government) and/or the Commission (but this time via political dialogue and not the EWS). More generally, this means that for anything beyond the EWS timeframe it is incumbent upon national parliaments themselves to keep track of the remainder of the legislative process, in the course of which amendments may be tabled and adopted.

Some might find it regrettable that the EWS only targets the initiation of the legislative process, but it should not be forgotten that the EWS is just that: an early warning system. To stay with the implied metaphor of missile defences, the system gives a warning of an incoming projectile: it is not a tracking system. Nor, of course, is it an anti-ballistic system that actually shoots missiles down itself: national parliaments' objections do not by themselves amount to a binding veto.

3.3.3 The standards of review: subsidiarity, proportionality and other principles

It is worth pointing out that the Protocol governing the EWS deals with subsidiarity and proportionality, but that reasoned opinions may, strictly speaking, be issued only as regards subsidiarity. Also other related or adjacent principles, notably the presence of a legal basis, are not covered. However, it has been frequently pointed out in the literature, as well as by practitioners, that subsidiarity and proportionality cannot neatly be separated from each other, and that legality review plays a role as well in what is essentially a three-stage test. In the next chapter,[21] we shall take a closer look at the theoretical delimitations of the subsidiarity principle and the definitions that national parliaments themselves appear to be using in EWS practice. It appears that parliaments have a need for a somewhat broader scope for the EWS, and it shall be argued that there are ways to interpret the EWS in a way that accommodates these needs without violating the letter of the law.

3.3.4 *The political dialogue*

The Commission's Barroso initiative proclaimed the establishment of the so-called political dialogue with national parliaments. The Commission is committed to respond to letters it receives from national parliaments. This plays an important role in the context of the EWS. First, the political dialogue is a sort of predecessor of the EWS, in the sense that it formed the basis of a dialogue at a time when the Treaty of Lisbon, and therefore the EWS, was not yet in force. Now that it is in force, the political dialogue remains as a parallel or auxiliary track, but also as an antecedent and subsequent form of communication between the Commission and national parliaments. The objects of the EWS are, after all, draft legislative acts. That by definition excludes consultation documents circulated before an actual proposal is tabled, and it also excludes amendments put forward in the course of the legislative process as well as legislation in force, about which national parliaments may surely have an opinion as well. Letters addressed to the Commission that do not deal with an actual draft legislative act within the EWS period, and letters that do not deal with subsidiarity but with broadly political considerations at any point in time, may be shifted from the EWS into the political dialogue and be answered as such. While national parliaments will still receive a reply, their letter will not count towards the EWS thresholds. It should furthermore be noted that the political dialogue applies only to the Commission and not to other initiators of EU legislation. If a group of Member States is confronted with non-subsidiarity related opinions, they are not obliged to count them as votes under the EWS, nor to answer them, especially if they originate in parliaments of Member States that did not join their initiative.

3.3.5 *Negative review*

It has been pointed out that the EWS review is negative, in that reasoned opinions are solicited only for perceived *breaches* of subsidiarity,[22] which strictly speaking is correct. While Article 3 of Protocol No. 1 broadly speaks of opinions 'whether' subsidiarity is respected, the *lex specialis* of Protocol No. 2

TEU/TFEU is phrased regatively. Some might wish for national parliaments to adopt a more constructive approach to the dialogue with the EU institutions. However, it is submitted that the negative wording of the EWS in fact fits very well with a system where an external actor is invited to check compliance with subsidiarity. Consider, by way of analogy, the judicial review of executive or legislative action in the light of the principle of proportionality: judges are not examining whether a contested action is *proportionate*, only whether it is *dis*proportionate. A verdict stating that a measure is *not* disproportionate may have a number of reasons: 'the court might think the primary decision is correct, or one that the decision-taker was entitled to take, or sufficiently plausible, or it might simply not know, and remain unconvinced by the claimant's case'.[23]

It is true that a number of times national parliaments have been adopting positive reasoned opinions in the context of the EWS, stating that they had found no breach of subsidiarity or agreeing with the Commission that the relevant principles have been observed. This has often occurred in COSAC-sponsored subsidiarity checks where parliaments or chambers had committed to reviewing a particular proposal and then found no breach, but it has also occurred in cases where parliaments or chambers had selected proposals for subsidiarity review on their own. One example of such a case was the proposed Reduced VAT Directive[24] which triggered three positive reasoned opinions, one from the two chambers of the Dutch parliament acting jointly and one from each of the two chambers of the Italian parliament. In that sense, even a negatively framed system may stimulate positive opinions. Still, there are good reasons to retain a negative setup. This also has consequences, of course. As shall be argued in this study, the negative setup is a factor that enhances the resemblance of the EWS to an advice procedure, as opposed to co-legislation,[25] and it even allows us to view it as an accountability mechanism vis-à-vis the Commission.[26]

3.3.6 *The adoption of reasoned opinions: internal parliamentary procedures*

While it might be tempting to take for granted that national parliaments or chambers adopt reasoned opinions, we should inquire whether EU law places any limitations, conditions or other procedural rules on who exactly counts as a national parliament or chamber, and on how such opinions must be adopted. Regarding the question how the term 'national parliaments' is defined for Treaty purposes, it shall be argued that this in fact cannot be an entirely national notion, that Member States, especially their governments, should not have unlimited discretion in assigning powers to internal constitutional bodies if they are meant for national parliaments in the sense of the Treaties, and that other Member States should not be obliged to accept decisions from entities that fall outside that scope.[27]

However, this does not mean that national parliaments should not have a certain margin of autonomy regarding internal procedures. This means above all that reasoned opinions should be deemed valid and admissible if under domestic law they are to be considered to have been adopted by the parliament or chamber as a whole. For example, it is absolutely possible for a national parliament or chamber to delegate the authority to cast a reasoned opinion to one of its committees, whether it is the European affairs committee or a sectoral committee. Nor is there a particular format in which reasoned opinions must be drawn up; they do not even have to be titled 'reasoned opinion' although it shall be recommended that parliaments do label them as such.[28] Thus, a reasoned opinion may take the form of e.g. a letter, motion, resolution or committee report, sent by e-mail or on paper. And EU law certainly does not regulate details such as what the quorum should be for the adoption of a reasoned opinion in a vote, or what kind of majority should apply for such adoption – absolute or relative majority, majorities of component members, of members present or of votes cast. In fact, nothing would preclude a parliament to adopt a procedure whereby the issuing of a reasoned opinion is turned into a minority right. The only precondition for this is that domestic law must stipulate: in other words the parliament as a whole must have authorised, that the minority opinion is deemed to be the opinion of parliament, or that parliament as a whole is obliged to act upon the initiative of a minority. There can then be no dissenting views from the majority. We shall come back to concrete examples of this configuration in the context of the minority's right in some parliaments to trigger an annulment action before the Court of Justice of the EU.[29] Either way, minorities should in no case be allowed to act in their own name and expect their vote to be counted: the minority within parliament is not parliament itself, unless the parliament itself acts upon the minority's initiative or otherwise endorses it.

It should be said that the receipt of minority opinions is not what the Commission seems to have in mind. In the context of the EWS it has in fact requested national parliaments to inform it 'how to ensure that the reasoned opinions the Commission receives represent the established opinion' of the relevant chamber.[30] The political assessment of opinions is indeed difficult if it is not clear whether an opinion came about in a majoritarian or consensual way and how diverging opinions actually were. Be that as it may, whereas 'parliament' usually means 'majority', a national rule stipulating that parliament as a whole must act if a minority so demands is lawful, it is submitted, as part of the domestic legal order.

Consider, as a contrast, German law, where the Basic Law gives State parliaments standing before the Federal Constitutional Court in certain competence questions, an unusual construction in a system based on executive federalism much like the EU's.[31] It is unclear whether a majority decision in a State parliament is required to bring such an action as a matter of federal prerequisite, or whether State (constitutional) legislatures are free to turn this into a minority right as well, and it has been argued that they are in fact not free to do that.[32] But even if they are not free, Germany is much more federal than the EU, in the sense that the federal constitution is much more dominant with respect to State constitutions. For example, the Basic Law requires States to have a representative assembly elected under a set of principles,[33] and these principles are enforceable by way of inter-institutional proceedings before the Federal Constitutional Court (though not by way of complaints by individuals).[34] This is something that the EU does not impose on Member States in such concreteness. Furthermore, German legal doctrine prohibits binding voting instructions from State parliaments to governments in the Bundesrat, arguing that the Bundesrat represents the governments and not the constituent peoples of the States. This, too, is something that the Union under the current setup could not possibly ban with respect to the Council: national parliaments may, and some of them routinely do, subject their own governments to binding instructions for Council meetings.

Thus, as far as the Union is concerned, greater leniency is in order than a federal nation-state might tolerate when it comes to internal voting procedures of national parliaments. We might even add that in some sense minority opinions have greater added value compared with a majority opinion, which tends to coincide with the government's opinion, at least in lower chambers and at least where a majority cabinet is in office. The reason why under national constitutional law certain acts, such as legislation, require parliamentary involvement is that, even while the government majority may ultimately prevail, at least the opposition can make its voice heard.[35] The Danish parliament, for example, routinely and rather helpfully includes accounts of internal deliberations in its reasoned opinions, indicating which political parties endorsed the majority viewpoint and which ones expressed a dissenting opinion. It is submitted that the Commission should be interested in hearing opposition views, if only for the utilitarian reason that this very opposition may be in power by the time a proposed directive is adopted and must be transposed into national law, but also because it is the opposition, as well as dissenting upper chambers, that can act as a healthy corrective and that are the actual engine behind pluralism. Legally, as long as a national parliament's opinion is uniform, it cannot matter to the EU whether it came about by majority, super-majority or minority vote.

3.4 Reasoned opinions: voting thresholds

As a general rule, the EWS is formally triggered if one-third of the votes constitute reasoned opinions against a proposal. The wording is important: it is not one-third of *parliaments*, as one sometimes hears in summaries for the sake of simplicity, but one-third of *votes*, i.e. 18 out of 54 total votes in the EU-27, two per Member State. The exception are proposals regarding the area of freedom, security and justice (AFSJ) where a lower threshold of one-quarter of votes, or 18 votes in the EU-27, applies. Both the general rule and the AFSJ exception had already been part of the original Draft Constitutional Treaty proposed by the Convention. The new element inserted by the Lisbon Treaty is the so-called orange card procedure which is triggered in the ordinary legislative procedure if more than half the votes constitute objections, i.e. 28 votes

Table 3.1 EWS voting thresholds and consequences

	Absolute number (EU-27)	Attained by, for example:	Consequence
One-quarter of total votes	14	7 parliaments; 4 parliaments and 6 chambers	Review of a proposal under Article 76 TFEU, statement of reasons for maintaining it
One-third of total votes	18	9 parliaments; 5 parliaments and 8 chambers	Review of any proposal, statement of reasons for maintaining it
Majority of total votes	28	14 parliaments; 7 parliaments and 14 chambers	Review of any proposal, statement of reasons for maintaining it; and, if ordinary legislative procedure applies: subsidiarity justification, review by EP and Council who may reject the proposal if it is maintained

in the EU-27. The most important result is that if the Commission chooses to maintain the proposal in such circumstances, the Council and the European Parliament may stop the consideration of the proposal before the conclusion of the first reading. The Protocol, by the way, does not provide for a lower total if not all Member States participate in a policy area, such as Schengen. Thus, even parliaments of non-participating Member States are entitled to cast a vote, and shares are still based on a total of 54 votes.

3.4.1 The yellow card

The consequence of the famous yellow card, as it had been inserted already in the Convention's original Draft Constitutional Treaty, is that the initiator of the contested draft legislative act must review the proposal. He may then maintain, withdraw or amend the proposal, but he must state reasons for maintaining it without amendment (and, less pertinently, also for amending or withdrawing it). This procedure is laid down in Article 7 of Protocol No. 2 TEU/TFEU:

> (2) Where reasoned opinions on a draft legislative act's non-compliance with the principle of subsidiarity represent at least one third of all the votes allocated to the national Parliaments in accordance with the second subparagraph of paragraph 1, the draft must be reviewed. This threshold shall be a quarter in the case of a draft legislative act submitted on the basis of Article 76 of the Treaty on the Functioning of the European Union on the area of freedom, security and justice.
>
> After such review, the Commission or, where appropriate, the group of Member States, the European Parliament, the Court of Justice, the

European Central Bank or the European Investment Bank, if the draft legislative act originates from them, may decide to maintain, amend or withdraw the draft. Reasons must be given for this decision.

No further consequences attach to the yellow card. The 'reasons' to be given for maintaining a proposal do not, strictly speaking, have to relate to subsidiarity, but there are valid arguments to hold that in fact the reasons *must* be a rebuttal explaining why in the initiator's opinion subsidiarity is nevertheless respected. It would defy the logic of the EWS as a means to extract more thorough justification regarding subsidiarity compliance if rebuttals could ignore the principle altogether, especially since the parliaments' reasoned opinions are expected to deal with subsidiarity only.

3.4.2 *The orange card*

The orange card has been a much-noted addition provided by the Lisbon Treaty with respect to the original Constitutional Treaty where the EWS was limited to the yellow card. Yet again, the wording of the provisions governing the orange card mechanism is important. First of all, unlike the yellow card, which applies to all draft legislative acts, the orange card applies to the ordinary legislative procedure only. Let us revisit the wording of the third paragraph of Article 7 of Protocol No. 2 TEU/TFEU:

(3) Furthermore, under the ordinary legislative procedure, where reasoned opinions on the non-compliance of a proposal for a legislative act with the principle of subsidiarity represent at least a simple majority of the votes allocated to the national Parliaments in accordance with the second subparagraph of paragraph 1, the proposal must be reviewed. After such review, the Commission may decide to maintain, amend or withdraw the proposal.

If it chooses to maintain the proposal, the Commission will have, in a reasoned opinion, to justify why it considers that the proposal complies with the principle of subsidiarity. This reasoned opinion, as well as the reasoned opinions of the national Parliaments, will have to be submitted to the Union legislator, for consideration in the procedure:

(a) before concluding the first reading, the legislator (the European Parliament and the Council) shall consider whether the legislative proposal is compatible with the principle of subsidiarity, taking particular account of the reasons expressed and shared by the majority of national Parliaments as well as the reasoned opinion of the Commission;

(b) if, by a majority of 55% of the members of the Council or a majority of the votes cast in the European Parliament, the legislator is of the opinion that the proposal is not compatible with the principle of subsidiarity, the legislative proposal shall not be given further consideration.

Regarding the threshold, the drafters of the Lisbon Treaty saw fit to use the word 'simple majority' in the relevant passage on the orange card procedure, presumably in order to make the mechanism appear easily triggered. However, the term 'simple majority' is misleading, because what it denotes here is in fact not a *simple* majority but an *absolute* majority. The reason is that the provision refers to 'at least a simple majority of the votes allocated to the national Parliaments in accordance with the second subparagraph of paragraph 1' of Article 7 of Protocol No. 2 TEU/TFEU, which in turn means two votes per national parliament, or 54 votes in a Union of 27 Member States. Consequently, this so-called 'simple majority' describes a share of the total votes available, not of the votes actually cast, and therefore cannot mean anything else than more than half of 54. And that is, of course, the famous 50% + 1 or, in other words, an absolute majority. Let us not allow ourselves to believe that the orange card procedure's threshold is any lower than it actually is simply because the Lisbon Treaty contains misleading terminology.

Regarding the consequences of the orange card procedure, its triggering imposes four distinct obligations. The first obligation is for the Commission to review the proposal. That obligation, of course, would arise already well before an absolute majority of votes is reached, namely under the yellow card already after one-quarter or one-third, depending on the subject-area. This obligation is therefore not unique to the orange card as it sets in already at a lower threshold.

The second obligation is for the Commission to adopt a reasoned opinion of its own, stating why subsidiarity is nonetheless respected, in order to justify that it maintains a proposal without amendment. Depending on the point of view, this may seem light since the Commission is obliged to provide such a justification anyway, and it may seem like the opposite: a stricter justification requirement that goes beyond the mere duty to state 'reasons' for maintaining a proposal as it applies under the yellow card. It is submitted that effectively the re-justification standard under the yellow and orange card is the same. The Commission cannot plausibly omit a justification on subsidiarity grounds in its yellow card 'reasons', while it cannot plausibly just repeat its original justification under the orange card either, without rebutting explicitly the opinions of the national parliaments.

The third obligation is for the European Parliament and the Council to review the proposal again in the light of subsidiarity if the Commission chooses to maintain it without amendment. This element deserves a closer look. The European Parliament and the Council are, in their legislative capacity, bound to respect the principle of subsidiarity in any case,[36] even if not a single national parliament objects, and the first reading is arguably a good moment to consider compliance with this principle anyway. Furthermore, it would be strange if the European Parliament and the Council were to review the proposal only if the Commission chooses to maintain the original proposal. What if the Commission does amend the proposal, but not in a satisfactory way? After all, there is a reason why reasoned opinions are sent not only to the Commission but also to the presidencies of the European Parliament and the

Council. Again, the general obligation to respect subsidiarity would require a review even if a proposal gets amended as a result of the EWS, not just if it is maintained. This holds true if the orange card is triggered, but also if only the yellow one is triggered and, indeed, if neither of them is triggered. The crucial addition may be a requirement of an additional justification: not just why the Commission maintains the proposal, or finds that it complies with subsidiarity, but also why the European Parliament and the Council agree (or disagree) with the Commission. How crucial exactly the addition is depends on how strict the duty to justify is taken, notably in judicial review. In a light scenario, the adoption by the Council and the European Parliament of a legislative act may be taken to simply imply their agreement with the Commission; if the review takes a more robust form, however, the act would not be valid without at least a recital in the preamble stating that the national parliaments' objections have been taken into account but were wholly or partly overruled. One of the main themes of this study is that much of the EWS revolves not around the right to veto but around the duty to justify. In that light, a more robust approach to the duty to justify would be very welcome.

The fourth obligation, or perhaps rather right, is for the European Parliament and the Council to stop the consideration of a proposal if one of them finds that a maintained proposal violates subsidiarity. Of course, again we should point out that under the general rule to comply with subsidiarity the duty to reject proposals that breach the principle does not end after the first reading. Article 1 of Protocol No. 2 TEU/TFEU commits each EU institution to 'constant respect' for the principles of subsidiarity and proportionality, whereby there is no reason to exclude the legislative process from 'constant'. If subsequent amendments to an initial proposal would result in a breach, the EU legislator is obliged to reject them just as well, also in the second and third reading. This is all the more important since the EWS applies to proposals but not to their subsequent amendments,[37] which may change the original version in such a way that it changes the implications for the draft's subsidiarity compliance.

What has to be borne in mind whenever the orange card is discussed is that the Council and the European Parliament act by (qualified) majority. In order to determine that a maintained proposal violates subsidiarity, the Council acts by a majority of 55% of its members and the European Parliament by a majority of votes cast. Do national parliamentary objections therefore make proposals any more vulnerable to defeat?

What is undoubtedly true is that the European Parliament can issue its veto against the Council more easily and earlier than usual. In the ordinary legislative procedure, the European Parliament may reject the Council's position and thereby veto the proposal only in second reading, and only by a majority of its component members.[38] With the orange card triggered, the rejection may take place already in the first reading and by a lighter majority, namely a majority of votes cast. Yet what is also true is that a triggered orange card does not make a proposal any more vulnerable to defeat by *minorities*.

After all, early rejection still requires a majority in the European Parliament, even though it is just a majority of votes cast, or a qualified majority in the Council, even though at just 55% of members and no further conditions it is a lighter qualified majority than the regular qualified majority under Article 16 TEU. Therefore, at a more practical level, it is fair to say that if 55% of Member States in the Council object to a proposal, it would never have been adopted anyway: with or without an orange card, neither in the first nor in the second or third reading. For if a qualified majority is opposed for whatever reason, there can by definition be no qualified majority in favour, which is what is needed for an act's endorsement in the Council in the ordinary procedure. To put it differently: '[D]ropping the proposal in the subsidiarity procedure requires majorities that would have [led] to [a] rejection of the proposal'.[39] Or, in other words, a usual blocking minority is still enough to shelve the proposal; the orange card does not change that fact.

Again, it should all come down to a duty to re-justify, notably the duty for the majority adopting the act to state in the preamble that the majority opinion under the EWS and the minority opinion in the Council and the European Parliament have not prevailed and, ideally, why it is that they have not prevailed. In the absence of such explicit justification under a triggered orange card regime, it is absolutely legitimate to raise the question whether the act is lawfully adopted at all, and thus whether defeated Member States and their national parliaments are really obliged to transpose it into national law and whether the European judiciary, including the Court of Justice as well as national (constitutional) courts, are really obliged to uphold it. The more seriously we take the EWS, and the duties to justify that the EWS protects, the more likely the answer should be no.

3.4.3 *Cumulative or alternative procedures*

As a matter of brief intermezzo, a few words should be devoted to the question of whether the yellow and orange cards are alternative variations of the EWS or whether the orange card is cumulatively added to the yellow card if it is triggered. The reason why this question is discussed is because it has been raised in a questionnaire for the purposes of the 2010 FIDE conference in Madrid and replies turned out to be surprisingly diverse.[40] The problem revolved around the word 'furthermore' at the beginning of Article 7 (3) of Protocol No. 2 TEU/TFEU which describes the orange card mechanism that, as said, applies to the ordinary legislative procedure only. What is then perceived as problematic is that the orange card restates the Commission's obligation to 'review' the proposal, like in the yellow card, but it does not restate its obligation to give reasons in case it maintains a proposal, whereas it does compel the Commission to issue a reasoned opinion of its own stating why it believes that subsidiarity is nevertheless respected. The Hungarian and Irish replies to the FIDE questionnaire stated that there was no clear consensus on whether the orange card produces effects on top of the yellow card consequences or whether yellow and orange cards were alternatives whereby the yellow card would not apply to the ordinary legislative procedure.[41] The Cypriot reply argued that they were clearly alternative mechanisms;[42] but the replies from Portugal,[43] Luxembourg,[44] Germany,[45] Slovenia[46] and the Czech Republic[47] – all correctly, it is submitted – indicated that the two were considered as cumulative facilities.

The reason why some authors even suspect the two cards may be alternatives is that they assume that the duty to give reasons for maintaining a proposal under the yellow card, and the duty to issue a reasoned opinion on subsidiarity compliance under the orange card, could be two different things. It is again submitted, however, that substantively these two types of re-justification cannot differ from each other. In both cases the Commission will have to press its point about subsidiarity compliance in order to maintain a proposal. The two types of justification could only be different things if under the yellow card the Commission were allowed to put forward reasons for a proposal's maintenance which are *not* related to subsidiarity: for example, if the Commission would state that it maintains a proposal due to political expediency. It is hard to accept that such a non-subsidiarity justification would be valid in the EWS system, even under the yellow card that merely requires reasons in general. It would not be plausible either if the Commission were to give as a yellow card reason that it deemed that the EWS threshold had not been reached because some national parliamentary opinions were inadmissible. For if the Commission does not consider the EWS to have been triggered, there is no duty for it to give reasons in the first place. Nor could the Commission limit itself, in its orange card justification, to simply repeating the subsidiarity reasons that it had been obliged to furnish under Article 5 of the Protocol in the first place, and that the Council and the European Parliament are already aware of, without violating the object and purpose of the EWS. Also here, subsidiarity-related arguments that explicitly address the subsidiarity-related objections brought forward by national parliaments are in order.

Thus, the yellow card applies to all procedures and the orange card only to the ordinary procedure. Where a proposal under a special procedure is challenged by a third of the votes, the yellow card applies as usual and where it is challenged by more than half the votes, then still only the yellow card will have been triggered, because it is not the ordinary procedure. And this does make sense. If a special procedure does not include the European Parliament as a co-legislator, then in the prevailing logic of the Treaties there is little reason to give it the right to veto proposals under subsidiarity or otherwise; if a special procedure does not envisage the Commission as the initiator of proposals, it would be absurd to force it to review or maintain a proposal that it had not authored in the first place.

It may well be that the orange card, grafted as it is by the Lisbon Treaty on top of the yellow card that had existed already under the Constitutional Treaty, had been formulated a bit hastily. Still, there is no reason for us to assume that the two cards are alternatives. They are cumulative procedures, and they are triggered depending on how many reasoned opinions are cast, with the exception that the orange card can only be triggered in the ordinary legislative procedure.

3.4.4 Partial breaches

Theoretically an EU legislative proposal can violate the subsidiarity principle either in its entirety or by virtue of one or several individual provisions. Protocol No. 2 TEU/TFEU does not regulate the distinctions between wholesale and partial breaches. A reasoned opinion may however very well challenge only one aspect of a proposal. The empirical record shows that this is in fact quite common, in that national parliaments would argue that in one respect a proposal goes too far. An example is the EU succession certificate proposal to which several parliaments had objections specifically to the extent that the proposal might undermine the mandatory minimum inheritance share for privileged categories of heirs.[48] Similarly, in its opinion on an EU proposal on jurisdiction in matrimonial matters,[49] the Hungarian parliament pointed out very aptly:

> A problem stubbornly persists in so far that, when presenting justifications for proposals, the application of the subsidiarity principle is only ever examined in relation to the proposal as a whole, even though individual parts or provisions may equally be in breach of the subsidiarity principle. In the current case, for example, the amendment of provisions relating to jurisdiction and the introduction of new rules pertaining to applicable law should clearly have been treated separately.

And also the UK House of Commons European Scrutiny Committee stresses that breaches by the whole proposal are 'very rare' whereas breaches by one of the provisions are 'less rare'.[50] As far as the EWS is concerned, it appears neither from the text of Protocol No. 2 TEU/TFEU nor from the Commission's responses to reasoned opinions in practice that allegations of partial breaches as such are somehow inadmissible. To the contrary: the definition of subsidiarity in Article 5 (3) TEU allows for EU action not only 'if' but also 'in so far as' the criteria are complied with, and the EWS stipulates that the initiator may *amend* the proposal,[51] indicating that the EWS does foresee partial rectification and thus, evidently, partial objections in the first place. The vote value of a partial objection is still two for unicameral parliaments and one for chambers of bicameral parliaments. Partial breaches are to be counted as breaches by the proposal as a whole. Separate justifications of individual provisions of a proposal might be welcome for many reasons, if only to bolster a more diligent attitude towards the justification of proposals in general, but even then a negative reasoned opinion regarding one such provision would not diminish that opinion's vote value under the EWS.

3.4.5 *Objections for diverging reasons*

One question that the provisions on the EWS leave somewhat open is what happens if one and the same proposal is challenged for different reasons. Protocol No. 2 TEU/TFEU does not explicitly regulate such an event, but the empirical record indicates that this happens regularly whenever several parliaments respond to the same proposal. That in turn is usually the case when COSAC conducts a collective review, but it occasionally happens, albeit on a much smaller scale, outside the COSAC framework as well. The Commission has indicated to national parliaments that it considers all incoming reasoned opinions under the EWS as counting towards the relevant thresholds even when they are based on divergent grounds.[52] And in the light of the logic of the EWS, this is indeed the correct thing to do. The alternative would be an artificial splitting up of the vote with several counts per type of objection, which would not appear to be justified by the rather broad wording of the relevant provisions of Protocol No. 2 TEU/TFEU. It should be pointed out, though, that the Commission's undertaking to keep only one count per proposal, and not per type of objection, is not binding upon the other initiators of draft legislative acts within the meaning of the EWS. These also include a group of Member States, the European Parliament, the Court of Justice, the European Central Bank and the European Investment Bank.[53]

3.5 Timeframe

In principle the time period during which the EWS may be triggered with respect to an EU legislative proposal is, in a nutshell, eight weeks. The Constitutional Treaty, as well as the Convention's Draft Constitutional Treaty, still stipulated a period of six weeks, which corresponds with the six weeks of minimum scrutiny delay that had been introduced by the Treaty of Amsterdam. The period has, however, been extended to eight weeks by the Treaty of Lisbon. Yet there is more to the timeframe than that, and it is crucial to have clarity on this considering how tight a national parliament's agenda is. Every day counts. We shall therefore consider the following practicalities: when exactly do the eight weeks start; when do they end; and what are the specific rules governing the summer month of August, which the Commission has agreed to not count?

3.5.1 *The start of the period. I: The availability of language versions*

When exactly do the eight weeks start? In the English version of Protocol No. 2 TEU/TFEU we are confronted with a rather alarming case of confusing punctuation. This may sound pedantic, and it probably is, but here a glitch in the translation actually alters the meaning of the text. The first sentence of Article 6 of the Protocol reads:

> Any national Parliament (. . .) may, within eight weeks from the date of transmission of a draft legislative act, in the official languages of the Union, send (. . .) a reasoned opinion (. . .)

The question is: what does the sub-clause 'in the official languages of the Union' refer to? Does it refer to the transmission of the act in the official languages, or to the languages in which reasoned opinions may be drafted? The problem is the second comma, after the word 'act'. Without the comma, it would be clear that the eight-week period starts after the transmission of a proposal in the official languages of the Union, meaning as soon as the last language version has been transmitted. With the comma in place, though, the sentence appears to say that for each parliament the eight weeks count individually starting with the transmission, and that each parliament is merely entitled to send a reasoned opinion in any official language of the Union. True, this would be an odd thing to stipulate, for it is hard to imagine why a parliament would write a letter in a language other than its own, but it might also mean that parliaments actually *are* free to write in their own language as opposed to just English or French.

The provision's German version contains no commas in the relevant clause whatsoever and can therefore mean both things, but the punctuation in the French version is absolutely clear: the sub-clause refers to the transmission of the act, so that the eight-week period starts with the last language version transmitted. After all:

> Tout parlement national (. . .) peut, dans un délai de huit semaines à compter de la date de transmission d'un projet d'acte législatif dans les langues officielles de l'Union, adresser (. . .) un avis motivé (. . .)

The punctuation in the Dutch and Portuguese versions of Article 6 mirrors the English version, implying that parliaments may write their opinions in any official language. The Bulgarian, Czech, Italian, Polish, Romanian, Spanish and Swedish versions however mirror the French one, implying that the eight-week period starts when all language versions have been transmitted.

For the Commission, as well as from a common sense point of view, the answer is clear and has been communicated to the national parliaments: the eight weeks start when the last language version has been transmitted.[54] This is also supported by the parallelism with Article 4 of Protocol No. 1 TEU/TFEU, which stipulates an eight-week scrutiny delay and which does not contain any superfluous commas in the English version:

> An eight-week period shall elapse between a draft legislative act being made available to national Parliaments in the official languages of the Union and the date when it is placed on a provisional agenda for the Council (. . .)

Furthermore, we should note the contrast with the equivalent text of the current Article 6 of Protocol No. 2 TEU/TFEU in the Constitutional Treaty,[55] Lisbon's immediate predecessor, which did not contain any reference to the language versions at all and simply stated:

> Any national Parliament (. . .) may, within six weeks from the date of transmission of a draft European legislative act, send (. . .) a reasoned opinion (. . .)

It is most likely that, without any bad faith on the part of the drafters, this wording of the Constitutional Treaty simply failed to take into account the fact that in practice the transmission of proposals is not simultaneous in all language versions. COSAC had noted this already in October 2005, stating that the review period, which at the time was six weeks rather than eight, 'should begin when the proposal has been published in all languages'.[56] And such a provision is surely justified empirically, for the disparities can be significant. The Cypriot parliament reported a two-week delay in the transmission of the Greek translation of the 2006 postal services directive dated 18 October 2006,[57] receiving it only on 31 October 2006. Under the current EWS, if these delays were not to be taken into account, this would have deprived the parliament of a quarter of the allocated time. The Czech version of the same proposal, according to the Czech Senate, was made available even later, on 7 November 2006.

Still, once more the quality of legal translation is highlighted. The Union would be well advised to adopt a corrigendum to fix the punctuation in Article 6 of Protocol No. 2 TEU/TFEU where it distorts the meaning of the text and leads to discrepancies between language versions, all of which are supposedly equally authentic. This is advisable especially since the Commission's letter is not binding on the other categories of initiators of draft legislative acts: a group of Member States, the European Parliament, the Court of Justice, the European Central Bank and the European Investment Bank.[58]

3.5.2 *The start of the period. II: The transmission of acts*

From a lawyer's point of view, Protocol No. 2 TEU/TFEU may furthermore have been clearer as to when exactly the period starts in another respect. Is it when the last language version has been *sent* or when it has been *received*? The text stipulates as a reference, eight weeks 'from the date of transmission' of proposals,[59] so neither of their posting nor of their receipt.

The Commission stated in a letter to the national parliaments that it starts counting the eight weeks 'with the transmission of the *lettre de saisine*', the formal transmission letter that is sent to all national parliaments informing them that the last language version of a document has been transmitted.[60] The Commission clarified upon enquiry that the date of that last transmission is considered to be the date that is stated on the transmission letter.[61] This means that the reference point is the sending rather than the receipt of the reference letter. To be on the safe side, the Commission committed itself to circulating weekly inventories of documents sent to national parliaments with the request to notify it if not all of the items in the inventory have been received, extending in case of non-receipt of legislative proposals the EWS deadline for that particular parliament – though not for the other parliaments – to compensate for the delay.[62]

Private law scholars might argue whether the 'transmission' of a document, by analogy with an offer and acceptance for a contract, is only complete when the document has been received or when it has been dispatched. But as far as the Commission is concerned all this will surely not matter much since it put in place the described confirmation safeguards, and anyway the transmission of documents is meant to be electronic, and hence near-instantaneous. The Commission has asked all national parliaments to designate a functional mailbox for this purpose,[63] and it also confirmed upon enquiry that it indeed communicates with all national parliaments via e-mail.[64] Practically, the only problem in this regard might arise where e-mail malfunctions or where communication otherwise takes place by regular mail, and where the initiator of legislation is not the Commission. After all, the Commission's transmission facilities and safeguards are not binding upon, for example, groups of Member States in their capacity as initiators of draft legislative acts.

3.5.3 The end of the period. I: The regular procedure

A related question regarding the timeframe is when exactly the eight-week period ends. What is decisive: whether a national parliament sent, or whether the Commission received a reasoned opinion within the eight-week period? On this the Protocol[65] does provide something of a guideline, though:

> Any national Parliament (. . .) may, within eight weeks (. . .) *send* to the Presidents of the European Parliament, the Council and the Commission a reasoned opinion (. . .) [emphasis added]

which implies that for the response the date of the posting of the reasoned opinion is decisive, not the date of receipt. The Commission confirmed upon enquiry that reasoned opinions are admissible if they have been sent in time even if they arrive too late, but it also noted that this situation is hypothetical as communication is effected via e-mail.[66] Still, national parliaments would be well-advised to notify the Commission by direct means if it chose to send a reasoned opinion on the very last day of the period by regular mail.

Incidentally, the *sending* of a reasoned opinion is decisive, not the day of its adoption by a committee or the plenary. Otherwise the delayed and eventually tardy transmission of adopted reasoned opinions would undermine the EWS timeframe as regulated by Protocol No. 2 TEU/TFEU and make it vulnerable to potential manipulation through backdating.

3.5.4 *The end of the period. II: Urgency override*

Article 6 of Protocol No. 2 TEU/TFEU by itself does guarantee the national parliaments an eight-week period for the purposes of the EWS. However it must be noted that Article 4 of Protocol No. 1 TEU/TFEU, which mirrors the EWS in that it also requires an eight-week scrutiny delay, contains an urgency clause that the EWS provision does not have. It reads:

> An eight-week period shall elapse between a draft legislative act being made available to national Parliaments in the official languages of the Union and the date when it is placed on a provisional agenda for the Council for its adoption or for adoption of a position under a legislative procedure. Exceptions shall be possible in cases of urgency, the reasons for which shall be stated in the act or position of the Council. Save in urgent cases for which due reasons have been given, no agreement may be reached on a draft legislative act during those eight weeks. Save in urgent cases for which due reasons have been given, a ten-day period shall elapse between the placing of a draft legislative act on the provisional agenda for the Council and the adoption of a position.

Technically, the eight weeks for the EWS from Protocol No. 2 are left unaffected by the fact that the eight weeks for general scrutiny from Protocol No. 1 have been overridden for reasons of urgency. Practically, however, it might make little sense for national parliaments to continue with subsidiarity review under the EWS if the Council and/or the European Parliament have already expressed a position or where the act itself has already been adopted.[67] This is either an accidental discrepancy between the two Protocols, in that both of them envisage the same time period but one of them contains an escape clause, or a deliberate decision to make the EWS subject to an urgency override. In either case, the practical outcome is the same. With the modest exception of the last-minute amendment of an already-tabled proposal under Article 293 (2) TFEU, proposals that have entered the legislative process proper cannot plausibly be halted in the manner foreseen by the yellow and orange cards of the EWS, even though all institutions of course remain bound to respect subsidiarity at all times, including the legislative process.

It must be concluded that the EWS is effectively subject to an emergency override. What legal consequences should follow from such override, then? If the act has been adopted and national parliaments did not have the full eight weeks at their disposal to conduct subsidiarity review due to the urgency override from Protocol No. 1, then it would be absurd to only count the votes of those parliaments and chambers that had managed to express reasoned opinions in time and go on to conclude that the EWS has not been triggered. Instead, it must be concluded that subsidiarity review was abortive and did not take place for reasons outside the parliaments' control. Parliamentarians or chambers which feel they have been unlawfully deprived of their opportunity to express themselves should be encouraged to press, if domestic arrangements are in place, for an annulment action within two months of the act's publication invoking Article 8 of Protocol No. 2 TEU/ TFEU.[68] They should then allege an infringement of the principle of subsidiarity on procedural grounds. The Court of Justice should in such case be invited to review whether reasons for the urgency pursuant to Article 4 of Protocol No. 1 TEU/TFEU have been given and whether those reasons are sufficient, for those are the same reasons that would have to justify the cutting short of not only the general scrutiny delay but also the EWS. If the reasons are deemed sufficient, both Protocol No. 1 and Protocol No. 2 will have been respected; if not, both should be considered breached.

3.5.5 *Means to buy extra time*

National parliaments can gain additional time in several ways. Of course, in the interest of fostering mutual trust in inter-institutional relations, tricks effected in bad faith, such as wrongly claiming that a draft act has not been received, or fraudulently backdating reasoned opinions, shall not be given consideration here. For there are also legitimate ways.

First, as noted, some language versions of EU legislative proposals take longer to produce than others, so the receipt of a proposal in a parliament's own official language does not necessarily mean that it is the last one to receive its version. This in turn means that from the date of receipt there may be more than eight weeks available. Second, if a parliament, its support staff or committee are able and willing to consider proposals in a language other than their own, they gain additional time as they can start reviewing them even before their own version has arrived. After all, proposals are published online as well. Still more time can be gained by considering consultation documents at early stages of decision-making, as some parliaments do routinely, although such exercises would not fall under EWS but, if letters are sent, would be considered as part of the political dialogue.

More generally, command of languages is crucial to active national parliaments for other reasons as well. Communication with other national parliaments, via the IPEX inter-parliamentary database or otherwise, is greatly facilitated if it takes place in languages that are mutually understood. Moreover, impact assessments are typically available in English and French, but in other EU languages only short summaries are available. This the Lithuanian parliament pointed out rather dryly when reviewing a proposal for a new framework decision on the fight against terrorism:[69]

> The Lithuanian version of the Impact Assessment was a 5-page summary of the 107 pages in the English language.

Since impact assessments may contain crucial reasoning and evidence not contained in the legislative proposal proper, its consideration should add to the depth of the review – even though it is submitted that it is incumbent upon the initiator of legislation to sufficiently justify proposals under subsidiarity headings in all official languages, and not just via a brief reference to other documents that are available only in some languages.

Finally, if a national parliament or chamber wishes to enjoy some more time for its ex ante consideration of EU initiatives, apart from starting earlier, it remains free to impose, if the necessary arrangements under domestic law and practice are in place, a scrutiny reserve upon its own government in the Council. This will not prevent an act's transmission to the Council and the European Parliament but may at least somewhat delay the Council vote.

3.5.6 *The month of August*

For the Commission, August does not count for EWS purposes so that the parliamentary summer recess – as well as the Commission's own holidays – can be taken into account.[70] Is it legal for the Commission to agree to such an arrangement unilaterally? If we adopt a teleological interpretation of the EWS, the extension of the eight-week period does not amount to a violation of the Protocol because the object and purpose of the period is to guarantee a *minimum* delay, not an exact or maximum delay, for the benefit of national parliamentary scrutiny. The eight weeks from Article 6 of Protocol No. 2 TEU/TFEU correspond with the eight weeks guaranteed under Article 4 of Protocol No. 1 TEU/TFEU on the role of national parliaments in the EU, which had been there since before the EWS was introduced, namely in the form of the six-week minimum scrutiny delay introduced with the Treaty of Amsterdam.

Still, we should not forget two important consequences of this arrangement. First, while the Commission has declared its willingness to not count August for EWS purposes, other initiators of EU draft legislative acts in the sense of the EWS are not bound by this commitment. These are a group of Member States,[71] the European Parliament, the Court of Justice, the European Central Bank and the European Investment Bank.[72] Second, the non-counting of August applies to August only, not to other periods when a national parliament may be in recess. The Christmas recess for instance, which became relevant in the COSAC review of a proposal of December 2008,[73] is not covered. And more generally, the EWS periods are not halted if one or more parliaments or chambers are otherwise prevented from participating in the EWS due to not being in session or due to being dissolved awaiting elections. On the bright side, August is not counted even if a national parliament should not actually be in recess, e.g. because its European affairs committee keeps working through the summer.

3.6 The EWS and regional parliaments

The parliaments of regions with legislative powers are a separate category of institutions mentioned by the EWS. Article 6 of Protocol No. 2 TEU/TFEU envisages that national parliaments or chambers may consult, 'where appropriate', regional parliaments with legislative powers before issuing a reasoned opinion. It does make sense to include at least a reference to regions in the context of the subsidiarity principle, considering that Article 5 (3) TEU is not based on a simple juxtaposition between the Union and the Member States' national level, but explicitly stipulates the possibility that some competences can in fact be better exercised at regional or local level. It is also presumably for that reason that the Committee of the Regions has the right to bring annulment actions against EU legislation for breaches of subsidiarity before the Court of Justice if it had to be consulted in the legislative process.[74] The Protocol does however not grant regional parliaments the right to submit reasoned opinions (or bring annulment actions, for that matter) in their own right, which is an issue to which we shall return below when discussing the peculiar case of Belgium.[75] As far as the text of Protocol No. 2 TEU/TFEU is concerned, the provisions on the EWS address *national* parliaments, which in turn may, where applicable and where appropriate, but by no means by way of an obligation, consult the parliaments of regions with legislative powers. It might be added that they may consult assemblies of regions *without* legislative powers as well, just like they may consult municipalities or, in fact, anyone they want.

A relatively literal implementation of the idea of ex ante consultation of regional parliaments has been carried out in Spain, where the parliaments of autonomous communities have four weeks, out of the total eight weeks, to provide an opinion to the national parliament.[76] However, a report commissioned by the Committee of the Regions highlights the fact that, even though there is much enthusiasm about the EWS, most regional parliaments in the EU are ill-equipped and understaffed to perform subsidiarity checks within time constraints that are even tighter than those of national parliaments.[77] In that light, it is submitted that the EWS proper may not be the best means of making regional voices heard. First, in the light of scarce time and resources, for a region as a whole it might make sense to maximise input by letting the regional *government* rather than the regional parliament formulate a regional opinion. Second, for a region as a whole, it might make sense to submit its regional opinion directly to the national government rather than the national parliament, and directly to the Commission and the Council presidency, to the parliaments and governments of other Member States, especially neighbouring ones with which close ties exist, to the European Parliament as well as to individual MEPs, especially MEPs elected in the relevant region where applicable. There is no reason why regional opinions should be relayed, especially if they do not count as EWS votes anyway. And again, it should be recalled that pursuant to Article 8 of Protocol No. 2 TEU/TFEU the Committee of the Regions, though again not the regions or their parliaments in their own right, also has standing to bring direct annulment actions on subsidiarity grounds before the Court of Justice of the EU, an aspect of subsidiarity enforcement that shall also be discussed hereafter.

3.7 The EWS and the judiciary

While the discussion so far has focused on the carrying out of subsidiarity review by parliaments, our considerations would not be complete without taking into account the judiciary as well. Courts may in fact play a quite active role in the context of the EWS. Their involvement can be triggered under three separate headings. First, national courts may be involved by national parliaments in the drawing up of reasoned opinions. Second, under the most visible but arguably not the most relevant heading, once EU legislation has entered into force, the Court of Justice of the EU has jurisdiction to hear annulment actions for alleged breaches of subsidiarity to be brought by Member States or 'notified by them in accordance with their legal order on behalf of their national Parliament or a chamber thereof'.[78] Third, the Court of Justice might take into account reasoned opinions in any other type of procedure, notably in preliminary reference procedures, in order to rule on the validity of EU legislation. The same applies to national (constitutional) courts if they were ever to carry out their threat of reviewing secondary EU legislation.

3.7.1 *National courts in the EWS*

Whereas the EWS is meant to be used by national parliaments rather than courts, there is no legal reason why judicial opinion should be excluded from parliamentary will-formation. Judicial review does not necessarily have to be limited to the ex post stage. Claes rightly notes that EC/EU secondary law acquires its special characteristics, notably its supremacy, from the moment of its entry into force, not from the moment of its initiation. And there is no reason to assume that a preliminary review of proposals, if it is readily accepted and even encouraged regarding national parliaments, would be inadmissible if it were to be carried out by national courts.[79] In fact, the parliament of Lithuania reports that the national supreme court already is a contributor of advisory opinions in the context of the EWS.[80]

Thus, there is nothing to preclude courts from conducting preventive review of the legality, whether or not specifically the subsidiarity compliance, of proposed EU legislation. Actually, this study shall argue that there is furthermore nothing to prevent parliaments *themselves* from checking the legality of EU proposals, as opposed to their political merits.[81] A normative concern regarding the judiciary might be that while it is not unlawful for national courts to supply advisory opinions if domestic law allows for it, this might result in awkward and perhaps needlessly confrontational situations where a court, especially a constitutional court, is asked to pronounce itself ex post on the validity of EU legislation on which, at the ex ante stage, it had already issued an opinion. This might needlessly juridicise political decision-making at EU level, provoke litigation and make it hard for national courts to revise their own opinion afterwards. This might furthermore explicitly turn courts into co-legislators which, constitutionally speaking, is not unproblematic to begin with.[82] Thus, a national court seized to supply an advisory opinion and forced to give an answer might be wise, and might in fact be expected, to limit its opinion to very general observations based on very lenient review.

3.7.2 Annulment actions

The first paragraph of Article 8 of Protocol No. 2 TEU/TFEU reads as follows:

> The Court of Justice of the European Union shall have jurisdiction in actions on grounds of infringement of the principle of subsidiarity by a legislative act, brought in accordance with the rules laid down in Article 263 of the Treaty on the Functioning of the European Union by Member States, or notified by them in accordance with their legal order on behalf of their national Parliament or a chamber thereof.

This provision should strike us as somewhat odd, for two reasons. First, it deals with possible annulment actions under Article 263 TFEU (the successor of former Article 230 TEC) regarding legislation already in force. Even though in the literature it is readily discussed in the immediate context of the EWS,[83] it is not actually part of the EWS since the EWS is an ex ante procedure. Furthermore, where a national parliament presses for an annulment action it is irrelevant whether that parliament had adopted a reasoned opinion at the ex ante stage or not. In other words, not having participated in the EWS is no ground for holding an annulment action initiated by a national parliament inadmissible. In fact, it is not even necessary that the EWS had been triggered by other parliaments. Wyrzykowski et al. put this rather cautiously, noting that it is 'unclear' whether having filed a reasoned opinion is a prerequisite for demanding that an annulment action be brought, but that *de lege lata* it is not a prerequisite.[84] However, in fact there is nothing unclear about it and there is no reason to be cautious: it is manifestly not a prerequisite. Even where not a single reasoned opinion had been filed ex ante, an annulment action can still be brought ex post. It arguably helps if a chamber has had subsidiarity concerns in the first place since that would allow it to act more quickly after an act's adoption: the deadline for annulment actions under Article 263 TFEU is, after all, two months. But that is a different matter. Legally, the EWS and annulment actions are detached from one another.

The second oddity of Article 8 of Protocol No. 2 TEU/TFEU is the indirect construction regarding the right to bring an annulment action. We should note that national parliaments or chambers thereof are *not* awarded standing as privileged applicants on their own. Instead, actions may be filed by Member States, i.e. governments, 'in accordance with their legal order *on behalf of* their national Parliament or a chamber thereof [emphasis added]'. It is true that the provision distinguishes between 'bringing' an action and merely 'notifying', whereby the latter would mean that it is not the government itself that takes the initiative. Still, this provision only formulates a right for governments to act on behalf of their parliaments or chambers, which arguably is a right they have anyway. Sure enough, some authors found it regrettable that national parliaments have not been awarded standing on their own.[85] In fact, the provision does not even formulate a *duty* for governments to act on behalf of parliaments or chambers since actions may be notified by Member States 'in accordance with their legal order'. That national legal order may well exclude government action on behalf of parliaments, most pertinently on behalf of senates which are controlled by a majority hostile to the incumbent government but to which the government is not accountable.

In the Dutch case, a legal obligation of the government to bring an action upon a parliamentary initiative might have been inserted into the Lisbon ratification act, but it was not; instead, the government announced its (political) willingness to bring actions upon parliamentary motions, which are legally not binding.[86] France, by contrast, goes further in that the parliamentary right to initiate an action is codified even in the Constitution, and in that this right is effectively turned into a minority right. Sixty members of either chamber have the right to initiate annulment actions on subsidiarity grounds. Germany goes further still: not only is the right laid down in the Basic Law, and not only is this a minority right, in that case for one-quarter of Bundestag members: the Bundestag or its European affairs committee is even in charge of the subsequent conduct of court proceedings including the formulation of annulment grounds and the appointment of an agent to act before the Court.[87]

Is it lawful to turn the provisions of Article 8 of Protocol No. 2 TEU/TFEU into a minority right? Indeed, Wyrzykowski et al. contemplated the question whether these provisions might also apply to bodies, like committees, or groups, like opposition parties, *within* a parliament or chamber, concluding that this issue was 'open to enquiry'.[88] The following reply shall be submitted here. First, the question is moot since national governments are in any case entitled to bring actions on behalf, or upon the initiative, of whomever they like. So the pressure of finding a legally correct answer is greatly reduced since it is a matter of national political and constitutional choice. Even so, we could tentatively hypothesise that an *opinio iuris* on the part of the Member States exists holding that they are not allowed to let internal bodies or parliamentary minorities act in their own name. Thus, internal bodies or groups are not entitled to initiate annulment actions unless under domestic law these internal bodies or groups are considered to prompt an action that then counts as an action by the chamber as a whole.

In the German case, for example, it should be noted that the minority's initiative is not an action brought by the opposition in its own name, but an action of the Bundestag as a constitutional organ which is merely compelled to act as a whole, only this time not pursuant to a majority vote but pursuant to a minority vote.[89] The newly inserted paragraph 1a in Article 23 of the Basic Law states:

The Bundestag and the Bundesrat have the right to bring an action before the Court of Justice of the European Union if a legislative act of the European Union infringes upon the principle of subsidiarity. The Bundestag is obliged to do so on application by a quarter of its members. (. . .)

Access to judicial review for parliamentary minorities is nothing new under German law. Article 93 (1) (2) of the Basic Law provides for abstract review of federal legislation by the Federal Constitutional Court upon a minority's request as well: traditionally one-third of the Bundestag and now, since the Lisbon Treaty, in an amendment that was part of a package deal, upon the request of one-quarter of Bundestag members. However, in domestic constitutional review the minority acts in its own name; in the case of EU annulment actions it causes the Bundestag to act. Also where the Bundestag's European affairs committee, in other words an internal body, launches such an initiative, it does so on behalf of the Bundestag as a whole, substituting the plenary.[90] Something similar applies in France. The second and third paragraphs of Article 88-6 of the French Constitution read:

Each chamber may bring an action before the Court of Justice of the European Union against a European legislative act for a violation of the principle of subsidiarity. The action is transmitted to the Court of Justice of the European Union by the Government.

To that end, resolutions may be adopted, also outside sessions where appropriate, in accordance with the terms on initiative and debate set by the rules of procedure of each chamber. Upon request of sixty deputies or of sixty senators, the action is brought by operation of law.

'The action' ('le recours') in the last paragraph refers to the 'action' from the preceding paragraph, which is an action brought by 'each chamber'. Also here, like in the German case, the construction is not merely a copy of the minority right that applies to the reference of domestic bills for constitutional review by the Constitutional Council, where the same threshold of sixty deputies or sixty senators applies.[91] For also here, the minority does not act in its own name but causes an action to be initiated by the chamber as a whole. The action is then transmitted by the chamber's speaker to the government.[92]

And also in the other German legislative chamber, the Bundesrat, this view seems to be prevailing. The premiers of the German States have politically agreed among themselves that they would support an annulment initiative of individual States within the framework of the Bundesrat.[93] Why? Because whereas individual States, as regional entities, are not covered by Article 8 of Protocol No. 2 TEU/TFEU, the Bundesrat, where the governments of those States are gathered, does count as a chamber of the national parliament. As such, it is much more entitled, at least in a moral sense, to compel the federal government to bring an action before the Court of Justice of the EU.

And again, even without a codification of domestic rules, a national government is free to bring annulment actions on behalf of minorities or majorities in upper or lower chambers, as it can also be politically or legally prompted to act on behalf of a region or municipality. Even the Belgian construction of triggering an annulment action if one competent assembly (out of the seven parliamentary assemblies that exist within Belgium) so demands,[94] is in that light unproblematic. As far as Article 8 of Protocol No. 2 TEU/TFEU is concerned, with its passive grammatical construction whereby the subject of the clause is the Court, and with its 'legal order' escape clause, it does not impose any obligation on national governments. Legally, and again in the light of the syntax, it does not actually so much deal with the identity of the possible applicants as with the jurisdiction of the Court of Justice.

It has been argued that the reiteration of subsidiarity as a ground for annulment actions in the Protocol is there to encourage the Court to take a less restrained stance on judicial review of subsidiarity compliance.[95] Legally, however, rather than being an extension of the EWS, Article 8 of Protocol No. 2 TEU/TFEU is simply a *lex specialis* of Article 263 TFEU: 'The Court of Justice of the European Union shall review the legality of legislative acts' and shall for this purpose 'have jurisdiction in actions brought by a Member State (. . .) on grounds of (. . .) infringement of the Treaties or of any rule of law relating to their application', which evidently includes the principle of subsidiarity. The Protocol creates no entitlements beyond what is already laid down in Article 263 TFEU.

The true practical challenge under Article 8 of Protocol No. 2 TEU/TFEU is therefore not so much the question to what extent parliaments or chambers may force the government to act but the question to what extent the government 'notifying' and the chamber actually triggering the action can bring forward arguments separately or concurrently. German law provides that the Bundestag *bringing* the action, not the government *notifying* the action, is in charge of the conduct of proceedings.[96] In other Member States this may well be more complicated, and primary EU law is indeed silent on the point of who represents the Member State beyond the notification stage. A strong case can be made that unless domestic law provides that the parliament or chamber itself assumes the representation of the Member State, and that the Member State 'agent' in the meaning of Article 19 of the Statute of the Court of Justice[97] actually answers to the parliament or chamber or a committee thereof, such representation continues to be effected by the government. Thus, the 'Member State' (meaning the government) first notifies an action on behalf of a parliament or chamber but then goes on to actually conduct proceedings, for it still remains 'the Member State' within the meaning of conventional Treaty law, unless it has agreed, or has been bound by domestic constitutional law, to cede this right of conduct to its own parliament or a chamber thereof. Convention member Palacio had unsuccessfully proposed to replace the term 'on behalf of' a national parliament ('au nom') with 'upon the request of' ('à la demande'), to ensure the unitary representation of Member States before the

Court.[98] But even with the notification taking place 'on behalf', the name of the case would still have to be, for example, *Germany* v *European Parliament and Council*, and not *Bundestag* v *European Parliament and Council*. For we are still talking about a Member State action, not a national parliamentary action.

It is interesting to note that already in the Convention process it has been suggested to delete the notification of annulment actions on behalf of national parliaments from the text of Article 8. The reasoning was clear:[99]

> Only Member States should be able to bring actions to the Court of Justice on the grounds of infringement of the principle of subsidiarity. As such an action may, if appropriate, also be brought at the request of a national parliament, the last sentence of the proposed [clause] appears superfluous and should thus be deleted. Whether and how this might be done is a purely internal matter, and should therefore not be included in the Constitution.

But it cannot be denied that the existence of the clause has given a political impulse, making it easier for national parliamentarians to insist, vis-à-vis their governments, that some internal arrangements must be found in the first place. Otherwise, chances are that no, or few, procedures for the parliamentary initiation of annulment actions would have been adopted.

3.7.3 *Reasoned opinions as arguments in other procedures*

It is empirically established that the Court of Justice is highly reluctant to apply the principle of subsidiarity and instead prefers to use the principle of proportionality in annulment actions or preliminary rulings.[100] At the same time we do notice an increasing readiness on the part of the Court to take into consideration the Commission's impact assessments when reviewing the institutions' exercise of policy discretion.[101] The ex ante stage thus provides useful evidence for judicial review ex post. There is no reason why reasoned opinions, which after all, also form part of the ex ante stage of EU legislation and which often have a direct link to impact assessments in that they either refer to them or in that the Commission refers to them in its replies to national parliaments, should not also be used as evidence.[102] One possible use by applicants or parties to domestic proceedings contesting the validity of EU legislation can be to plead, as a matter of supplementary argument, that certain reasoned opinions contained persuasive grounds for doubting the legislation's substantive compliance with subsidiarity or, perhaps more pertinently, with proportionality or the requirement of the presence of a legal basis, already at the ex ante stage. In such context, the quality of reasoned opinions is crucial, much more crucial than its origin: even unelected upper chambers may thus make a valuable contribution to judicial discourse. Another use would be to contest legislation based on a procedural breach of the EWS itself, and therefore of the rules on the legislative process, e.g. by arguing that an urgency override of the eight-week period under Article 4 of Protocol No. 1 TEU/TFEU, which effectively cuts short the EWS as well, has been insufficiently justified.

Of course, in the light of the Court's subsidiarity case-law thus far,[103] an actual annulment or invalidation of EU legislation based on a breach of subsidiarity or a breach of the duty to justify is still very unlikely. But if reasoned opinions were to be given a more prominent role in judicial reasoning, for instance in the context of the proportionality – necessity, suitability and proportionality proper – or of the reasonableness test, it would nevertheless enrich the discourse. The Court might also for strategic reasons be well-advised to take a more robust stance on subsidiarity enforcement.[104] And such approach would also facilitate judicial review since the Court, when confronted with a task of assessing the quality of, say, an impact assessment, could rely on readily available external evidence without even requesting new submissions.

3.8 On the definition of national parliaments

While Article 12 (b) TEU as a master provision, and Protocol No. 2 TEU/ TFEU as the detailed schedule on the enforcement of the EWS, base the system on information privileges and the distribution of votes among national parliaments, there is no provision in the Treaties or Protocols that would provide for a definition of what the term 'national parliament' actually means. Nor is there an annex or other list of national chambers that are addressed by the EWS. The same holds true for all the other instances where Treaty provisions mention national parliaments.[105] It would be perfectly legitimate to adopt such a list as a Treaty annex; the main drawback would only be that this annex would have to be changed each time a Member State would undergo internal constitutional reform, so a simplified, non-unanimity based revision procedure would be in order. As the law stands now, however, there is no such list, only a term: 'the national parliaments'.

Intuitively, it might be clear which bodies are meant by 'national parliaments'. Legally, however, there can be only two possible ways to define what does and what does not fall within the scope of the term. Either the Member States, notably their governments, are free to determine themselves what they consider to be their national parliament or chamber thereof, or alternatively, the term 'national parliaments' as mentioned in the Treaties and Protocols is a Union concept, what we would have called Community concept in the past, or at least a concept that puts certain constraints on individual Member States' creativity.

The reason why this question is relevant is that, if the EWS is taken seriously as a legally framed feature of primary EU law in the adoption of secondary EU law, the question may arise whether a reasoned opinion issued by a certain national or sub-national entity will be counted as a vote towards the thresholds defined in the EWS or not. This in turn is also relevant for the scope of the term 'national parliaments' for EU purposes other than the EWS, such as for the right to receive draft legislative acts and consultation documents in the first place or, probably most pertinently of all instances, the right to cast a binding veto against the application of the general passerelle in the simplified Treaty revision procedure under Article 48 (7) TEU and the special passerelle for family law under Article 81 (3) TFEU. The general passerelle allows the European Council, unanimously and with the assent of the European Parliament, to move to co-decision with the European Parliament or to introduce qualified majority voting in the Council for future legislation in areas where these rules do not yet apply, but such decision cannot be adopted if even one national parliament 'makes known its opposition within six months' of the date of the notification of the intention to apply the general passerelle. The family law passerelle is framed in a similar way, except that it is the Council that acts, that it acts upon a proposal from the Commission, and that the European Parliament is merely consulted, but the national parliamentary veto right is the same: any one national parliament can block the Council decision within six months of notification.

Therefore the delimitation of the scope of the term 'national parliament' is neither self-evident nor irrelevant. And there is no reason why it could not end up in court where, e.g., the validity of secondary legislation or of a simplified Treaty amendment is contested because certain bodies were ignored. For example, the validity of a regulation adopted under the flexibility clause might be contested because the Commission had not drawn the attention of institution X to it, or because QMV in the Council had applied only thanks to an adopted passerelle against which that institution X had, unsuccessfully, tried to cast a veto as a national parliament. The European Parliament could, conversely, bring inter-institutional proceedings against the Council, or the Commission or another Member State could bring infringement proceedings against a Member State, for accepting as a binding veto the opinion of institution X in the passerelle procedure in the area of family law; applicants could argue that a regulation on Europol's structure, operation, field of action and tasks is void or invalid since it does not involve institution X in the evaluation of Europol's activities.

The following paragraphs shall offer possible lines of reasoning to arrive at a definition of the term 'national parliaments' for EU purposes. Should it come to court proceedings and the question of a definition arises, then parties, Advocates-General and the judges at the Court of Justice are invited to consider the various options. We shall distinguish five approaches: (1) a deferential approach, which would make the term an entirely autonomous Member State concept; (2) a semi-deferential, minimalist approach that would still rely on national autonomy but with due regard to Union law limitations; (3) an approach that would rely on circumstantial evidence to identify a common Union perception of what are 'national parliaments'; (4) a completely deductive approach that would seek to define the term as an autonomous Union concept from pure grammatical reasoning; and (5) an approach based on constitutional borrowing, whereby the Union concept of 'national parliaments' would be based on common traditions in interpreting the term 'legislature' under the European Convention on Human Rights.

It is submitted that the last approach is the most sophisticated but also the most predictable, whereas a more minimalist approach is more flexible, presumably more to the liking of the Court of Justice, but also more casuistic. To illustrate this, the different approaches shall be tested for their practical outcome in two of the most relevant grey-area cases: the Belgian scenario where a regional parliament seeks to be recognised as part of a national parliament, and the more common scenario where an individual chamber of a bicameral parliament seeks to issue a veto against the application of the general passerelle or the special passerelle in the area of family law even though the respective provisions mention only parliaments, not individual chambers.

When Belgium signed the EU Constitutional Treaty, it issued a unilateral Declaration[106] which it repeated when it signed the Treaty of Lisbon.[107] The Declaration, now numbered Declaration 51 to the Lisbon Final Act, states that:

> Belgium wishes to make clear that, in accordance with its constitutional law, not only the Chamber of Representatives and Senate of the Federal Parliament but also the parliamentary assemblies of the Communities and the Regions act, in terms of the competences exercised by the Union, as components of the national parliamentary system or chambers of the national Parliament.

In other words, Belgium among other things expects that for EWS purposes votes cast by the Flemish parliament, the Walloon parliament, the parliament of the Brussels-Capital region, the French-speaking community parliament, the Flemish parliament acting in its capacity as the Dutch-speaking community parliament, and the German-speaking community parliament be counted as Belgian votes on the same level as votes cast by the two chambers of the Belgian federal parliament. Presumably this would also imply that regional and community parliaments should be able to veto the application of passerelles, although this is contested in Belgium itself. The background to this Declaration is that in Belgium's constitutional order federal law does not enjoy supremacy over the law of regions and communities: instead any one legislative competence can be exercised by one authority at a time, without there being a hierarchical relationship between them.

As far as the European Commission is concerned, it appears that it does recognise the system stipulated in Declaration 51. The seven Belgian assemblies concluded a cooperation agreement between themselves already in 2005, stipulating that each assembly is entitled to issue a reasoned opinion and that these opinions would be gathered by the secretariat of the Conference of Speakers of the various assemblies, the so-called C7A, in order to convert them into EWS votes.[108] The agreement was meant to enter into force with the entry into force of the Constitutional Treaty, but effectively it is still the instrument that governs the internal procedures for Belgian EWS participation. The agreement prescribes exactly how many votes are deemed to have been issued depending on who would be competent in a matter domestically and who casts an opinion. In matters of federal competence, the two votes are shared out between the two chambers of the federal parliament; in matters affecting both federal and regional or community competences, two votes are cast only if (at least) one of the two federal chambers and (at least) one of the other assemblies casts a vote; in matters affecting only the regions and/or communities, two votes are cast only if they have been issued by two assemblies belonging to different language regimes: Dutch, French, Bilingual and German. Thus, it would not be possible for the Walloon regional parliament and the French-speaking community parliament to cast two votes together because they both belong to the same language regime, namely French. Their opinions would count as one vote only, and another vote would have to be cast by an assembly of another language regime: the Flemish parliament, the bilingual manifestations of the Brussels assembly, or the German-speaking community parliament.

Upon enquiry, the Commission confirmed that so far no regional or community assembly opinions have been received, only opinions from the federal chambers, but if it were to translate such opinions into votes under the EWS, it would count them in accordance with the internal Belgian cooperation agreement.[109] There is a crucial detail, though. The Belgian reasoned opinions that the Commission receives are accompanied by the statement that they are issued 'Pour le système parlementaire national de Belgique'. This means that they are issued not by individual assemblies in their own name but by the Belgian parliamentary system as a whole including the federal, regional and community assemblies.

Still, all this is not entirely unproblematic, even without taking into account possible implications for the distribution of passerelle vetoes, which has far graver effects than the EWS. Declaration No. 51 is a unilateral statement outside the scope of the Treaties proper and has not been endorsed by the IGC as a whole, even though no counter-declarations have been made by other Member States either. And regarding possible claims to Belgian constitutional identity, there is at close inspection nothing particularly special about the Belgian arrangement compared with other, more classical federal systems. What sets Belgium apart from, say, Germany, is that the latter relies on a rather conventional model of vertical power distribution: a competence catalogue defines federal legislative powers, residual powers remain with the States, federal law where lawfully adopted enjoys supremacy over conflicting State law. However, also in Germany there are policy areas, namely exclusive State competences, where the federal level is not competent to legislate at all, e.g. primary schooling, and where supremacy therefore does not apply either. In that sense, the federal legislature of both systems is restricted in its competences in one way or another. Meanwhile, the assemblies of the States in Germany, and of the regions and communities in Belgium, remain regional parliaments: irrespective of their hierarchical rank in the constitutional system, the jurisdiction of each of them is quite simply geographically limited to a part of the country. In both Germany and Belgium, only federal competence extends to the entire national territory. If German State parliaments are therefore considered to be regional parliaments with legislative powers for the purposes of the EWS, which they are, then there is no reason why the same should not apply to Belgian regional and community assemblies. The Belgian Council of State was of roughly the same opinion when it issued its advice on the Constitutional Treaty, stating that what was then Declaration No. 49 was not binding upon the EU institutions or other Member States.[110]

The other borderline scenario, one-house vetoes against the passerelle, may meanwhile be illustrated with a comparison between Germany and France. French law stipulates that the veto against the passerelle must be adopted by the National Assembly and the Senate in identical terms.[111] This seems absolutely correct, as one chamber by itself cannot be the same as the whole parliament, and the French Constitution even explicitly defines parliament to be composed of these two chambers.[112] German law, by contrast, allows the Bundestag alone to cast a veto against the passerelle if mainly exclusive federal competences as opposed to Länder competences are concerned, otherwise either of these two chambers may cast a veto on their own.[113] One could say that in the German case this question is moot anyway since the German government's subsequent consent to the application of the passerelle in the European Council requires prior statutory approval from both chambers anyway, pursuant to German law as adapted to the Constitutional Court's *Lisbon* ruling.[114] As a matter of principle, the admissibility of one-house vetoes, also in systems other than Germany, is nevertheless not a trivial matter.

The scenario of turning parliamentary rights into minority rights we have already discussed in greater detail in the context of the right of parliaments and chambers to initiate annulment actions before the Court of Justice on subsidiarity grounds.[115] This is, it is submitted, justified in any case, since it is a matter of internal procedural autonomy for parliaments and chambers to decide on decision-making rules, so long as the resulting decision counts as the uniform attributable opinion of the parliament or chamber as a whole.

3.8.1 *The deferential approach: a Member State concept*

A very simple and very deferential approach to the definition of the term 'national parliament' would be to consider it to be a purely national constitutional concept. In such case, each Member State, particularly its government, would decide on its own what its national parliament is. Such an approach would at first glance seem to be consistent with the very principle of subsidiarity that the EWS itself seeks to protect: even the definition of the relevant actors takes places closest to home. Wyrzykowski et al. argue, in the context of the definition of a national parliament for the purposes of the right to veto the application of the general passerelle under simplified Treaty revision, that it is 'difficult to consider that the notion should have an autonomous European interpretation', and that 'the matter should therefore be resolved in domestic legislation'.[116] The question they discussed was whether an individual, say upper, chamber could count as a national parliament since, unlike Protocol No. 2 TEU/TFEU, Article 48 TEU does not contemplate individual chambers in bicameral systems and might therefore require both chambers to act in concert in order to count as a full parliament. The authors' conclusion was that EU law cannot require joint or concurrent opinions if national law allows for the veto to be cast by one of the chambers.

It could sure enough be argued that respect for national constitutional autonomy, or constitutional identity under Article 4 (2) TEU, requires such deference to the Member States. However, I submit that unqualified deference in this context would not be compatible with the logic of the Treaty system since it would allow legally binding rights, including veto powers for EU purposes, to be spread unpredictably. There is a difference, for example, between who is a 'national authority' for the purpose of implementing directives, which is of almost no concern to the Union because all that counts is the result, and who is a 'national parliament' for the purpose of enjoying privileges and exercising binding rights awarded under EU law. There is no reason why other Member States should be forced to accept interference by a Member State's domestic bodies that are e.g. regional parliaments rather than national parliaments, or only half a parliament, or not a parliament at all. A few admittedly crass examples may illustrate the point by way of exploring the possible boundaries of the concept. What if a national government casts a reasoned opinion under the EWS and expects it to be counted as a vote, arguing that the subject-matter of the EU proposal concerns legislative powers that had at domestic level already been delegated to the government, or one that the constitution attributes to the government even without delegation from the parliament, and that the government should thus be considered to be the national parliament in this case? What if a regional assembly does the same in matters of partly regional competences? What if it does so in wholly regional competences? What if a senate seeks to veto the passerelle, implying that it is 'a' or 'the' national parliament? What if a head of state seeks to do the same, arguing that he is sufficiently involved in the domestic legislative process, e.g. by his rights to issue decrees and to veto bills, to count as part of the national legislature? What if Luxembourg divides its EWS votes between the Chamber of Deputies – conventionally the unicameral parliament – and the Council of State – conventionally an advisory body but with an observer status at the Association of European Senates? And what if, in all these cases, a domestic body with a competing claim to be, or speak on behalf of, the national parliament objects to such a move?

A strong case can be made that the Union is entitled to have a measure of control over the definition of the term 'national parliament'. Such control can take the form of outer boundaries, notably to prevent an abuse of the freedom to define the term, or it can take the form of a completely autonomous Union concept that draws on various sources of inspiration.

3.8.2 *The minimalist approach: qualified national autonomy*

A pragmatic and at the same time very liberal way to deal with the interpretation of the term 'national parliament' would be that of a qualified national autonomy. It would assume national constitutional autonomy as a starting point. Thus, Member States would be free to declare as their national parliament whatever they consider to come closest to the definition under their domestic realities. This autonomy would not be unfettered, though: it would have to be exercised with due regard to Union law. An analogy may be drawn with the acquisition of national citizenship, a core sovereign matter that Member States are free to regulate themselves but 'with due regard' to Union law.[117]

Applying this approach to the interpretation of the term 'national parliament', this would presumably allow Member States to apply even unusual definitions if they thereby do not obtain any unfair advantage or cause any disruptions to EU decision-making. For instance, Belgium's unilateral Declaration No. 51 declaring regional and community parliaments to be part of a composite national parliament could be acceptable for the purposes of the EWS, since by sharing out EWS votes Belgium does not gain any more votes than other Member States. Member States would be precluded, though, from violating the principle of loyal or sincere cooperation under Article 4 (3) TEU by making choices that border bad faith, such as declaring every city council, or every individual citizen, to be a national parliament for the purpose of vetoing the application of the passerelle.

But there is a grey area. It could be argued that parliamentary rights cannot be assigned to domestic bodies that are manifestly un-parliamentary in nature, such as courts or the government itself, since then the grammatical meaning of a provision of Union law would be disregarded. And what about individual chambers, or again regional parliaments, casting a veto against a passerelle? Unlike Protocol No. 2 TEU/TFEU, Article 48 TEU does not mention individual chambers and only speaks of (whole) parliaments that can cast vetoes. If the term 'national parliament' were simply a Union concept, one could argue more easily that Article 48 TEU must be read in the light of the Protocol, meaning that the Union is perfectly able to address individual chambers if it so wishes. If the term is a qualified Member State concept, though, one would have to show that due regard to Union law has not been had.

The main argument in favour of regional parliamentary vetoes in Belgium, and one-house vetoes from other Member States, might be that the approval of the bodies in question is also necessary in ordinary Treaty amendment ratifications, so they are veto players either way, even in normal circumstances. No unfair advantage is therefore gained. The other side might argue, though, that other Member States would suffer *dis*advantages as their attempts at simplified Treaty reform are frustrated by what is effectively not a national parliament but only a *chamber* of a national parliament, or not even a national assembly but a regional parliament. A case could then be made that, if the term 'national parliament' is a qualified national concept, the cavalier sharing out of veto rights would violate the principle of loyal cooperation in the EU or at least disregard the concept of 'national parliament' under Union law.

3.8.3 A Union concept based on circumstantial evidence

The more we find it justified to limit Member States' creativity, the further we move from a qualified or unqualified Member State concept towards an autonomous Union definition of the term 'national parliaments'. Arguably, a Union concept becomes more justified the more seriously we take the rights that the Treaties confer upon national parliaments.

The concept of autonomy of Union law as such is nothing new.[118] Nor is the application of autonomous Union definitions to heterogeneous groups of national bodies anything new. We may recall that the term 'court or tribunal of a Member State' for the purposes of the preliminary reference procedure under the old Article 234 TEC and the new Article 267 TFEU is also subject to an autonomous Union interpretation.[119] This means that Member States are not free to, say, exempt certain judicial or quasi-judicial bodies from the EU obligation to refer questions. In the case of national parliaments, one way of arriving at such an autonomous Union interpretation would be to consider, as circumstantial evidence, the composition of various EU bodies that are intended to represent national parliaments.

One possibility here is to identify who attended the Conventions which drafted the EU Charter of Fundamental Rights and the Draft Constitutional Treaty, respectively. Both Conventions comprised representatives of national parliaments, which might give an indication of what was deemed to be a national parliament in the first place. The drawback here is that, indeed, these members were *representatives* of national parliaments, not necessarily actual MPs, and many Conventioneers could have obtained a seat on various tickets. Another possibility would be to consider who is a member of COSAC. Here the drawback is that the composition of COSAC is not necessarily authoritative since it started as a more or less spontaneous, informal, self-governing conference that was only later endorsed by EU law. Still, it would offer already one important clue regarding sub-national parliaments: Belgian regional and community assemblies were not accepted as COSAC members. Upon enquiry, the European Department of the Belgian federal lower chamber confirmed that COSAC at one point considered allowing non-national assemblies to join but 'did not deem it necessary to take this discussion further'. COSAC instead noted that the Committee of the Regions would be a more suitable forum for regional assemblies, also because the Committee of the Regions is a fully-fledged EU institution whereas COSAC was not.[120] In the meantime, representation in COSAC could be ensured indirectly as some Belgian members of community assemblies are at the same time senators, and therefore members of the national parliament proper.

Thus, based on this line of reasoning, the enjoyment of parliamentary rights by Belgian regional or community assemblies, and other bodies that neither are, nor are eligible to be, members of COSAC would be excluded. Their EWS votes and passerelle vetoes could be duly disregarded by the Union unless it could be shown that the federal parliament, or one of the two chambers of the federal parliament, i.e. the national parliament proper, actively endorses such actions, thus making them their own.

3.8.4 Grammatical interpretation

An attempt to define a national parliament or chamber thereof for the purpose of a purely deductive conclusion is highly difficult. A straightforward grammatical interpretation is near-impossible. For often terms describing parliaments are used interchangeably, even though they actually highlight different aspects. We might consider the introduction to an ambitious survey of national legislatures of the world, where we read the following two consecutive sentences, with emphases added: 'We therefore set out to assess the powers of the central *representative institution* of national politics, and do so for all countries of the world. We knew (. . .) that measuring the powers of *legislatures* perfectly is a vain hope'.[121] The problem is that not all representative institutions have legislative powers, and not all legislatures or co-legislators are representative institutions. Other experts sometimes use the terms 'parliament' and 'legislature' interchangeably,[122] which may not be a problem if we all know what we are talking about but which strictly speaking may not always be warranted. Yet as soon as we focus on one particular aspect of what seems to define a national parliament, we frequently end up excluding bodies that are at least intuitively considered to be parliamentary chambers, or including those that are not.

Direct election of the body which we might consider to be a parliamentary chamber cannot be a requirement as this would quite simply exclude the UK House of Lords and those senates that are indirectly elected, such as the Austrian, the French or the Dutch one. Government accountability to the body in question cannot be a requirement either, although the option may seem appealing. Article 10 (2) TEU, second clause, after all proclaims the Union's attachment to representative democracy in the following terms:

> Member States are represented in the European Council by their Heads of State or Government and in the Council by their governments, themselves democratically accountable either to their national Parliaments, or to their citizens.

From this one might infer that a national parliament is the body to which the government is accountable unless (as in the case in Cyprus, which is a presidential system, or with some qualifications in systems with a directly elected executive presidency in a semi-parliamentary setting) the government is directly accountable to the citizens. Such definition would even include the Belgian regional and community parliaments to the extent that regional or community ministers participate in Council votes, who in turn are accountable to their regional or community assemblies.[123] However, such a definition would clearly exclude all senates except Italy's, as government accountability in bicameral systems is typically linked to the lower chamber only. It would therefore be of little use for the purposes of the EWS, which anyway, at least on the face of it, has little to do with calling national governments to account – although it can be used to call the Commission to account[124] – and instead relates much more closely to legislative involvement.

The only more or less promising autonomous definition of national parliaments as a Union concept in fact would aim in the direction of the legislative or co-legislative capacity of bodies. It cannot be enough that a body is 'involved' in national legislation, for that would arguably include advisory bodies like the Council of State in Luxembourg or Spain. The definition however cannot be so strict as to demand that the *consent* of the body in question be required for the adoption of national legislation. After all, that would again exclude most senates and, arguably, perhaps even the National Assembly of France. If consent were to be required *in principle*, i.e. always and, in the case of senates, always except when the lower chamber overrules the upper chamber's veto, this would cover most of what is intuitively understood to be a parliamentary chamber. However, it would also exclude the German Bundesrat, whose consent is in principle *not* required to pass federal legislation even though it may, by absolute majority of votes, object to bills. Conversely, the presence of veto power alone is not workable as a criterion either because some heads of state and, say, the French Constitutional Council, do have a sort of veto power as well.

Still, the term 'legislature' is in this context much more promising than the term 'parliament'. Consider the two chambers that stand out in their extraordinary character and composition: the House of Lords of the UK and the German Bundesrat. The House of Lords is the only upper chamber in the EU that is entirely unelected: the award of peerages is a royal prerogative exercised effectively by the Prime Minister. The Bundesrat is composed of regional executives and is, notwithstanding the hemicycle setting of seats in the plenary room, manifestly un-parliamentary in nature. Its democratic legitimacy depends on the accountability of the sixteen State governments to their State parliaments, who are probably in an even weaker position with respect to the Bundesrat than national parliaments are vis-à-vis the Council of the EU.[125] German language usage does not even call the Bundesrat a parliament or even part of a parliament: the actual parliament is the directly elected Bundestag. And the Lords and the Bundesrat are not negligible fringe cases, but the upper chambers of two Member States which together are home to almost 30% of the EU population. They also happen to be among the most prolific writers in the EWS, producing all or almost all of the reasoned opinions from their respective Member State.[126] One of them is, as said, not a parliament and the other is conventionally called a House of Parliament but is not elected. What both chambers have in common is that they are national (co-)legislators. And that is, it is submitted, what qualifies them to participate in the EWS and be considered a part of a national parliament.

Based on such functional approach of examining whether a body is at least part of the legislature, a case could be made that regional parliaments, particularly in federal Member States, are not categorically ruled out from enjoying the status of being at least part of a composite national parliament, nor are individual legislative chambers. Limitations would have to be sought in the letter of the Treaties themselves, such as where they explicitly exclude regional parliaments or individual chambers from certain rights. Sadly, this brings us back to square one. Article 6 of Protocol No. 2 TEU/TFEU makes a clear distinction between national and regional parliaments, so does this exclusion of regional parliaments also apply to the scope of the passerelle veto? When interpreting the term 'national parliament' for the purposes of the passerelle, does it matter that the EWS distinguishes between individual chambers and whole parliaments whereas the passerelle provisions do not? In the end, pure deduction cannot really help.

3.8.5 Constitutional borrowing: common traditions under the ECHR

Assuming for a little longer that the term 'legislature' is a much more usable concept than the term 'parliament', because it focuses on a body's concrete functional characteristic rather than its abstract and somewhat arbitrary description, a standard would have to be identified how to determine what is a legislature and what is not. One option would be to borrow from another body of European law: the European Convention on Human Rights (ECHR).

The European Court of Human Rights provides some measure of guidance in its interpretation of the term 'legislature' for the purposes of the right to vote as protected by Article 3 of Protocol No. 1 to the ECHR:

> The High Contracting Parties undertake to hold free elections at reasonable intervals by secret ballot, under conditions which will ensure the free expression of the opinion of the people in the choice of the legislature.

True, in the ECHR the term 'legislature' is used not to denote as a body that is awarded certain rights, like it is the case with 'parliaments' in the EU. But the term 'legislature' has nevertheless been interpreted to identify what exactly is a body that can be called a legislature and to which, consequently, the right to vote must apply. Thus, there is a body of ECHR law that attempts to define the term 'legislature'. If this definition could be used, in fact borrowed, for EU purposes, it would have three important advantages. The first is that the Court of Justice of the EU would not have to re-invent the wheel, since decades of Strasbourg case-law have already resulted in some ready-made definitions. The second is that the concept, even if it is borrowed from Strasbourg, would remain an autonomous Union concept, allowing the Court, and the Member States, to uphold most effectively the integrity of the letter of the EU Treaties and above all the predictability of their effect. The third is that this approach would enjoy a great amount of legitimacy since the concept would not be imposed top-down but would be rooted in constitutional traditions common to the Member States, as they are in this case expressed in the ECHR.

What would this mean concretely? Admittedly, Strasbourg case-law on the term 'legislature' is a bit intuitive and sometimes very much ad hoc. Two approaches are, however, distinguishable in the case-law of the Strasbourg Court. First, bodies that are *prima facie* parliaments (including sub-national assemblies) are tested for what competences they enjoy. On that basis, provincial assemblies in Italy do not qualify whereas regional assemblies do.[127] Second, bodies that are *prima facie* not parliaments, or whose characterisation is doubtful, are tested for the degree to which they are involved in the legislative process. On that basis, the European Parliament does qualify,[128] but so might, at least potentially, heads of state, if their involvement goes beyond checks and balances and truly amounts to a co-legislative role.[129]

Of course, a borrowed definition from the ECHR would have to be adapted to the realities of EU law, which would make it a slightly more complicated exercise. The guiding principle would be that the EU term 'national parliament' must be read in the light of the ECHR definition of the 'legislature', and it still would be an autonomous concept of Union law, but the definition cannot apply where Union law itself excludes certain entities from the relevant scope even though under the ECHR they might be legislatures. For example, heads of state may be ECHR 'legislatures' but they are not EU 'parliaments'. This approach of borrow-then-subtract has a great advantage in that it would much more clearly resolve the borderline cases because it would be based on single definitions of the term 'national parliament' throughout the Treaties, instead of an article-by-article weighing of autonomy versus loyalty.

What would have to be subtracted from the ECHR term 'legislature'? As said, heads of state are potentially part of the legislature for ECHR purposes but are, in EU law, mentioned explicitly as possible members of the European Council in Article 10 (2) TEU, a provision that also refers to national parliaments separately, so that the two cannot coincide for EU purposes. Also the governments themselves, even if they were covered by Strasbourg case-law, would never be counted as national parliaments since both Article 10 (2) TEU and the Preamble to Protocol No. 1 TEU/TFEU juxtapose national parliaments and national governments explicitly, so they cannot coincide for EU purposes. The European Parliament is recognised under ECHR case-law as a 'legislature' but under EU law, such as Article 9 of Protocol No. 1 TEU/TFEU ('The European Parliament and national Parliaments shall together . . .') it is evidently not a national parliament. Local (municipal) parliaments simply do not qualify as legislatures under ECHR case-law.

Regional parliaments are routinely considered part of the legislature for ECHR purposes but they are separately covered by Article 6 of Protocol No. 2 TEU/TFEU: 'It will be for each national Parliament or each chamber of a national Parliament to consult, where appropriate, regional parliaments with legislative powers'. Since the present approach is based on unitary definitions, not case-by-case analysis, this would exclude regional parliaments from *all* instances where national parliaments are mentioned in the Treaties, including the passerelle veto. The same would hold true for individual chambers in bicameral systems. The EWS distinguishes between parliaments and individual chambers specifically. For the purpose of the passerelle veto, 'national parliament' under Article 48 (7) TEU can be equally read in the light of the definition of that term in Articles 6, 7 (1) and 8 of Protocol No. 2 TEU/TFEU all of which envisage two or more chambers together forming one parliament. Individual chambers are therefore, pursuant to primary EU law, a subset of national parliaments and therefore cannot be identical to them.

A measure of lenience would be derived from the fact that while the Union enjoys autonomy to define what national parliaments *are*, national parliaments still enjoy internal procedural autonomy in determining how they exercise their EU rights, including how they vote and whom they authorise to exercise these rights on their behalf. Internal procedural autonomy is crucial as it would be illusory for the Union to determine how exactly, e.g. in how many readings, a national chamber adopts its decision. Instead the Union would have to refer to what national constitutional law defines as a validly taken decision *of the parliament or chamber as a whole*. If domestic law provides that a chamber acts through a parliamentary committee, that is legitimate, for the decision counts as a decision of the chamber as a whole. Where domestic law provides that a chamber is obliged to act upon the initiative of a parliamentary minority, that is legitimate as well, for again the chamber as a whole has essentially agreed to act upon a minority's behalf.

The same holds true where one chamber is authorised to speak on behalf of the whole parliament if the parliament is bicameral. The German one-house passerelle veto would be acceptable: not because either of the two chambers alone is a national parliament in the sense of Article 48 (7) TEU, but because both chambers have agreed, by statute that has received bicameral approval, that each of them may act on behalf of the national parliament as a whole. It is as if a right can be exercised by a married couple and both spouses have agreed that any one of them can act on behalf of the other and therefore for the couple. That too does not mean that one spouse is the couple. It only means that each of them is authorised to act on the couple's behalf. It would furthermore be acceptable for regional parliaments to exercise EU rights such as EWS votes and passerelle vetoes, but only if the national parliament proper can be deemed to endorse the regional actions thus making them their own.

What would not be acceptable is for a minority to act in its own right and demand recognition at Union level as the voice of the chamber, or for a chamber in its own right to claim to represent parliament as a whole, certainly where the majority or the other chamber dissent. And it would not be acceptable for parliaments or chambers to delegate the exercise of rights that, pursuant to EU law, were meant for them and them only, to extra-parliamentary entities: the government, councils of state, national courts, regional assemblies. The prohibition of delegation of certain parliamentary powers, notably legislative powers, is well-known in national constitutional systems, such as the US and all those European systems whose constitutions stipulate that certain actions, like the limitation of fundamental rights, may only take place by statutory legislation. It should be seen in a similar way as regards rights that EU law reserves for national parliaments: Article 12 TEU addresses specifically national parliaments, with a view to their active contribution to a good functioning of the Union, and not any national authorities as the Member States deem fit to designate. Again, this does not exclude that certain extra-parliamentary entities may adopt opinions which, in each case, are endorsed by the national parliament or chamber. For then the opinion can still be attributable to the national parliament or chamber itself.

3.8.6 Summary

The EU Treaties do not provide for an exhaustive list of bodies that are meant to be 'national parliaments' for the purpose of EU law. The Court of Justice of the EU should therefore not act as if they did, and it should not impose a rigid and inflexible definition of the term 'national parliament' upon the Member States. At the same time it is readily apparent that national constitutional autonomy cannot mean a free-for-all. National governments should not be able to define what is a national parliament without any restraints whatsoever.

The solution lies somewhere in the middle, and can take essentially two forms. One is to allow for national autonomy to define the term 'national parliament' but with due regard to Union law. This would grant Member States great discretion but would rule out flagrant violations of the principle of loyal cooperation, for example where national definitions would mean an abuse of such discretion to the advantage of the Member State in question or to the disadvantage of other Member States. EWS votes for regional parliaments would contradict the letter of the Treaties but would be relatively harmless, especially if a Member State has been as open and consistent about it as Belgium has been; a passerelle veto, strictly meant for 'national parliaments', could also be cast by regional parliaments or individual chambers if they would have been veto players in ordinary Treaty ratification, otherwise probably not.

The other option would be to construct an autonomous, less casuistic Union concept of 'national parliament' that would apply throughout the body of EU law. A grammatical interpretation based on pure reason is not really possible, but sources of inspiration can be found in various corners. The membership of COSAC and the two European Conventions held thus far could offer clues, although reliance on such circumstantial evidence alone could give undue weight to the composition of informal and ad hoc bodies.

If a more robust Union concept is to be constructed, this might be done in the light of the Member States' common constitutional traditions of defining the term 'legislature' as expressed in Article 3 of Protocol No. 1 to the ECHR, except where Union law itself explicitly excludes certain bodies from the scope of the term 'national parliament' even though they might be legislatures for ECHR purposes. The principle would be borrow-then-subtract. This approach, since it refers back to common constitutional traditions, offers a considerable degree of respect for the Member States' constitutional identity under Article 4 (2) TEU. But it would allow the Union to effectively uphold the letter and spirit of the Treaties in a field where binding powers are conferred to a certain set of institutions. Heads of state, regional parliaments with legislative powers, municipal parliaments, national governments, the European Parliament would all be excluded from the definition of 'national parliaments'; individual chambers in bicameral systems would also be excluded unless EU law explicitly envisages individual chambers. At the same time, national parliaments would continue to enjoy internal procedural autonomy in determining how they exercise their EU rights, e.g. by which majorities they vote, or whether they let a committee or even a minority speak on the chamber's behalf, as long as the resulting opinion is uniform. Member States would be barred from sharing out EU rights to bodies other than the national parliament proper, e.g. to regional parliaments, unless the national parliament endorses each and every regional opinion, thus making it its own.

Chances are that the Court of Justice of the EU will prefer something more pragmatic, casting the net widely and then defining exceptions on a case-by-case basis. Still, it is recommended that Member State autonomy be restricted, via a review against EU law or by defining the term 'national parliaments' as an autonomous Union concept, much like the term 'court or tribunal' which rightly is a Union concept as well.

3.9 The logic of the distribution of votes

The EWS as it entered into force with the Lisbon Treaty distributes two votes per national parliament, to be shared out between chambers where a parliament is not unicameral, and to be distributed equally among both chambers if a parliament is bicameral.[130] From a technical but also from a doctrinal point of view, both positive and negative remarks can be made about this choice. Two issues are pertinent: the question whether the distribution of an equal number of votes for all parliaments is justified; and whether the equal sharing out of votes between chambers in bicameral systems is justified.

3.9.1 On the equality of parliaments

The EWS assigns two votes per national parliament irrespective of the Member States' respective population sizes. In contrast with the breakup of the European Parliament by national delegations of uneven size[131] and with the qualified majority formula in the Council,[132] both of which do take into account population size, the EWS is based on unqualified equality of Member States. In areas that are no longer governed by unanimity, this gives parliaments of small Member States a weight that exceeds their, or rather their governments', weight in the Council. Practically, where the political colour of the government and the majority in the parliament or at least the lower chamber coincide, as they normally do, government parties enjoy a larger share of the vote at the EWS stage than they do later on in the Council.

While this would seem inconsistent with the progressive introduction of majoritarian elements in the European institutional arena, this egalitarian approach to national parliaments nevertheless seems justified. The equality of the vote under the EWS can be seen as a form of minority protection, giving small Member State parliaments a disproportionate weight. This would be consistent with the understanding of the principle of subsidiarity as a brake on excessive regulation by European majorities in the Council and the European Parliament, and with the fact that the 'yellow card' is in itself literally a minority right, triggered as it is by one-third or one-quarter of total votes. Furthermore, it would seem healthy to treat and count parliaments on a different footing from the governments: a simple extension of the QMV formula to the EWS would merely make the EWS a mirror for Council proceedings rather than a review mechanism in its own right, with the exception that senates might profit more from such involvement since EWS opinions are not relayed through the governments. Finally, on the assumption that subsidiarity review is to verify that EU bodies stay within the scope of powers conferred by the Treaties, and that these Treaties have been ratified by unanimity between Member States as well, there would be little reason to limit the opportunities of small conferring Member States to verify whether the scope of their conferral is still being respected. For large Member State parliaments, of course, this means that minorities in terms of population size can impose a disproportionate weight on such interpretation; however, that is no different from Treaty ratification in the first place, where small Member States enjoy disproportionate weight as well, which at least from the point of view of public international law is absolutely legitimate. Incidentally, the reverse of this argument would be that the EWS could be interpreted as a tool for at least primarily *legal* scrutiny on the admissibility rather than the political desirability of legislation, as shall be argued later on.[133] After all, for exchanges of purely political opinions, equal votes for all Member States would be misplaced; for legal scrutiny concerning the delimitation and exercise of competences once conferred, it makes sense to apply the same equality of Member States as it reigned at the Treaty ratification stage in the first place.

3.9.2 *On the equality of chambers*

Of the 27 EU Member States, 13 feature a bicameral system. These are Austria, Belgium, the Czech Republic, France, Germany, Italy, Ireland, the Netherlands, Poland, Romania, Slovenia, Spain and the United Kingdom. The remaining 14 Member States are unicameral, namely Bulgaria, Cyprus, Denmark, Estonia, Finland, Greece, Hungary, Latvia, Lithuania, Luxembourg, Malta, Portugal, Slovakia and Sweden. Of the 13 senates in the EU Member States, two – the German and the Austrian Bundesrat – exist for the purpose of representing the component entities in a federal system. The other 11 can be said to exist for various idiosyncratic reasons but generally for the sake of bicameralism itself, as chambers of reflection or as a check and balance against lower chambers.[134]

In that context, Article 7 (1) of Protocol No. 2 TEU/TFEU differs from the version as originally proposed by the European Convention as part of the Draft Constitutional Treaty in one crucial respect. The Convention version distinguished only between unicameral and bicameral parliaments:[135]

> The national Parliaments of Member States with unicameral Parliamentary systems shall have two votes, while each of the chambers of a bicameral Parliamentary system shall have one vote.

The version as it was adopted by the 2004 Intergovernmental Conference as part of the Constitutional Treaty[136] and subsequently by the IGC that adopted the Treaty of Lisbon,[137] by contrast, refers to parliaments that are either unicameral or not unicameral, in which case votes are 'shared out', and prescribes equality in the case of bicameral parliaments:

> Each national Parliament shall have two votes, shared out on the basis of the national Parliamentary system. In the case of a bicameral Parliamentary system, each of the two chambers shall have one vote.

The effect of this provision is two-fold. The first is that, in contrast to the Convention version, the EWS now applies theoretically to parliaments that have not only one or two, but also more than two chambers. For Belgium, this looks like an endorsement of multicameral parliamentary systems in the way Belgium sees itself – with a bicameral federal and a plethora of regional and community parliaments forming part of a multi-faceted whole – although it is submitted that this should not escape close scrutiny from an EU law point of view and cannot be acceptable in all cases.[138] But more generally, the change from the Convention version to the IGC version is, from a constitutional law point of view, to be applauded. For this means that Member States are not restricted in adding chambers to their national legislature: the possible future introduction of a tricameral parliament, say, would still be compatible with the EWS as long as the two votes are shared out somehow. This prospect is not completely outlandish. France briefly had a tricameral legislature during the Napoleonic Consulate; much more recently, Slovenia, when it still was a constituent republic of the Socialist Federal Republic of Yugoslavia, featured a tricameral legislature as well. The EWS is in that case much more durable, compared with the Convention version, since it can now accommodate future constitutional reforms within the Member States without there being a need to change the formula. It might in that sense be compared with the formula for QMV introduced by the Lisbon Treaty for Council votes.[139] The formula – 55% of Council members, at least fifteen of them, representing 65% of the EU population, with a blocking minority comprising at least four members – is also much more durable than earlier QMV formulas which still used tables to assign absolute numbers of votes per Member State. In the Council, the Lisbon formula can continue to apply irrespective of how many states eventually join or leave the Union; in the EWS it can apply no matter how many chambers their parliaments have.

The second effect of the cited Article 6 of Protocol No. 2 TEU/TFEU is that, where a parliament is bicameral, both chambers must have one vote. This was already the case in the Convention version, as cited above. This means that Member States are not free to assign one of their chambers a fraction of one vote, for example half a vote, and to then award one and a half votes to the other chamber. In the light of the fact that in most bicameral systems the lower chamber is the dominant one and the senate is inferior to it, this equality of lower and upper chambers might appear problematic. Not only does the cabinet rely on the confidence of the lower chamber and not the senate (only in Italy can the senate oust the cabinet as well). Among the 13 bicameral systems in the European Union, the Netherlands is the only one that grants its upper chamber an absolute veto in the legislative process in all cases, and even then the upper chamber votes only *after* the lower chamber has adopted a bill, and technically the upper chamber may only approve or reject a bill and does not enjoy the power of initiative or amendment.[140] Due to the strict wording of Article 6 of Protocol No. 2 TEU/TFEU, Member States cannot even do what might often be the fairest solution of all: allow the lower chamber to cast both votes, irrespective of what the senate does, while reserving one vote to the senate in case it wants to act alone. This way lower chambers, after all in most cases and for most practical purposes the functional equivalents of unicameral parliaments, would not be penalised for being trapped inside a bicameral system. But again, under the current EWS this solution is ruled out: the chambers must have one vote each. If we reason that subsidiarity enforcement is about keeping the exercise of legislative competences domestic where possible, under the EWS senates enjoy a voice that is completely out of proportion with the voice that they have when legislative competences actually *are* domestic.

To be sure, the senates themselves welcome their equality with lower chambers under the EWS very much.[141] It would certainly leave the Member States greater constitutional autonomy if they were able to freely dispose of the votes they have as they wish, as long as they do not claim more votes than other Member States just because they happen to have more chambers. But there are in fact grounds to justify mandatory equality of upper and lower chambers. A first argument may be – although it is not particularly strong since it does not have to apply to all bicameral systems – that even where senates are inferior to lower chambers in domestic lawmaking, they usually have an equal veto power when it comes to ratifying EU Treaties and thus conferring new competences upon the EU in the first place. This is typically the case when under domestic law such transfer requires, or is treated on par with, constitutional amendment. This would justify e.g. the equal status of the German Bundesrat, whose assent is required for the transfer of sovereign competences to the EU but not for all domestic bills. It would, however, not justify the equal status of the House of Lords, which can be overruled by the Commons in virtually all cases including in the course of Treaty ratification.

A second, stronger but very pragmatic and somewhat opportunistic argument derives from the empirical reality of the EWS. It would appear that the equality of chambers under the EWS is an acceptable price to pay for the active participation by senates. In several bicameral Member States, the upper chambers are far more active than the lower chambers in formulating and issuing reasoned opinions, and it would be a shame to lose this source of input by undervaluing it in terms of votes. For instance, regarding EU proposals launched in 2009, all 11 British letters in response originated in the House of Lords, not a single one in the Commons; seven out of eight French letters came from the Senate; the Czech Senate was the one to respond to 22 out of the 23 EU proposals that triggered a Czech parliamentary reaction; six out of ten Austrian letters came from the federal-senatorial Bundesrat; and the German Bundesrat authored 15 out of 17 German letters over this period. Senates which are more independent from the cabinet than lower chambers in fact offer a greater prospect that their opinion will not merely be a repetition of what the government thinks already, and they can thus potentially add fresher ideas to the discourse.

Finally, we should consider the alternative to Treaty-mandated co-equality. Without it, either the Commission and the other initiators of a draft legislative act would have to weigh the vote of a senate themselves, possibly with different values for different senates, or each bicameral Member State would be compelled to indicate what exact value it allocates with its senate. These are choices on thorny constitutional issues that surely none of the actors involved would be too keen to make.

A 'Rise of the Senates' is one of the possible phenomena that we may well witness as the EWS becomes more established.[142] The EWS grants the senates co-equality with lower chambers in terms of vote weight so that they do not have to fight for it themselves. While it could be argued that this is not always justified on the ground, an even stronger case can be made that this is in fact a rather smart design for reasons of both principle and practical effect.

3.10 Conclusion

No matter how we qualify the EWS politically, we must face the reality that it is a complex mechanism and that it functions in accordance with legal rules. It is not a loose dialogue but a system that operates on the basis of legally binding rights and obligations, admissibility criteria, deadlines and other procedural and substantive constraints. It also follows a certain deeper institutional logic. The present chapter sought to dissect those rules, and to make explicit this logic. As regards the procedural complexity, it suffices to point out the formal requirements for reasoned opinions under Article 6 of Protocol No. 2 TEU/TFEU. In effect, five admissibility requirements must be complied with:

- Opinions must originate in a national parliament or chamber;
- they must concern a draft legislative act;
- they must be sent in time;
- reasons must be given, i.e. a blank objection is inadmissible; and
- the opinion must concern an alleged breach of the principle of subsidiarity.

All this may sound straightforward, but we have seen that it is anything but. First of all, the EWS accords rights and privileges to national parliaments without defining what that term means. But, it is submitted, Member States should not be able to interpret the term completely autonomously; it must be constructed as a Union concept, at least as a national concept under Union law constraints, although in either case as one that leaves parliaments and chambers procedural autonomy in how exactly they adopt their decisions. Then, reasoned opinions must concern a draft legislative act, so it is worth pointing out that this excludes, for example, consultation documents but also amended drafts. This means that the EWS is not placed at the very beginning of a legislative process, nor does it extend to its very end. National parliaments that seek to be fully involved are therefore advised to start their involvement earlier and not to quit after the EWS stage. Reasoned opinions must also be sent in time, but what is 'in time'? The famous eight-week period may for individual parliaments be both longer than eight weeks, due to the fact that some language versions arrive earlier than others, and shorter, if the urgency override from Protocol No. 1 TEU/TFEU is invoked. Reasons must be given in reasoned opinions, which does not seem problematic in practice. What is problematic, though, is the definition of subsidiarity. The following chapter shall consider in greater detail how the principle can be defined, how national parliaments define it themselves, and how the EWS can be interpreted in such a way that the letter of the law is respected but the needs of national parliaments are taken into account as well.[143]

What about the constitutional logic of the EWS? The system accords each national parliament the same amount of votes, which is justified if we consider subsidiarity enforcement as a form of policing of the boundaries of competences conferred upon the EU by Treaties. In Treaty ratification, after all, all Member States have an equal vote as well. The EWS furthermore insists that in bicameral parliaments both chambers must have one vote each; this does not reflect the constitutional law of bicameral Member States where senates are typically inferior to lower chambers, but as senates have turned out to be very active EWS participants, this distortion appears to be an acceptable price to pay. The effect of the EWS never does amount to a 'red card' for national parliaments, so it preserves the logic of the classical Community method of lawmaking. However, the EWS should not exclusively be assessed a veto right, as there are other reasons to have it. And indirectly national parliaments' reasoned opinions, whether the EWS is actually triggered or not, can produce tangible results.

4 The material scope of the early warning system

Subsidiarity and other criteria

4.1 Introduction

The introduction of the principle of subsidiarity in EU Treaty law has spawned an entire branch of academic literature seeking to translate the principle into a workable assessment framework. While the principle itself is relatively straightforward, prescribing as it does regulation at the lowest sensible level, it is nevertheless fiendishly hard to establish criteria to conclude when the principle is actually breached. The current study provides us with a unique opportunity to empirically observe how, based on correspondence within the early warning system (EWS), national parliaments *themselves* seem to be defining the subsidiarity principle in real life. Thus, next to deductive definitions and conceptualisations deriving from theoretical academic effort, we can attempt to construct a 'bottom-up' definition of subsidiarity that is based on actual acceptance and needs on the ground. Where practical needs seem to extend beyond what the EWS is offering, an attempt shall be made to formulate lines of legal reasoning that would nevertheless accommodate those needs by carefully adapting the definition of the term 'subsidiarity'.

4.2 Subsidiarity: a legal analysis

Legally, the subsidiarity test is part of a sequence of cumulative tests which the Union must pass in order to exercise its competences. These are legality, subsidiarity and, finally, proportionality, and they are all consolidated in Article 5 TEU:

1. The limits of Union competences are governed by the principle of conferral. The use of Union competences is governed by the principles of subsidiarity and proportionality.
2. Under the principle of conferral, the Union shall act only within the limits of the competences conferred upon it by the Member States in the Treaties to attain the objectives set out therein. Competences not conferred upon the Union in the Treaties remain with the Member States.

3. Under the principle of subsidiarity, in areas which do not fall within its exclusive competence, the Union shall act only if and in so far as the objectives of the proposed action cannot be sufficiently achieved by the Member States, either at central level or at regional and local level, but can rather, by reason of the scale or effects of the proposed action, be better achieved at Union level.

    The institutions of the Union shall apply the principle of subsidiarity as laid down in the Protocol on the application of the principles of subsidiarity and proportionality. National Parliaments ensure compliance with the principle of subsidiarity in accordance with the procedure set out in that Protocol.

4. Under the principle of proportionality, the content and form of Union action shall not exceed what is necessary to achieve the objectives of the Treaties.

    The institutions of the Union shall apply the principle of proportionality as laid down in the Protocol on the application of the principles of subsidiarity and proportionality.

First, the Union must therefore have competence to act in the first place, i.e. possess a sufficient legal basis in the Treaties. This reflects the principle of legality in line with the principle of conferral and enumeration whereby Member States confer powers upon the Union. Without legal basis there is no reason to apply the subsequent tests: a measure may be proportionate, but without legal basis that is irrelevant. Second, if the legality test is passed, one needs to determine whether the competence is exclusive or not. If the Union is exclusively competent, subsidiarity does not apply since there is no way Member States could exercise the competence, and immediately the proportionality test ensues. If the competence is anything other than exclusive, the subsidiarity test must be passed first. The subsidiarity test itself consists of two sub-tests, one negative and one positive. The first is that the objectives of the proposed action *cannot* be sufficiently achieved by the Member States, at whatever internal level of government (negative criterion). If they can, the test is over and the Union is not entitled to exercise its competences even though it might have a legal basis, and even though the measure might be proportionate. Then, it must be shown that the objectives can rather, by reason of the scale or effects of the proposed action, be better achieved at Union level (positive criterion). This means that even where Member State action is insufficient, the Union would still need to show that it can achieve better results. Finally, proportionality applies to both the content of the Union action, e.g. the scope of a regulation, and the form thereof, e.g. the choice of a regulation over a directive.

Coming back to subsidiarity, Article 5 of Protocol No. 2 TEU/TFEU elaborates the various aspects that the initiator of EU legislative acts. i.e. not just the Commission, must justify:

Draft legislative acts shall be justified with regard to the principles of subsidiarity and proportionality. Any draft legislative act should contain a detailed statement making it possible to appraise compliance with the principles of subsidiarity and proportionality. This statement should contain some assessment of the proposal's financial impact and, in the case of a directive, of its implications for the rules to be put in place by Member States, including, where necessary, the regional legislation. The reasons for concluding that a Union objective can be better achieved at Union level shall be substantiated by qualitative and, wherever possible, quantitative indicators. Draft legislative acts shall take account of the need for any burden, whether financial or administrative, falling upon the Union, national governments, regional or local authorities, economic operators and citizens, to be minimised and commensurate with the objective to be achieved.

The detailed duties of justification had originally been inserted by the Treaty of Amsterdam and constituted a strengthening of the procedural aspect of subsidiarity compliance.[1] Indeed, we could very well view this provision from the Protocol as a *lex specialis* of both Article 5 TEU and the general duty to state reasons under the second clause of Article 296 TFEU, which stipulates that:

Legal acts shall state the reasons on which they are based and shall refer to any proposals, initiatives, recommendations, requests or opinions required by the Treaties.

4.3 The difficulties of applying subsidiarity in practice

While the black-letter law analysis of subsidiarity is relatively neat, the problem arises with its actual application in real life. All three principles from Article 5 TEU – legality or conferral, subsidiarity and proportionality – are clearly justiciable.[2] Still, as far as subsidiarity is concerned, both its judicial application by the Court of Justice and its application in the EU legislative process are far from easy. This is exactly why our empirical findings below will be of such value, since they allow us to formulate methods of operationalising the principle in line with what seems to be practical and accepted on the ground. It may well be that the introduction of subsidiarity in the Maastricht Treaty in the first place was a compromise to paper over some deep divisions between various factions in the EU, and that from the beginning there was no clear and authoritative understanding of what the principle really was supposed to mean.[3] At its most fundamental, subsidiarity can be seen as a brake on integration in that it restricts the exercise of Union powers to those cases where Member State action is insufficient, but also at least potentially as a justification for further integration *wherever* Union action is better than national action.[4] Article 5 TEU provides for two cumulative and not alternative criteria, of course, so in the end it appears to be meant at least primarily as a safeguard against excessive EU regulation: the inadequacy of purely national action alone is not enough to justify EU action. Still, that by itself does not make the application of subsidiarity much easier. Now that the principle is there, and now that the EWS has been set up to enforce it, we simply need to make sense of it. That in turn requires us to identify the concrete difficulties in the principle's application.

One aspect that arguably at least inhibits the judicial application of subsidiarity by courts, as well as its more or less objective application by political institutions, is the principle's political dimension.[5] The European Convention itself had a political exercise in mind when proposing the EWS,[6] and the Commission has declared that it favoured a 'political' approach to the EWS as well,[7] although there it means that the Commission should review, and respond to, any reasoned opinion irrespective of how many votes have been cast.

Indeed, if we think about it pragmatically, when one is opposed to a policy in general, this opposition would include the policy's manifestation as an EU measure as well. Conversely, there is little reason why one would support a national policy but object to its Union-wide extension. We need to differentiate by policy areas and types of measures, of course, for example where Union action threatens to contradict established policies or to lower domestic standards. Still, it should be fairly evident how an alleged infringement on subsidiarity can be just another way of saying that one is opposed to a measure politically. The UK House of Lords aptly remarked, in their opinion on a proposal in the area of inheritance law,[8] that:

> in practice the determination whether a measure complies [with the principle of subsidiarity] includes a significant political assessment based on the evidence as a whole.

Another argument why subsidiarity enforcement is so difficult relates to the perception that subsidiarity cannot plausibly be divorced from the principle of conferral and from proportionality, certainly not in the way the EWS does where it prescribes a review on subsidiarity and proportionality but allows for reasoned opinions on subsidiarity only. As Schütze aptly points out, the question *whether* the Union may legislate is already answered by the principle of conferral, whereas the question *how* it should legislate, and whether it should adopt a *particular* measure, is a matter of proportionality.[9] De Búrca has argued as well that not only subsidiarity and proportionality but also conferral are interlinked.[10] In the practical context of the EWS, when submitting reasoned opinions for the purpose of COSAC-sponsored reviews, a host of parliaments or chambers have pointed out that the various relevant principles cannot be neatly separated from each other, and many chambers simply address proportionality and legality explicitly even though the COSAC secretariat so far keeps insisting that the EWS is meant for subsidiarity only. The Irish parliament should be cited in particular for its consistency in pressing for a common definition of subsidiarity, expecting that otherwise the EWS will never be triggered.

In the literature there are in fact several attempts to provide definitions for the principle of subsidiarity and to translate it into a workable tool that can actually be used by regulators and courts. Calliess, for instance, proposes to distinguish between two manifestations of subsidiarity in EU context.[11] One is what he calls conservative subsidiarity, meant as a brake on integration, whereby a competence is to be exercised by either the Union or the Member States and where the test to be passed for the exercise of Union competence is strict. The other manifestation would be progressive subsidiarity whereby the Union would set frameworks, or minimum standards, leaving Member States the option to dynamically go beyond those standards. Here subsidiarity would be fulfilled as a rebuttable assumption that the EU is competent to regulate as long as Member States are free to complement the EU policy progressively. The former type of either/or policy sector is illustrated with the example of corporate cross-border merger control, where it would need to be shown that in trying to achieve the objective, Member States reach the limits of what they can do. The latter, dynamic type, is illustrated with EU minimum environmental standards that prevent a rat race while leaving Member States discretion to complement those standards. In both cases, proportionality cannot wholly be separated from subsidiarity, though. Schütze goes further and proposes to treat subsidiarity explicitly as a form of federal proportionality: one that protects national autonomy whereas proportionality proper is to protect liberal values. Both national and individual autonomy can thus be interfered with disproportionately.[12]

Another reason for the less-than-enthusiastic endorsement of subsidiarity in practice is that it can be fiendishly difficult to objectively prove or disprove that the Union is in a better position to regulate compared with the Member States individually. Professors Dashwood and Hix and former Commissioner Wallström are cited as agreeing that objective subsidiarity review criteria are impossible to spell out, and the British minister for Europe Murphy as saying that such objective criteria are not even needed.[13] What appears to be called for on the face of it is a test of comparative efficiency.[14] That, however, is difficult. First, the objects of comparison are hypothetical – a proposed EU measure versus potential and presumably very diverse national measures.[15] This is what would make even the principle of proportionality hardly enforceable: proportionality cannot be assessed purely in the abstract.[16] Second, the terms 'scale' and 'effect' in Article 5 TEU are very broad so that it appears to be relatively easy to formulate a fitting justification for more or less any measure desired. There may of course be areas of EU regulation that are more evidently in line with subsidiarity than others. The EU protection of migratory birds is, for example, easier to justify than the protection of birds that stay put in their home Member State. But even here a justification can be found.[17]

Yet another factor may be psychological in nature. In assessing subsidiarity in the context of the EWS, national parliamentarians are asked not only to review the negative aspect of what Member States themselves cannot sufficiently achieve but also what Europe can achieve better than they themselves could. Reviewing the 2006 postal services directive, the Hungarian parliament sought to objectify its review by making explicit three criteria: (1) a meaningful connection between the proposed actions and Community objectives; (2) the Community/cross-border scope of the problem; and (3) the added value of legislation on a European level and the inadequacy of purely national legislation. In addition the parliament considered the fact that the proposal at hand was an amendment of existing EU legislation, presumably a factor justifying more lenient review.[18] But there may also well be a certain reluctance on the part of national parliaments to being co-opted into confirming that EU regulation would outperform national regulation, considering that national parliamentarians may not see conveying legitimacy to EU-wide measures as their primary mandate. A passage from the opinion of the Belgian Senate on the same postal services directive is illustrative in its internal contradiction.[19] The question in a COSAC questionnaire was whether the Commission's subsidiarity justification was considered sufficient, to which the answer was:

> Oui, mais il est évident que les justifications faites par la Commission s'appliquent à l'Europe. Nos parlementaires doivent encore évaluer si ces justifications peuvent également être valable pour la Belgique.

Naturally, the Commission is not going to justify subsidiarity country by country: the object of comparison is – again hypothetical – regulation at national level in general, not particular sets of regulation. The only object that is specific is the proposal that is being tabled by the Commission itself. To be fair, the Belgian Senate's reply also applied to its assessment of the quality of the reasoning under proportionality, and here one could very well imagine that what is proportional in one Member State is less so in another. Presumably that depends on the degree to which a proposal actually affects certain Member States and the degree to which it would subsequently generate misfits with existing law: the Irish parliament was much more open to a liberalisation of postal services based on the country's readiness for such a move than its Belgian counterpart was.

A more fundamental reason why the Court of Justice and the EU legislator in particular might be disinclined to give effect to subsidiarity is that it is designed to constrain measures of EU integration by these very institutions. This is what Estella identifies as the classical legal critique of subsidiarity: not only is the principle said to be a-legal, it is also distinctly anti-integrationist.[20] This, however, is exactly one of the main reasons to involve national parliaments as external actors in subsidiarity enforcement in the first place.

4.4 The quality of the justification

Meanwhile, there are also arguments to cease trying to establish subsidiarity as a substantive principle and instead to focus on what its procedural safeguards can mean to lawmaking. Cooper, for example, has argued that the

EWS sets up the Commission and the national parliaments as interlocutors in a constructive argument rather than in typical legislative bargaining, even though the system's focus on subsidiarity to the exclusion of proportionality appears inhibitive.[21] We shall return to this point shortly as our empirical findings on the use of the EWS would actually very much support a stronger emphasis on justification, argument and the system's deliberative value.

Writing in the context of accountability theory in public administration, rather than of legislative studies, Behn draws our attention to an important aspect of accountability. The question is not just who holds whom to account and for what and how, but also who sets the standards, in other words the expectations, against which an actor's performance is to be measured?[22] Behn notes that all too often it is the civil servants themselves who define what results should be produced, even though they would typically deny that they are actually making policy. If we transfer this thought to the EU legislative process, then legally the Commission is of course obliged to 'promote the general interest of the Union',[23] while refraining from breaching the principles of conferred powers, proportionality and subsidiarity.[24] Yet evidently a monopoly on defining the general interest, or specifically the scope of the Union's enumerated objectives,[25] will give any institution a relatively easy opportunity to justify any of its proposed measures in that light.

We should remember that subsidiarity applies to the reaching of a *measure*'s objective, in other words to the question at which level an aim can better be reached which is set out in the measure itself. And it is easy to imagine that only an EU measure can achieve the aims of an EU measure. It is presumably for that reason that under the EWS the Hungarian parliament seeks to verify whether there is a sufficient link between a proposal's aim and an EU Treaty objective. Indeed, it would appear natural that debates should cover not only the appropriateness of the means but also the appropriateness of the ends. Since the exact definition of measures' immediate objectives and of the Union's broader objectives is rather discretionary, and therefore primarily political, we witness another instance where subsidiarity discussions potentially border, or intrude into, the realm of sheer political desirability. If we wish to keep the discussions about means and ends separate, though, which is what the Treaty regime on subsidiarity enforcement clearly implies, and concentrate on the appropriateness of the means only, then it becomes all the more important to verify whether at least an attempt has been made to *justify* those means.

Of course, a sharpened focus on the quality of justification means to take the duty to state reasons seriously. Specifically, the approach would have to be a lot more robust than what can so far be observed in the case-law of the Court of Justice of the EU. The Court's approach can safely be summarised as lenient, generous, prudent, restrained, deferential. On the substance, the Court is not willing to second-guess the EU legislature's assessment of the necessity of legislative action unless a manifest error is apparent; regarding formal compliance, the Court does not even require legislation to actually mention the word subsidiarity, it is enough that on the whole it can be inferred that the legislature has given it a thought.[26] Such leniency may well be criticised, and it has been.[27] Attempts have also been made to explain the Court's restraint, in that as an EU court it may be neither well-placed to, nor strategically interested in, defeating EU legislation on subsidiarity grounds.[28] And a restrained review by courts, including a limited focus on whether consultation procedures have been followed and whether arguments of comparative efficiency have been provided at all, has in fact also been hailed as welcome moderation to avoid undue judicial activism.[29]

As far as national parliaments are concerned, though, we can safely say that the strategic interests that might prompt self-restraint on the part of the Court of Justice do not apply to the same extent. Even though a significant part of national mainstream political parties are, on the whole and financial and migration crises notwithstanding, pro-EU and generally more so than their own electorate,[30] in principle national parliaments do not have a vested interest in simply giving away competences. Again, this is exactly the reason to put the national parliaments rather than EU institutions in charge of the EWS.

The suitability of subsidiarity as a review standard of choice is a rather more complex issue. Intuitively we could be tempted to say that if subsidiarity is a political principle, one which is not legal enough for courts to handle, then parliamentarians as political animals par excellence should certainly not feel uncomfortable using it. The empirical evidence suggests, however, that the opposite tends to be the case. Significant numbers of national parliaments do attempt to formulate their reasoned opinions in an objective way and in one that is tailored to the EWS, in that concerns are consciously phrased as matters of subsidiarity. Strikingly, then, we see that national parliaments, which are conventionally called political institutions, in fact engage in what can be best described as legal review. Parliaments thus behave in a court-like manner, accepting or at least attempting to use subsidiarity as a legal principle. We shall return to this point in the analysis of the practical use of the EWS by national parliaments, as well as in the conceptualisation of the EWS as a legal accountability tool.[31]

4.5 The empirical reality of the subsidiarity principle

One of the most frequently raised concerns about the practicability of the EWS relates to the elusive definition of the principle of subsidiarity itself. The principle, and the means to justify an act's compliance with it, are of course defined in Article 5 TEU and Article 5 of Protocol No. 2 TEU/TFEU. Nevertheless, the principle does not seem to be clear enough in that it is highly debatable when exactly it has been breached. Now, instead of trying to derive a workable definition from legal theory, the present chapter shall follow an inductive method to establish how national parliaments *themselves* seem to define subsidiarity, whether explicitly or implicitly. Below we shall take stock of existing reasoned opinions, both negative and positive, with a view to distilling common characteristics regarding the scope of subsidiarity as it is evidently perceived by national parliaments. Most – and the most diverse – opinions are generated when a proposal has been selected by COSAC for a collective review. We shall therefore consider the opinions on those proposals. Between 2004 and 2011 eight such reviews have been carried out. For the empirical analysis reference is made to the reports and annexes compiled by the COSAC secretariat rather than the Commission's database of incoming reasoned opinions. The reason is that, first, at the time of writing the Commission's database did not yet reach back to 2004 and, second, not all parliaments that participated in COSAC reviews did actually send their reasoned opinions to the Commission, reporting instead only to COSAC itself. Arguments are mentioned only where an opinion explains why exactly subsidiarity is breached or why exactly it is complied with, not where a parliament confirms compliance without saying why.

4.5.1 *The Third Railway Package*

During the XXXII COSAC meeting in The Hague on 23 November 2004, the conference decided to subject the so-called Third Railway Package to a collective subsidiarity check as a pilot project. Results were presented at the XXXIII COSAC meeting in Luxembourg in May 2005.[32] The package included four legislative proposals on, respectively, the development of the Community's railways,[33] on the certification of train crews operating locomotives and trains on the Community's rail network,[34] on international rail passengers' rights and obligations[35] and on compensation in cases of non-compliance with contractual quality requirements for rail freight services.[36] The idea of the pilot project was to simulate the use of the EWS as if it was in force: at the time, the parliaments were still anticipating the entry into force of the Constitutional Treaty. It was (rightly) observed that nothing precluded national parliaments from carrying out such review even before the EWS's entry into force. Out of the then 37 parliaments or individual chambers, 31 participated in the review.

The proposal on non-compliance in freight services triggered 10 explicitly negative reasoned opinions regarding subsidiarity. The train crew certification proposal provoked five negative reasoned opinions, the passengers' rights proposal triggered four, and the railway development proposal triggered three.

In the case of train crew certification, the Swedish parliament, the Czech Senate and both chambers of the parliament of the United Kingdom contested the compliance with subsidiarity because the measure would apply also to crews that do not actually cross any international borders. The two chambers of the French parliament and the German Bundesrat challenged the freight services proposal on the same ground, namely its applicability also to non-international traffic. The Hungarian parliament and the two chambers of the Irish parliament, again on the same basis, expressed doubts regarding both train crew certification and freight services, without, however, adopting a formal and outright negative reasoned opinion. The Italian Senate contested the freight services proposal for being applicable to purely domestic transportation.

The Belgian Senate also raised as a subsidiarity objection that the certification of train crews would apply to train crews operating within the national territory of one and the same Member State, but added itself that it would be unrealistic to envisage two categories of train conductor only one of which is qualified to cross national borders. The Finnish parliament was also more nuanced, questioning the merit of applying certification to crews not actually crossing borders but eventually recognising the merit of, and the Commission's efficiency justification for, Union-wide regulation. It did largely the same in the context of the freight services proposal, whereby the consideration that a national rail system is part of a larger network outweighed the intrusiveness of EU regulation of purely domestic rail traffic.

The Czech lower chamber demanded subsidiarity justification for any transfer of powers to a 'higher level' including not only national to EU level but also from the private sector to the state. Similarly, in the context of the freight services proposal, the two chambers of the Dutch parliament criticised the choice for (European) public regulation over self-regulation. It also expressed a concern, much like the parliament of Luxembourg and the transport committee of the parliament of Sweden (though not the constitutional affairs committee eventually in charge of the review), about the potential threat of a deterioration of the competitiveness of rail transportation in comparison to sea or road transportation.

The Czech Senate stated on the railway development proposal that it agreed that 'opening the rail carriage market between Member States cannot be achieved through independent actions of the European Union's Member States'. The Finnish parliament and the two chambers of the Irish parliament stated essentially the same thing. On the train crew certification proposal the Czech Senate argued that the introduction of new licensing authorities and accreditation of medical doctors was not necessary and that use could be made of pre-existing structures. Harmonised professional examinations were accepted; harmonised training as such was considered excessive. The Finnish parliament made a comparable point, noting that Finland's only railroad link to another EU Member State was with Sweden which did not even use the same gauge, so the imposition of common standards on Finland would not be justified, but unlike the Czech Senate the Finnish parliament expressly stated that this was a proportionality rather than a subsidiarity argument. The Luxembourg parliament submitted an inverse argument in that nearly all rail links in Luxembourg were international as they crossed borders to reach border towns in the neighbouring countries, so that EU regulation, and liberalisation, under the railway development proposal would apply to nearly the entire domestic railway system. But the Luxembourg parliament, too, noted that this affected proportionality if not subsidiarity.

The passengers' rights proposal and the non-compliance in freight services proposal were seen by the Czech Senate to be in breach of subsidiarity as complicating overlaps were predicted with an already existing international convention outside EU framework to which virtually all EU Member States were party. The Luxembourg parliament saw complications in that area as well, arguing that the envisaged objectives had already been achieved outside EU context. The Estonian parliament found that passengers' rights and non-compliance in freight services were in fact better regulated by the Member States through international agreements that take 'better account of the circumstances in the Member States'. This view was essentially shared by the Polish Senate. The Finnish parliament, by contrast, pointed out that the alternative to EU regulation of international train traffic would be regulation by another international private or public regulator: for the purposes of subsidiarity review, purely national regulation of international travel or freight transportation by train was considered inconceivable.

The Czech and Polish lower chambers found a formal breach of subsidiarity in that they did not receive a translated version of the proposals, which made an appraisal of the question impossible. Indeed, the Third Railway Package had been introduced before the 2004 enlargement of the EU. Other Central and Eastern European parliaments and chambers noted the same, without however establishing a breach on that ground.

4.5.2 *Divorce regulation*

The Commission's proposal for a Council regulation amending regulation 2201/2003/EC as regards jurisdiction and introducing rules concerning applicable law in matrimonial matters[37] was selected by the COSAC chairpersons in February 2006 for a collective review, and results were presented in November that year at the XXXVI COSAC meeting in Helsinki.[38] The review was completed within the deadline by 11 parliamentary chambers from nine Member States, but more parliaments and chambers submitted opinions after the deadline. A breach of subsidiarity was explicitly alleged by the Belgian Senate, the two chambers of the Dutch parliament, the Czech lower chamber and the UK House of Lords.

The Commission itself had justified the proposal in the light of subsidiarity as follows:

> The objectives of the Proposal cannot be accomplished by the Member States but require action at Community level in the form of common rules on jurisdiction and applicable law. Jurisdiction rules as well as conflict-of-law rules must be identical to ensure the objective of legal certainty and predictability for the citizens. Unilateral action by Member States would therefore run counter this objective. There is no international convention in force between Member States on the question of applicable law in matrimonial matters. The public consultation and the impact assessment have demonstrated that the scale of the problems addressed in this proposal is significant and that it concerns thousands of citizens each year. In light of the nature and the scale of the problem, the objectives can only be achieved at Community level.

The Belgian Senate in fact found a breach of both subsidiarity, mostly because existing Belgian private international law rules seemed to suffice, and of proportionality because an EU recommendation or directive was preferred over a regulation. The parliament of Cyprus found a breach of proportionality in that it was opposed to the idea of letting spouses choose the applicable law, including law that is 'totally foreign to the domestic legal order'. The Czech lower chamber doubted the applicability of the Commission's chosen legal basis in that it was not clear how the unification of private international law rules in matrimonial matters would contribute to the proper functioning of the internal market. It furthermore found a breach of subsidiarity in that the added value of an EU measure was not sufficiently shown, and found the proposal's compliance with proportionality 'disputable' in that an EU measure seemed inappropriate to tackle an international problem that reaches also beyond Europe. The Czech Senate found the tabling of a new proposal too premature for a proper subsidiarity review, as insufficient evidence had been collected regarding actual judicial practice.

The parliaments of Finland and Hungary and the French Senate found no breach of subsidiarity or proportionality but did find the Commission's justification too general and inadequate; the Lithuanian parliament found the reasoning 'not fully' satisfactory. The French National Assembly put this disarmingly politely with respect to the justification in the light of the principle of proportionality: 'Il gagnerait à être plus approfondi.' The chambers of the Irish parliament, by contrast, were more acidic. They noted that the subsidiarity justification was 'rather thin, particularly given that it had been flagged that national parliaments would be giving the proposal consideration in the context of a COSAC test.' Indeed, the proposal was introduced by the Commission in July 2006 but had been selected for COSAC review already in February. The German Bundestag as well as the Hungarian parliament demanded a more thorough justification of the internal-market relevance of the proposal for the purpose of the choice of legal basis; the chambers of the Dutch parliaments questioned the availability of the legal basis more directly on that ground. And like the Dutch parliament, the UK Lords found both a breach of law and established an insufficient justification. The Czech parliament complained of the poor quality of the translation of the proposal's text into Czech.

The most persuasive reasoning was probably provided in the opinion of the two chambers of the Dutch parliament, an excerpt from which was also directly quoted in the summary report drawn up by the COSAC secretariat and which is worth citing here as well. Proportionality was said to have been breached, among other things, because:

> According to the figures of the European Commission, an estimated 170,000 'international' divorce proceedings take place each year. It follows that approximately 340,000 people are faced each year with the conflict-of-law rules of the Member States, which is equivalent to some

0.074% of the EU population (about 457 million). The possible scope of the (potential) obstacles to the free movement of persons in the internal market should therefore not be overestimated. The question of in what percentage of these 170,000 cases the differences between national conflict-of-law rules actually result in the problems identified by the European Commission, including lack of legal certainty and the 'rush to court', is disregarded.

Thus, statistical proof for a cause of action was missing, an allegation also put forward by the UK Lords and, in essence, the Belgian Senate. Subsidiarity was, according to the Dutch parliament, breached because ultimately the only means to address the problems identified by the Commission was a harmonisation of substantive family law, for which the Union lacks the competence, whereas mere private international law rules provided insufficient added value. Indeed, several parliaments and chambers that did adopt reasoned opinions pointed out the cultural and emotional sensitivity of the regulation of national family law, fearing that the proposal was a step towards an EU-wide unification of this area of law as cross-border discrepancies could in the long run conceivably be avoided only by tackling substantive family law and not just conflict-of-law rules on the applicable jurisdiction.

4.5.3 Postal services directive

The Commission's proposal for a directive of the European Parliament and of the Council amending Directive 97/67/EC concerning the full accomplishment of the internal market of Community postal services[39] was selected for a COSAC review in February 2006 at the same time as the proposal on jurisdiction in matrimonial matters. Results were presented to the COSAC chairpersons meeting on 12 February 2007 in Berlin.[40] Again, chambers from nine Member States completed the review by the agreed deadline in December 2006 while more opinions were received afterwards, so that by the end of January 2007 parliaments or chambers from 21 Member States had completed the check.

The Commission's own justification regarding subsidiarity read as follows:

> The objectives of the proposed action are to achieve an internal market for postal services through the removal of exclusive and special rights in the postal sector, safeguard a common level of universal services for all users in all EU countries and set harmonised principles for the regulation of postal services in an open market environment, with the aim of reducing other obstacles to the functioning of the internal market. These objectives cannot be sufficiently achieved by Member States alone. The most striking example of this is that a number of Member States retain monopolies of varying scope over the provision of certain postal services in order to finance universal service, while others have completely or partly removed service monopolies or have firm plans to do so before 2009. These objectives can,

by the reason of the scale or effects of the proposed action, be better achieved at Community level and it is submitted that the Community can therefore adopt measures in accordance with the principle of subsidiarity as set out in Article 5 of the EC Treaty.

The only chamber to allege an outright breach of subsidiarity (and proportionality) was the parliament of Luxembourg. The parliament first of all criticised the Commission for limiting its justification to 'generalities'. It went on to point out that the Commission had not taken into account a report drawn up by a consultancy highlighting the problems that would face Luxembourg specifically in case of a liberalisation of postal services, and concluded that in particular the financing of universal postal services – letters lighter than 50 g – could be more efficiently regulated at national level. Regarding proportionality, it conceded that the proposal left plenty of room for Member States to decide how to finance those universal services, but the abolition of the exemption from liberalisation nevertheless went too far in its view, especially since the setting up of alternative means of financing might create more bureaucracy compared with simply keeping universal services a 'reserved area'.

Also the Belgian lower chamber with the Senate largely concurring, the French National Assembly, and the French Senate, demanded a more thorough justification regarding the proportionality principle, especially the necessity of the proposed measure, as well as further explorations regarding alternative means of financing universal postal services where operators may come under pressure in case of liberalisation. The Czech lower chamber mainly focused on the financing of universal services as well, without however establishing a subsidiarity or proportionality breach. The Lithuanian and the Portuguese parliament found the justification of how the proposal would smooth the operation of the internal market, respectively how the legal bases relate to the observance of the subsidiarity principle, wanting.

The German Bundesrat established a breach of subsidiarity – or rather legality and necessity – in one single provision of the proposal, regarding the obligation for postal sector and competition law regulators to cooperate and regarding a detail of appeal procedures against regulators' decisions, but not in the proposal as a whole. The Latvian parliament pointed out that another provision in the proposal should fall under personal data protection rather than services liberalisation and it had questions about the exact definition of the term 'address database', but conceded that these were not strictly subsidiarity or proportionality questions.

4.5.4 Anti-Terrorism framework decision

The proposal for a Council framework decision amending framework decision 2002/475/JHA on combating terrorism,[41] which at the time fell under the separate Third Pillar procedure but to which subsidiarity equally applies, was selected by the COSAC chairpersons for review on 12 July 2007. Following the proposal's introduction in November that year, the test was conducted, using eight weeks in anticipation of the regime under the Lisbon Treaty rather than the six weeks under the Constitutional Treaty, and results were presented in February 2008, parliaments or chambers from 20 Member States having concluded the review before the deadline.[42]

The UK House of Commons formally established a breach of subsidiarity, mainly on the ground that it was not convinced that an EU framework decision would achieve any better results than an already existing convention concluded in the framework of the Council of Europe, and apparently because the competent British minister, who had endorsed the Commission's viewpoint, in the Commons' view had had difficulties explaining the actual need for the measure as well. The German Bundestag made a similar remark regarding the added value with respect to the Council of Europe convention, but it did so in the context of proportionality and without alleging a subsidiarity breach.

The Austrian Bundesrat and the Belgian Senate, without establishing a breach of subsidiarity or proportionality, still found the Commission's justification wanting, based essentially on the notion that substantive criminal law remained a national competence where the need for an EU intervention must be justified particularly convincingly. Also the chambers of the Irish parliament found the Commission's justification 'incomplete', pointing out a lack of a thorough impact assessment and of a comparative analysis where exactly national law was deemed insufficient. The European affairs committee of the German Bundestag (though not its legal affairs committee) also missed, in the context of subsidiarity justification, a demonstration that loopholes actually existed in the criminal codes of the Member States. The chambers of the Dutch parliament even formulated a counter-questionnaire to the Commission, stating that the proposal complied with subsidiarity and proportionality 'in a strict sense' but that several questions were still left unanswered, including the exact scope of the term 'public provocation' of terrorist offences in the light of the narrower wording of the Council of Europe convention, a point that other parliaments had raised as well. The Greek parliament would have preferred a more thorough justification as well but put this, in the COSAC questionnaire, under the heading of 'other observations'. The Hungarian and Swedish parliament stated that they would have expected greater attention to the human rights dimension of the proposed new instances of criminal offences.

4.5.5 Equal treatment directive

The 2008 proposal for a new equal treatment directive, namely a Council directive on implementing the principle of equal treatment between persons irrespective of religion or belief, disability, age or sexual orientation,[43] was selected by the COSAC chairpersons in February 2008, and this choice was confirmed by the XXXIX COSAC in Brdo, Slovenia, in May; the proposal itself was launched in July that year and findings of the subsidiarity review were presented at the XL COSAC meeting in Paris in November.[44] Parliaments and chambers from 13 Member States submitted opinions within the deadline, but many more followed afterwards as the review period coincided with the summer recess period of July and August – there was then no rule yet that August would be discounted, but the findings stressed again the need for such rule which in the end indeed did get adopted.

The only parliament to expressly find a breach of subsidiarity within the deadline was the Irish one, and even then the opinion was nuanced, stating that there 'may be certain aspects of the scope of the proposed directive that may be best left to Member States, while others have clear advantage if action is taken at Community level'. This opinion was based on the observation that in some sectors the EU had more competences than in others. The parliament added, however, that subsidiarity compliance in its view in any event required prior consultation which in this case, at least with respect to Ireland, had not taken place. The Czech Senate submitted its opinion too late but also found a breach of subsidiarity in that Member State action in the area of anti-discrimination law could take better account of national norms and customs while avoiding the risk of an infringement upon exclusive national competences by the EU, which is why EU action should be limited to non-legislative means. The chambers of the Dutch parliament stated that until greater clarity regarding the meaning and implications of certain provisions of the proposal itself was provided, no definitive assessment – and therefore no positive clearance – on subsidiary grounds could be given. The UK Commons did not object on subsidiarity grounds provided that the EU had competence to regulate in the first place and stayed within those competences.

And yet again, while many parliaments were unable to process the proposal in time due to the summer recess, several parliaments or chambers found the Commission's justification insufficient as providing too few details item by item and inadequate qualitative and quantitative arguments. The core of the Commission's subsidiarity justification was that:

> The objectives of the proposal cannot be sufficiently achieved by the Member States acting alone because only a Community-wide measure can ensure that there is a minimum standard level of protection against discrimination based on religion or belief, disability, age or sexual orientation in all the Member States. A Community legal act provides legal certainty as to the rights and obligations of economic operators and citizens, including for those moving between the Member States.

The French Senate made a particularly apt observation in this regard. It rejected as invalid – essentially as tautological – the argument that only EU measures could ensure uniform minimum standards throughout the EU: while this is self-evident, such argument would justify basically anything, depriving the subsidiarity principle of any effectiveness. On a positive note, the Senate went on to note that the Commission's other argument was much more convincing, namely that common European standards were beneficial to the cross-border mobility of economic actors who could then expect comparable minimum norms throughout the EU.

4.5.6 Organ Transplantation Directive

The proposal for a directive of the European Parliament and of the Council on standards of quality and safety of human organs intended for transplantation[45] was selected by the COSAC chairpersons for review in July 2008, which was confirmed by the XL COSAC in Paris in November; the review was carried out immediately following the proposal's publication in December 2008 and findings were presented at the XLI COSAC in Prague in May 2009. From 20 Member States, 27 parliaments or chambers completed the check before the deadline, and four more did so afterwards.[46]

Again, only one chamber expressly found an outright breach of subsidiarity within the deadline, this time it was the Austrian Bundesrat. It put forward a number of concerns with reference to the proposal, including the ethical implications commanding caution on the part of the EU, the national prerogatives in the organisation of health care, the risk of a decline in organ donations in Member States with well-functioning systems if such Member States were to be forced to export organs to Member States with inadequate systems, the hazards of organ transplant tourism for which no incentives should be created, and the administrative burden. The Bundesrat referred specifically to subsidiarity when noting that one provision authorised the Commission in a comitology procedure to determine detailed implementation procedures which, according to the Bundesrat, violated subsidiarity, as such procedures can be 'determined and agreed in the normal way by the collaborating national organisations themselves in accordance with the state of the art'.

The UK Commons, the German Bundestag and the chambers of the Dutch parliament requested further clarification on the proposal while reserving their definitive assessment. The Italian Senate insisted, for the purpose of compliance with subsidiarity, on the insertion of clauses protecting Member States' right to impose higher standards and ensuring that national rules on the donation or medical use of organs and blood are not affected. The German Bundesrat questioned the Union's competence regarding some of the proposal's provisions and awaited details on the proposal's administrative impact for the purposes of proportionality review.

And yet again, a host of parliaments and chambers – roughly half of those participating – criticised the Commission's rudimentary justification, which stated that:

> [s]ince the objectives of this Directive, namely laying down quality and safety standards for human organs intended for transplantation, cannot be sufficiently achieved by the Member States and can therefore, by reason of

the scale of the action, be better achieved at Community level, the Community may adopt measures, in accordance with the principle of subsidiarity as set out in Article 5 of the Treaty.

The French Senate for instance remarked that this justification by the Commission comprised only meaningless standard formulations ('une de ses formules-type qui ne démontrent rien'). The Hungarian parliament described the reasoning as 'formal' and only repeating 'the relevant wording of the EC Treaty without any further explanation'. And in the words of the Irish parliament:

> [i]n order to be in compliance with its obligations under the Protocol, the Commission should complete a detailed comparative analysis of how the objectives of the Proposal could be effected at national level, outlining its possible advantages as well as shortcomings. There should be a comparison with other possible choices of actions other than at EU level. The Commission should explain in greater detail why regional and national parliaments are not in the position to take similar effective action in a specific policy area.

The impact assessment was not much more helpful, by the way, in fact the subsidiarity justification there was even rather obscure:[47]

> 1) The European Community has a clear opportunity and obligation to implement binding measures laying down high standards of quality and safety for the use of blood, organs, and substances of human origin.
> 2) European Community action is likely to contribute to public value by providing a platform for implementation and mutual learning which combines standardisation of reporting with diversity of service.

The UK Lords, for instance, quite dryly disagreed with the assertion that the EU had a duty to act. But the justification in the proposal itself could indeed be described as formalistic. In fact, this is not the only case where a national parliament supplied more elaborate reasons for supporting a proposal than the Commission did itself.[48] Here for example the Bulgarian parliament, which issued a positive opinion, observed that:

> [t]he Draft Directive unifies quality and safety standards of human organs transplantation in the EU Member States and will facilitate trans-border exchange. It will lead to standardization of collecting data on organs, donors and recipients and will create a mechanism of providing this information. These objectives and trans-border organ exchange in particular cannot be met effectively at national level and a regulation at EU level is required. The proposal does not regulate the ways of obtaining donor permission in procuring organs and does not contain regulations about

the clinical evaluation regarding organ compatibility and transplant-ation. (. . .) That is why it can be said that the proposal does not breach the principle of subsidiarity.

However the Bulgarian parliament did not find the Commission's own justi-fication inadequate. Also the opinion of the Estonian parliament was one that was much more elaborate than the Commission's initial justification, and the Finnish parliament's summary in the COSAC questionnaire, while it was not longer than the Commission's justification, was much more to-the-point:

> The shortage of suitable organs is a problem in all the Member States. Efficient use of transplantations requires organ exchange across borders between the Member States. The Commission proposal ensures the high quality and safety for patients at EU level and enhances the mutual trust between national authorities and safety of their transplantation system. These results could not be achieved as effectively by national measures.

Still, as can be seen with reference to the Bulgarian and Finnish parliamentary opinions, not all positive subsidiarity opinions were positive for the same reasons. The Greek parliament's opinion was, to cite yet another and quite different example, positive since:

> in the case in question the Union takes action within its limits of jurisdic-tion [and] the selection of a Directive as legal means leaves member-states with room to take further measures towards that direction if desired, whereas there is a possibility for selection of penalties applicable in case of legislation infringement.

These grounds appear to be less of an active endorsement of the proposal and are rather an acknowledgement of the fact that it complies with the principle of conferral and is not over-intrusive. The opinion of the parliament of Luxembourg, by contrast, noted that the simple coexistence of various national quality protection regimes precluded a harmonisation of such rules at the highest quality levels.

4.5.7 *Translation in criminal proceedings*

The proposal for a Council framework decision on the right to interpretation and translation in criminal proceedings[49] was selected for collective review by the COSAC chairpersons in February 2009, which was confirmed at the XLI COSAC on 12 May 2009 in Prague; the proposal was launched in July and results of the subsidiarity check were presented at the XLII COSAC meeting on 4–6 October 2009 in Stockholm. From 17 Member States, 21 parliaments or individual chambers completed the subsidiarity check in time, and COSAC received replies from 30 parliaments or chambers from 24 Member States in total.[50]

The proposal was designed as a step towards establishing a catalogue of minimum norms in criminal proceedings, starting with the regulation of cases where a defendant in criminal proceedings does not understand the language in which the proceedings against him are conducted. The Commission itself had justified the proposal under the subsidiarity heading as follows:[51]

> The objective of the proposal cannot be sufficiently achieved by Member States alone, since the aim of the proposal is to promote trust between them and it is therefore important to agree on a common minimum standard that applies throughout the whole of the European Union. The proposal will approximate Member States' substantive procedural rules in respect of interpretation and translation in criminal proceedings in order to build mutual trust. The proposal therefore complies with the subsidiarity principle.

The Austrian Nationalrat and Bundesrat established a breach of subsidiarity but did not in fact explicitly discuss subsidiarity in their reasoned opinion. Their objections were mainly based on the consideration that the European Convention on Human Rights (ECHR) already provides minimum standards so that there did not appear to be any urgent necessity for EU regulation, especially since the cost of the facilities proposed would have to be borne by the Member States themselves. The Czech Senate submitted largely the same objections, conceding however that this did not in fact relate to subsidiarity. It added that the Commission's justification for a measure in such a sensitive area was entirely unsatisfactory. The German Bundesrat declared that it had found no breach of subsidiarity and that it found the Commission's justification sufficient, but added that on the substance the proposal went beyond the standards already applicable under the ECHR. The Slovene lower chamber also considered the proposal superfluous as its content was already covered by Slovene law, but did add that the Commission's justification was not satisfactory.

The Irish parliament's main objection related to the fact that minimum standards would be applicable to criminal suspects in all proceedings, and not just cross-border cases. The Maltese parliament even rejected the proposal relatively harshly as 'an instance of overregulation and duplication', noting that the legal basis invoked did not relate to fair trial standards and that those fair trial standards were already covered by national law in conformity with the ECHR, further strengthened by the EU Charter of Fundamental Rights. It concluded that the proposal went 'beyond the issue of subsidiarity and constitutes an unwarranted measure at the level of the EU'.

The parliament of Bulgaria established no overall breach of subsidiarity adding, however, that it had difficulty assessing compliance with subsidiarity and proportionality in the case of one provision which was worded too broadly. In its report to COSAC it noted that the Commission's justification on compliance was not backed up with sufficient quantitative and qualitative indicators. Similarly to its Bulgarian counterpart, the parliament of Cyprus, the Polish Senate, and the House of Commons and House of Lords of the UK found no breach of subsidiarity but noted that the Commission's justification was too meager. The Hungarian parliament and the two chambers of the Romanian parliament were in principle satisfied by the Commission's subsidiarity justification although they noted that it was rather short and that they would have appreciated more detailed impact assessments regarding the administrative and financial burden on the Member States. The Hungarian parliament found no breach of subsidiarity 'since the Proposal seems to respect the relevant competence of the Member States'. The senatorial Dutch First Chamber found no breach either but sent a letter to the Commission politely requesting a more detailed reasoning, reporting to COSAC that the original justification was indeed insufficient. The French National Assembly found no breach but found the Commission's justification concerning legal basis wanting.

The parliaments of Denmark, Estonia, Finland, Latvia, Lithuania, Luxembourg, Portugal, Slovakia, Sweden, the two chambers of the Spanish parliament acting jointly, the German Bundestag, the Slovene upper chamber, the Polish Sejm and the French Senate, by contrast, found no breach of subsidiarity and even found the Commission's reasoning satisfactory. However, the Danish report included, rather helpfully, a minority opinion from an opposition party that largely overlapped with the objections of some of the other parliaments or chambers who had submitted critical opinions. The Italian Senate issued a positive reply stating that the proposal complied with the principle of subsidiarity, 'in that the goal of establishing minimum common standards may not be achieved individually by member States, and can only be attained by action at community level'. It is worth noting that this was not exactly the reasoning the Commission employed, which justified common standards not as the goal but as a means to build trust between criminal jurisdictions.

4.5.8 Succession regulation

The proposal for a regulation of the European Parliament and of the Council on jurisdiction, applicable law, recognition and enforcement of decisions and authentic instruments in matters of succession and the creation of a European Certificate of Succession[52] had already been selected by the COSAC chairpersons in February 2008, which was confirmed by subsequent COSAC meetings; the proposal was published in October 2009, a collective review was carried out and findings were presented at the XLIII COSAC of 31 May and 1 June 2010 in Madrid. This proposal triggered the greatest participation of any COSAC test up until that time as 36 out of 40 national parliaments or chambers, covering 25 out of 27 Member States, took part in the exercise.[53]

In spite of the high participation rate, though, only one chamber, namely the Belgian Senate, explicitly alleged a breach of subsidiarity, and this finding was not so much based on the substance of the proposal but on the fact that different language versions of the proposal stated opposite things as a result of which the protection of an aspect of substantive Belgian law of succession was not guaranteed. The point of concern for the Belgian Senate was addressed by other parliaments and chambers as well, only not in the form of an alleged breach of subsidiarity, namely that the private international law rules contained in the proposal might undermine the statutory rights of heirs, notably the mandatory reserve to which certain categories of relatives are entitled by law. Also the regulation of the substance of family law or other substantive areas related to succession, such as inheritance tax or *inter vivos* gifts, were said to be problematic in general, or to violate specifically the principle of proportionality in that the proposal would then go too far, or to violate the principle of legality as the EU had no competence to regulate substantive family law. The French National Assembly and the Senate raised this concern as a possible infringement on proportionality, the Belgian lower chamber as a breach of both proportionality and competence, the Italian Senate and the German Bundestag as a point regarding competence, the Hungarian parliament as a comment on the justification of the proposal, the Austrian Bundesrat, the Italian lower chamber, the chambers of the Romanian parliament and the Greek and Portuguese parliament as a comment or reservation on the substance, and the UK Commons as a concern directed at its own government for the purpose of subsequent Council negotiations.

The Austrian Bundesrat, the Belgian Senate and the parliaments of Cyprus and Portugal furthermore found the Commission's subsidiarity justification inadequate, while the French Senate found the proportionality justification insufficient. The Commission's reasoning on subsidiarity read as follows in full:

> The objectives of the proposal can be met only by way of common rules governing international successions which must be identical in order to guarantee legal certainty and predictability for citizens. Unilateral action by Member States would therefore run counter to this objective. There is a Hague Convention concerning the law relating to successions ('the Convention') which has never entered into force. The Hague Convention of 5 October 1961 on the conflicts of laws relating to the form of testamentary dispositions has been ratified by 16 Member States. It would be desirable for the other Member States to ratify the Convention in the interests of the Community. All the consultations and studies have illustrated the amplitude of the problems with which this proposal deals.

The chambers of the Irish parliament, by contrast, found the Commission's justification 'to be far more complete than in some previous subsidiarity tests'. The UK Commons were satisfied as well 'on this occasion', and so were the Lords. The reason for this is probably these chambers' reliance on the impact assessment, which was available in English but not in all other EU languages.

It should be noted that the German Bundestag, although it made no differentiation between subsidiarity and proportionality, carried out a detailed comparison of what Member States can and what they cannot regulate individually (e.g. they can regulate the authentication of foreign documents on their own territory but not how their own documents are handled abroad).[54] This brief discussion certainly reached a greater depth than the Commission's own reasoning.

4.6 Analytical assessment of subsidiarity in action

Based on the empirical record of the use of the EWS within COSAC, it is possible to derive several analytical findings. The following paragraphs shall discuss, in turn, the findings regarding whether the EWS thresholds have been or can be reached, the forms in which reasoned opinions are drafted, and the formal and substantive compliance with subsidiarity as it appears to be assessed by national parliaments themselves. In the end, policy recommendations shall be formulated how to define subsidiarity and the EWS in such way that it accommodates national parliaments' preferences in reality.

4.6.1 Reaching the threshold

Probably the first question the observer will be curious about is whether the EWS thresholds have been reached. To recall, the formal thresholds are a quarter of all votes for proposals under Article 76 TFEU regarding the area of freedom, security and justice and one-third of all votes in all other cases to trigger the yellow card, and more than half of all votes in all cases under the ordinary legislative procedure to trigger the orange card. The answer to this question for the considered period actually depends on the definition of what counts as a valid negative reasoned opinion. In a narrow sense, which is the one adopted by the COSAC secretariat, a negative reasoned opinion is only one that is sent in time and contains an explicit allegation of a breach of subsidiarity. This means alleged breaches of subsidiarity as opposed to other principles like legality or proportionality, and it means explicit allegations as opposed to more cautiously worded concerns, e.g. stating that a national parliament is not sure or has reservations about subsidiarity compliance. In that case the answer is no, the threshold has never been reached, although at 10 out of then 50 votes the parliaments came close to the yellow card threshold of then 17 votes in the case of the rail freight services regulation, one of the elements of the Third Railway Package, the object of their very first EWS pilot project in 2004/2005. However, based on a somewhat broader understanding of the scope of the EWS, which shall be elaborated further below, the parliaments in that case fell merely one vote short of triggering the yellow card. This would include parliaments or chambers that formulated their objections in forms related to but not labeled as subsidiarity complaints. In the case of the succession regulation, in a narrow sense only one chamber representing one vote explicitly alleged a breach of subsidiarity; if we however include all those parliaments and chambers which formulated similar objections but under the headings of competence, proportionality or substantive issues and which found the Commission's justification inadequate, the parliaments would have cast 20 votes between them, which is enough to trigger the yellow card with its threshold of 18 out of 54 votes! Since much evidently depends on the scope of the EWS, it becomes clear once again that it is worth considering what arguments the national parliaments are using in their EWS practice.

4.6.2 Forms of reasoned opinions

From the practice of the EWS as considered above, a complex but intriguing picture emerges. Positive opinions, which confirm compliance with subsidiarity, are just as relevant as negative opinions alleging a breach. Why exactly is subsidiarity breached, or respected, according to the national parliaments themselves? The reasons why subsidiarity is *respected* range from the assertion that EU regulation is greatly needed, to the dry observation that a proposal does not infringe upon Member States' competences. However, many parliaments refrain from supplying reasons for their acceptance in the first place and explain their positive verdict with the absence of problems. *Negative* verdicts are not uniform either: in some cases a parliament or chamber alleges an outright breach, but in other cases the wording is more cautious, or concerns are phrased like requests for further information. The following table gives a schematic overview of types of responses identified, ranging between the most positive endorsement and the most negative rejection.

Table 4.1 Typical wordings in reasoned opinions

Nature of the reasoned opinion	Formulation
Positive	Finds that subsidiarity has been complied with
	Is unable to detect any breach of subsidiarity
	Has no reason to make any comments
Negative	Has some doubts, concerns or reservations
	Requires further information, withholds verdict
	Finds that subsidiarity has been breached

As far as black-letter law is concerned, it should be noted that strictly speaking the EWS does not require national parliaments to issue positive opinions. The biggest question therefore is what counts as a subsidiarity objection and what does not?

4.6.3 Substantive compliance with subsidiarity

There is no comprehensive and authoritative, let alone universally binding, working definition of the scope and meaning of the subsidiarity principle beyond Article 5 TEU and Article 5 of Protocol No. 2 TEU/TFEU. This point was observed in the very first COSAC pilot project in 2004/2005 and it should be said that so far no spontaneous consensus has emerged between national parliaments or chambers either. Based on the empirical record, however, it is at least possible to identify several clusters of arguments. This means that, based on the elements of proposals that attract greatest attention, of a subsidiarity type or otherwise, the following three kinds of EU action seem hardest to justify:

- EU action in areas with no cross-border elements (Third Railway Package, Divorce Regulation);
- EU action in areas that are already covered, or that could be covered, by international agreements between Member States outside the EU framework (Third Railway Package, Succession Regulation, Anti-Terrorism Framework Directive, Translation in Criminal Proceedings); and
- EU action which comes dangerously close to regulating an area of law in which the EU has no or limited competence (substantive family law in the cases of the Succession Regulation and the Divorce Regulation, the medical care system in the case of the Organ Transplantation Directive).

4.6.3.1 EU action with no cross-border elements

It is fair to say that only considerations regarding the first type of action – i.e. action in areas with no cross-border implications – falls unambiguously within even the narrowest recurring definition of the principle of subsidiarity. This does not mean that the absence of cross-border implications automatically leads to a breach of subsidiarity, that a measure cannot be justified or that a presence of such cross-border implications cannot be demonstrated nonetheless. Estella points out that plausible reasons can be formulated to justify even measures concerning noise abatement, waste disposal and the protection of non-migratory birds, which arguably all concern activities that produce cross-border effects only when they actually take place at or near a national frontier.[55] Instead, all that we conclude is that here national parliaments are hitting the nail on the head when they identify a problematic aspect of proposed EU measures with reference to the purely local, regional or national implications of the object of the envisaged regulation. Or, to put it in different terms, the theoretical concerns about subsidiarity compliance in case of EU action with no cross-border implications do bear out in practice.

4.6.3.2 EU action vs. international conventions

As regards the second type of action, concerning the choice between an EU measure and an international agreement between the Member States, the issue is more complex. It is true that not only national parliaments at times point out their preference for an international convention instead of an EU measure to regulate a certain area with cross-border implications or to set common minimum standards. Even the Commission itself at times employs as a justification a reference to the dissatisfactory effect of an existing international convention that is not part of EU law. All this is odd since subsidiarity, strictly speaking, manifestly does *not* occupy itself with the question whether transnational regulation is best achieved inside or outside the regulatory framework of the EU. In this light, an argument that certain cross-border arrangements are preferably concluded by the Member States via normal international agreements rather than via EU legislation cannot be a subsidiarity argument. The expression 'by the Member States' in Article 5 (3) TEU cannot be stretched so as to mean 'by the Member States cooperating with each other via international agreements'. For the provision expressly specifies that what is meant are 'Member States [acting] either at central level or at regional and local level', not at international level.

What is more, a national parliament arguing that a subject-matter should preferably be addressed by an international convention already concedes that some form of a transnational approach is required, meaning that individual Member State action is inadequate and that the negative subsidiarity criterion is already fulfilled. In the subsequent choice between an international convention and, say, a directive, it is implausible that a convention would be more effective: non-EU international conventions require unanimity, which makes them harder to adopt, and they do not come with the judicial enforcement mechanism of EU legislation. Of course qualified majority and direct or indirect effect of EU legislation is less sovereignty-friendly compared with a regular treaty, but that is something the Member States might have considered before ratifying the EU Treaties. If the field is covered by EU competence, it means that the Member States have entrusted at least the possibility of regulation to the Union.

There are two cases, though, where a preference for an international convention over EU action might be a legitimate argument in the context of the subsidiarity principle. One is where Member State action would be inadequate but EU action would not be any better either because the scale of the problem is global or at least transcends the territory of the Union. Here a case can be made to pursue an alternative approach that is based on classic external relations, whether within EU external relations, the common foreign and security policy, or channels outside the EU framework altogether. The second case where a preference for an international convention could legitimately be raised within the EWS concerns the existence of an international convention that is *already operational*, and to which ideally all Member States are party. For the observation that an international convention already covers the object of a proposed EU measure can very well be an argument to deny the *necessity* of any additional EU measures as a part of the proportionality test. The question then is to what extent proportionality can be considered under the EWS – it shall be submitted that there are valid grounds for including it. Either way, a preference for an international convention *to be yet concluded* between the Member

States and not with third parties, as a substitute for EU measures in the same field that are already tabled, is not a subsidiarity argument. If anything, it confirms the need for a transnational approach and only strengthens the Commission's case.

4.6.3.3 Potential breach of competence

The last type of EU action that proved sensitive with national parliaments in the EWS, namely measures that threaten to overstep the Union's competence boundaries, does not only touch upon the adjacent issue of proportionality but even on that of legality. In practice the most relevant areas proved to be substantive criminal law, substantive family law and healthcare, not because they are sensitive in the EWS specifically but because they are sensitive in general, and therefore do not fall under EU competences that are as self-evident and uncontested as, say, packaging requirements. Also here we would need to consider whether and to what extent competence arguments may be validly raised in the EWS, and again it shall be submitted that there are valid grounds for accepting them as part of a subsidiarity test.

4.6.3.4 Formal compliance with subsidiarity

One point on which there is relatively consistent criticism, or on which a considerable number of parliaments or chambers is ready to speak out, is the often dissatisfactory depth of the Commission's justifications under the subsidiarity heading. The quality of the reasoning did not seem to improve between the period when the EU was anticipating the entry into force of the Constitutional Treaty and the actual entry into force of the Lisbon Treaty. It has even been pointed out that the Commission does not take any additional efforts in justifying proposals even when it knows in advance that a particular proposal will come under collective scrutiny through COSAC.

The most frequently voiced criticism concerns the fact that the Commission's subsidiarity justification is often formalistic, in effect a copy-and-paste exercise reproducing a rather banal assertion based on the wording of Article 5 TEU. A more subtle observation would be that sometimes the justification is erratic because it is designed to match an available legal basis. Thus, the justification for the proposed framework decision on translation in criminal proceedings, which intuitively would appear to be a measure to consolidate human rights protection in the Member States via the imposition of minimum standards, was sold as a measure to build trust between national criminal jurisdictions.

Special attention should be devoted to the status of impact assessments. These documents sometimes contain more elaborate qualitative and quantitative reasoning, as pointed out by the British and Irish parliament in the case of the succession regulation, but sometimes they contain little more grounds, or different grounds than the proposal itself. What is crucial, though, is that even where an impact assessment offers what the proposal itself does not offer, these impact assessments are not available in all EU languages, as the Lithuanian parliament pointed out in the case of the divorce regulation. Considering the value that the EWS, certainly in its Lisbon version, attaches to the availability of legislative proposals in all EU languages – the EWS clock does not start ticking until the last version has been transmitted – an impact assessment in just two or three languages cannot substitute for the persuasiveness of the proposal itself. Therefore, it would appear essential that the proposals themselves incorporate the core reasoning from the impact assessments to a much greater extent, including quantitative indicators.

The practical question that now remains is what role an allegedly insufficient justification should play within the EWS. Unless a national parliament explicitly concludes that subsidiarity has been breached, the COSAC secretariat – or the Commission, for that matter – apparently has little reason to count the remark as a vote under the EWS. It shall be submitted, though, that the quality of justification is an integral part of the test of the compliance with the principle of subsidiarity, and that national parliaments should not hesitate to make this clear in the way they draft their reasoned opinions. The time has now come to translate the empirical analysis above into concrete policy recommendations based on a bottom-up approach to defining the scope of the EWS.

4.7 Defining subsidiarity: a bottom-up approach

The present study shall not be attempting to formulate any sort of checklist for subsidiarity compliance based on abstract thoughts, such as a questionnaire with boxes that parliamentary committees may tick or not. Parliamentarians may simply choose to refrain from participating in an exercise that is set up in an excessively narrow fashion. For in reality the consideration of EU proposals and the drawing up of reasoned opinions requires time and energy which will only be invested if there is enough critical political mass. This could be achieved because the parliament in question has committed itself to participating in COSAC-sponsored reviews, or because a proposal is sufficiently salient in its own right, or both. If that salience is not, or not directly, subsidiarity-related, and if opinions would therefore become inadmissible, the incentive for participation will be low. Whatever can be gained from a dialogue between parliaments and the Commission governed or prompted by the EWS would be lost. Of course it may be retorted that arguments falling outside the scope of the EWS would fall under the political dialogue. However, the political dialogue is not a perfect substitute for the EWS. First, it applies only to the Commission and not to the other initiators of draft legislative acts. Second, effects of opinions channelled into the political dialogue are much more likely to remain confined to a closed circuit of parliaments, governments and EU institutions. Far greater visibility to the general public, in the sense of headline-making events, can be achieved if EWS thresholds are reached and the initiator of a proposal must publicly re-justify a proposal: not because it has voluntarily agreed to engage in a dialogue, but because Treaty law compels it to. Thus, a bottom-up approach taking into account what parliaments are willing to use already would have a more realistic chance of succeeding at offering guidance to parliaments, their committees, or at least the parliamentary support staff that actually draw up opinions in an appropriate format.

4.7.1 *The effect of a reasoned opinion*

The European Commission and the other initiators of draft legislative acts should agree or be compelled to consider as a negative reasoned opinion under the EWS any letter where a national parliament or chamber has even the lightest criticism regarding a proposal's compliance with subsidiarity. This would mean that the EWS is considered like an ultra-sensitive alarm system, one that is set off even by the noise of a passing car, but one that only produces a shrill sound and does not, say, kill the intruder. The relative mildness of the effect is offset by the fact that even slight disturbances can trigger it, and vice versa. To support this approach, national parliaments or chambers should actually start calling their letters 'reasoned opinions'. At the moment only very few actually do this. A reasoned opinion may of course take different actual forms including a parliamentary statement, motion, resolution or committee report, but there is no reason to be coy about the meaning of a letter and the message it is meant to convey for the purposes of the EWS. Moreover, national parliaments or chambers should clearly include in their reasoned opinions an unambiguous formula along the following lines:

> We consider that the proposal breaches the principle of subsidiarity within the meaning of Article 5 TEU and Protocol No. 2.

National parliaments or chambers would then remain free to be more subtle, nuanced and diplomatic in the text of the reasoned opinion itself. For example, they may in the text continue, as they mostly do now, to employ formulations to the effect that they have doubts, reservations, concerns, or objections to just some parts of a proposal, or that they would appreciate a more thorough justification, or further explanations on the scope, meaning and impact of all or some of a proposal's elements. Often enough the Commission is formalistic in justifying proposals under the subsidiarity heading. National parliaments are not barred from using a similarly robust approach in making clear, for example in the cover letter to their statement, that theirs is – for the record – a negative reasoned opinion whatever subtlety it contains, and that it should be read, and counted, as such.

4.7.2 *The scope of a reasoned opinion*

The Commission noted that it prefers subsidiarity to be distinguished from other considerations in reasoned opinions but hastened to add that of course parliaments were free to formulate letters as they wished. Indeed, the empirical practice thus far shows that national parliaments and chambers require the EWS to be given a scope that is sufficiently broad. As a consequence, subsidiarity should be understood very broadly, even if it means a certain overlap with other criteria that national parliaments evidently find relevant to subsidiarity review as well, namely competence and proportionality. Legal analysis of the definition of subsidiarity provides sufficient justification for such an approach, meaning that even arguments that appear to be distinguishable from subsidiarity can in fact very well be covered by the EWS.

4.7.2.1 Competence

First, if the Union does not have the competence to regulate as intended, then subsidiarity cannot possibly be fulfilled since the antecedent test on the principle of conferral has not been passed.[56] We should recall that subsidiarity proper is only fulfilled if 'the objectives of the proposed action (. . .) can rather, by reason of the scale or effects of the proposed action, be better achieved at Union level'. However, if competence is missing, the Union cannot achieve the objectives any better than Member States, because it cannot achieve them at all. The German Bundesrat made this view explicit when reviewing the 2009 proposal for a Succession Regulation, stating that:

> the Bundesrat considers scrutiny of the legal basis to constitute part of its scrutiny of compliance with the subsidiarity principle. If a proposal for legislation or some of the provisions contained in such legislation do not fall within the ambit of EU legislative competence, the legislation in question cannot be considered to be in compliance with the principle of subsidiarity.

A breach of the principle of conferral is a valid allegation to make in the context of the EWS. However, in spite of its reasoning of the scope of their review, in the above case the Bundesrat nevertheless confirmed that subsidiarity has in fact *not* been breached. Again, national parliaments should be encouraged to make it absolutely clear that they have found a subsidiarity breach by virtue of a lack of legal basis. This they can do by calling their letter 'reasoned opinion' and by formally alleging a breach of the principle of subsidiarity within the meaning of Article 5 TEU. Hesitation to adopt a letter for fear of addressing the wrong principle, an excessively nuanced differentiation between principles in the opinion, or the feeding of the opinion into the political dialogue instead of the EWS, would in this case definitely be misplaced.

A lack of competence is particularly present where there is no meaningful connection between a proposed measure and an EU Treaty objective, where a relevant legal basis excludes a certain type of EU action, and where a different legal basis is called for than the one relied upon. The latter possibility is highly relevant where a different legal basis would imply a different legislative procedure. And it is in fact most relevant if an objective would require an invocation of the flexibility clause of Article 352 TFEU. For not only would it then require unanimity in the Council; it would also mean that the Commission must have drawn the national parliaments' attention to its plan in the first place.[57] It is not clear how attention is sufficiently drawn for these purposes, but it cannot simply mean the usual forwarding of the proposal to national parliaments, which is an EU obligation anyway; it would have to require some additional effort such as a special notification of the COSAC secretariat and/or the presidents of the parliaments and chambers. If Article 352 TFEU is not relied upon in the first place, such special notification is unlikely to have occurred, in which case the subsequent adoption of the act would be in breach of the Treaties.

Again, all this describes lines of reasoning which can be validly put forward under the EWS. Where there is no EU competence, there can be no comparative efficiency on the part of the Union, and therefore by definition no compliance with the principle of subsidiarity. To put it differently, if the Union already fails the competence test, a subsidiarity test even if conducted cannot possibly be positive.

4.7.2.2 *Proportionality*

Second, where a national parliament or chamber finds that subsidiarity is breached because a proposal 'goes too far' in whatever sense, this should also be considered a valid allegation of a breach of subsidiarity: it should not be ignored as falling under proportionality. On the one hand, subsidiarity can indeed be considered a manifestation of the same idea that underlies proportionality, only here the 'victim' of a breach is the intactness of national competence.[58] Under the principle of subsidiarity the Union may act not only 'if' but also 'in so far as' it passes the two subsidiarity tests of national inadequacy and comparative efficiency. The term 'in so far as' implies an element of gradation within subsidiarity as well, for the mere presence of comparative efficiency on the part of the Union cannot mean a carte blanche for just any form or extent of regulation desired.

It is not impossible to think of a subject area where it would be legitimate for the Union to issue recommendations to Member States, since the Union is in a much better position than individual countries to collect information from across the EU and to conduct a comparative analysis. That, however, does not mean that the adoption of binding legislation, let alone total harmonisation, is therefore automatically legitimised. Subsidiarity-based legitimacy may be enough for recommendations but may run out where the optimal form and level of binding regulation should be tailored to the divergent preferences of smaller communities, or where the quest for the optimal form and level of regulation may well be left to regulatory competition between Member States, regions and municipalities.

Of course, the Commission may argue, as it sometimes does, that only an EU measure can achieve the objectives of an EU measure. It has every reason to do this since Article 5 TEU itself demands subsidiarity compliance with respect to the attainment of the objectives of a proposed measure itself. And of course, Member States cannot on their own enforce an EU-wide standard which an EU measure proposes to set. The conclusion we should draw from this is, however, not that anything goes, but that the initiators of EU legislation should abstain from putting forward tautological arguments and instead identify the deeper purpose of the proposed action. Regulation is not, or at least should not be, adopted for the sake of regulation, but for the attainment of a fundamental aim which, in the case of the EU, is laid down in the Treaties. It is for this reason that it makes sense to verify, taking inspiration in the practice of the Hungarian parliament, whether a *measure*'s immediate objective, which surely can be fulfilled only by that measure, displays a meaningful link with the *Union*'s objectives.

And it is for this reason that national inadequacy and comparative efficiency can hold for one type of instrument but not for another, or for one degree of intrusiveness but not for another. In other words, even under the heading of subsidiarity, the Union may well go 'too far'. And no EU measure can enjoy comparative efficiency if it takes a form that goes outside the Union's competences, for then it could not lawfully exist. Under the EWS, national parliaments are not the final judges on whether the Union did go too far, but any allegations to that effect should not be dismissed as falling purely under proportionality or be shifted out of the EWS and into the political dialogue. National parliaments should insist on their right to raise such points under the EWS, and to have their votes counted, again by explicitly calling their letters 'reasoned opinions' and by including a formula that makes clear that the opinion contains an allegation that the principle of subsidiarity within the meaning of Article 5 TEU has been violated.

4.7.2.3 Adequate justification

The final point concerns the link between the quality of the justification and an act's substantive compliance with subsidiarity. It is, in that context, difficult to understand how it can be that a parliament would confirm that subsidiarity has been respected while at the same time finding, as several parliaments and chambers have, that the Commission's reasoning *why* exactly it has been respected is insufficient. Such an outcome is only possible if one takes an autonomous-review approach to the EWS whereby the substance of subsidiarity compliance is double-checked on its own merits, no matter what reasons, if any, the initiator adduces. Yet this would not seem to be in the interest of national parliaments, nor would this correspond with the other subsidiarity safeguards which require the initiator to justify adequately in the first place. It is legitimate to argue that inadequate justification means a breach of subsidiarity, for two reasons. First, national parliaments are expected to see to it that subsidiarity within the meaning of Article 5 TEU is respected in accordance with Protocol No. 2 TEU/TFEU. That Protocol includes duties for the initiator to justify, a breach of which leads to a breach of Article 5 TEU by default (formal ground). Second, if even the initiator himself is unable to demonstrate subsidiarity compliance, it is legitimate to conclude that therefore such compliance cannot be demonstrated at all. National parliaments are not required to provide (better) subsidiarity grounds – and nor is the Court of Justice afterwards – only to detect breaches. An inadequate justification can and should therefore be translated into a rebuttable presumption of breach. The presumption is rebuttable since the initiator is to re-justify proposals if they are formally challenged under the EWS. As with the other grounds, parliaments and chambers should be encouraged not to approve of EU drafts if they find the initiator's reasoning insufficient, but to draw conclusions into their final consequence and announce and label them as such: where they detect a breach, they should say so and call their letter 'reasoned opinion'.

Again, special consideration should be given to the role of impact assessments in the overall justification of proposals. Meuwese suggests that national parliaments may use impact assessments in the review of EU legislative proposals. She observes that the EU legislator can brush aside impact assessments and insist that such instruments do not substitute the making of discretionary political choices; however, she also points out how the *absence* of an impact assessment can be used to challenge a proposal.[59] There is no need for national parliaments to be drawn too deeply into the study of impact assessments, though. As long as they are not available in all EU languages – and the availability of all language versions of proposals is a requirement that had been added specifically to the EWS by the Treaty of Lisbon – national parliaments are entitled to expect a restatement of the most relevant conclusions from the impact assessments in the proposals themselves.

4.8 Conclusion

There is a fundamental case to be made for the initiators of EU legislative proposals to justify convincingly why they launch a particular piece of regulation. Majone, in his preface to the paperback edition of his book *Dilemmas of European Integration*, argues that '[u]nless the EU can actually demonstrate that it can add value to what individual member states, or subsets of member states, can achieve on their own, it will be impossible to resolve the legitimacy crisis which is currently threatening the stability, and possibly the very survival, of the EU'.[60] Even without resorting to such stark appeals, still a case can be made that the justification of EU proposals is a necessity. For the truth is that this is simply a legal obligation laid down in the Treaties. Now that this legal obligation has, in the Treaty of Lisbon, not only been maintained but even backed up by an additional review mechanism, namely the EWS, we must conclude that the necessity to justify is not diminishing but, if anything, increasing. This chapter sought to offer the national parliaments a means to use the EWS in such way that the letter of the law is respected but their needs are accommodated as well. Arguments about subsidiarity can legitimately be brought forward in reasoned opinions, for example, but not only where a cross-border aspect of a measure's objective is missing. Arguments about the EU's overstepping its competences can also be raised under the subsidiarity test: without EU competence there cannot possibly be a positive outcome of the subsidiarity test. Arguments about the EU's going 'too far' with a proposal do resemble proportionality concerns but they can in fact also be brought under the heading of subsidiarity: subsidiarity may after all justify one degree of regulation but not necessarily all types of regulation. And arguments about an insufficient reasoning on the part of the initiator of EU proposals are just as well part of the subsidiarity test. An inadequate justification violates not only the procedural aspect of subsidiarity compliance, it presumably also breaches the substantive aspect, for if even the initiator himself cannot give proper reasons for an intended piece of regulation, chances are that no-one can.

5 The early warning system as an accountability mechanism

5.1 Introduction

In the overall discussion of the European Union's institutional framework, a branch of literature has developed that occupies itself with the Union's accountability. It is true that the term 'accountability' as an umbrella term has come to mean all manner of good things, including transparency, responsiveness or simply ethical behaviour.[1] Yet it is also possible to narrow down accountability to a relationship between an actor and a forum whereby the forum may ask questions and the actor must justify his conduct under the threat of consequences in case of dissatisfactory answers. This is the definition Bovens has put forward and which has gained broad acceptance in the literature.[2]

When applying accountability theory to the European Union, some rather bleak pictures have been drawn. First of all, several developments already inhibit the exercise of accountability to national parliaments even without the complicating factor of the EU, such as new public management that addresses the citizen while bypassing parliaments, the agentification of governance and the deliberate depoliticisation of executive action.[3] As regards the EU, very prominently Harlow has made a strong case for a more cautious approach to European integration in the light of the structural accountability deficits that have emerged in that context.[4] Gustavsson et al. have even brought out an edited volume exploring what they term the 'illusion of accountability' in the EU.[5] In it, the gaps in sustaining accountability for the exercise of formally delegated but effectively irretrievable powers is highlighted,[6] especially if this exercise involves informal processes and civil servants acting as policy-makers.[7] Of course we may choose a nuanced approach, such as the one offered by Menon and Weatherill, who acknowledge the limitations of attempts to legitimise far-reaching delegation of powers to the EU by means of accountability models originally designed for nation-states.[8] Still, no matter which way we turn, it is fair to say that accountability is not the European Union's strong suit.

The present chapter shall seek to apply accountability theory to the early warning system (EWS) for subsidiarity, exploring whether the EWS might contribute to a strengthening of accountability in the EU. It is rather unusual to frame the EWS in terms of an accountability regime,[9] yet it would turn out that such a view is largely justified and may make a valuable contribution to the conceptualisation of accountability and, at a more practical level, to making the Union's accountability more robust than it currently is. The key institution that would be held to account, then, is mainly the Commission as the sole initiator of legislative proposals in the ordinary legislative procedure, but in fact any initiator of EU legislation;[10] national parliaments are the bodies holding it to account for that activity.

Of course we would be well advised to take into consideration that different EU bodies face different types of accountability dilemmas. For example, the democratic accountability of the European Central Bank, which is not uncontested,[11] is a rather idiosyncratic affair because the Bank's protection from political intervention in the area of monetary policy is instrumental to its functioning as an independent central bank. Meanwhile, far graver accountability gaps surely exist with respect to comitology committees and EU agencies which are still clouded in obscurity,[12] and which create acute problems of lacking parliamentary oversight of any kind.[13] As far as the EU legislative process proper is concerned, the role of the Council is also quite problematic from a parliamentary accountability viewpoint, as the body as a whole is not accountable to the European Parliament while only its component parts, i.e. the ministers, and to a far lesser extent the civil servants in Coreper and the working groups, are or can be called to account by national parliaments, each by their own. In that light, the accountability of the Commission in its capacity as the initiator of legislative proposals, which is perhaps a relatively innocuous activity compared with its autonomous legislation and the execution of law but which is the primary target of the EWS, may not even be the most pressing issue.[14] The Commission's policy choices are often suggested by the Council anyway and, as Craig notes, no important overall EU priority is set without having passed through one or more summit meetings.[15] In that sense, the EWS might be criticised for attempting to offer a remedy to one of the Union's lighter problems.

Still, this does not mean that accountability for the initiation of legislation is irrelevant. First, irrespective of the multi-annual agenda, it is well known how important the timing and framing of individual proposals, in other words agenda-setting, is to the eventual outcome of legislative projects. The issuing of proposals is therefore not all that innocuous. Second, as noted earlier, EWS participation on the part of national parliaments may well generate spillover effects and act as a catalyst for heightened activity on, or at least attention to, EU legislative projects and their follow-up. And that does have a bearing on areas where accountability gaps are wider than they are with the Commission.

Several questions shall be raised. The first question is whether a national parliament's participation in the EWS can indeed be seen as an instance of enforcing accountability vis-à-vis the Commission, using Bovens' sociological definition of the term as an actor–forum relationship. If the answer to the first question is at least partly affirmative, the follow-up questions shall probe more deeply into the theory and reality of the EWS from that point of view, namely:

- In which direction is accountability rendered to national parliaments under the EWS: is the relationship vertical, diagonal or horizontal, and is it based on a principal–agent relationship?
- How does the EWS fit in existing theoretical models of accountability to multiple forums, in particular redundancy models and accountability networks?
- What is the purpose of accountability under the EWS, considering that *democratic* accountability is not the only type of accountability and that it may not even be the most relevant here? And,
- What sort of accountability obtains under the EWS: *political* accountability, which is typically associated with parliaments, or *legal* accountability, which is usually seen as something that courts do?

It shall be argued that the EWS does fit the definition of an accountability relationship between national parliaments and the Commission, albeit imperfectly. Regarding directionality, a case can be made for each of the proposed conceptualisations, which makes the EWS a very multi-faceted institution, revealing more of the European Union's constitutional complexity than might appear. As far as the conceptual embedding of the EWS as a multiple-forum arrangement is concerned, redundancy is only a partly suitable model; meanwhile, national parliaments thus far form an accountability network that is rudimentary at best but one that might also acquire strength via informal contacts within a coalition of the most proactive chambers, including senates. Regarding the sort of accountability, it shall be argued that the EWS contributes to the checks and balances within the EU as well as to learning on the part of the Commission but that we should not be too eager to presume any meaningful boost to the regime's democratic dimension. Finally, in order to determine whether a case of legal or political accountability is at hand, we shall introduce a definition of the two terms that is sharper than what is used in the literature so far. In short, it will define accountability as legal or political, not based on the nature of the *forum* (parliament or court), which is only of limited help, but rather on the nature of the *criteria* that the forum employs in order to enforce accountability. Political criteria are rooted in the imposition of values and subjective desirability: in cases where two choices are available and both are lawful as such, the actor opts for one rather than the other in a discretionary manner. Legal criteria meanwhile distinguish between lawful and unlawful choices, which means that the actor must opt for the lawful ones or at least may not opt for the unlawful ones. To verify empirically the legal or political nature of the arguments employed by national parliaments in the context of the EWS, the responses of national parliaments to EU legislative proposals that were launched during the calendar year 2009 shall be examined in depth.

Adherence to legal review criteria makes a parliament's reasoning more narrow and, in a sense, more formalistic. This might appear restrictive on national parliaments where interactions tend to centre on the imposition of values, not on what is lawful and what is not. However, we should not forget the usual and surely justified stereotype about parliaments as rather path-dependent institutions.[16] Their endorsement of legal accountability as a tool under the EWS, instead of the political accountability patterns that they are used to, would make those parliaments appear to be much more innovative than we might initially have expected. This final notion shall not only conclude the present chapter, it shall also lead over to the next one (Chapter 6) where we shall make a further step and propose to compare the European role of national parliaments under the EWS with the domestic advisory role of French-style Councils of State.

5.2 The EWS as an accountability relationship

From an analytical point of view, the EWS gives rise to a fundamental question: of what nature the involvement of national parliaments is meant to be? More specifically, is the EWS a system of co-legislation, with parliaments acting at least in an advisory capacity, or is it a system allowing national parliaments to better enforce democratic accountability of the EU institutions? The relevant documentation is inconclusive on this point. The EWS is de facto a step in the ordinary EU legislative procedure, however it is enshrined in a separate Protocol to the European Treaties rather than in the central provisions setting out the legislative process in the TFEU itself. The Final Report of the working group on national parliaments of the European Convention, which in turn produced the Draft Treaty establishing a Constitution for Europe, mostly speaks of 'involvement' of national parliaments in a general sense.[17] At the same time, the concepts of legislative participation of national parliaments and those of democracy and accountability are, in the literature, often linked or perhaps even conflated.

Co-legislation, or at least participation in legislation in an advisory function, and accountability enforcement do not have to be mutually exclusive, though. It is true that when speaking of the constitutional functions of a parliament, one typically distinguishes between lawmaking and control.[18] Yet domestic experience suggests that even lawmaking contains an aspect of accountability. This is because almost all legislative proposals in Western parliamentary systems are drawn up and introduced by the government. The parliament's – especially the opposition's – response to these proposals may then call into question the need for such new legislation in the first place. This prompts the government to justify its proposal. The parliament's right of amendment then allows it to propose and discuss changes to the bill, but if the bill is originally drawn up by the government, such changes may become unacceptable to the government. In both cases, government–parliament relations, and the sustained confidence of parliament in the government, may become an issue even where actually 'only' a bill is being debated.

The European Union's EWS shall here be considered as a hybrid mechanism between (mostly) advisory participation in legislation and (a weak form of) accountability enforcement as against the Commission, the initiator of most EU legislation as the sole initiator of secondary law in the ordinary European legislative procedure. Both aspects are present, like they are present even in a domestic legislative procedure where the government initiates bills. We shall discuss the advisory role of parliaments under the EWS – parliaments as Councils of State – in the following chapter.[19] Here we shall focus on the accountability dimension of the EWS. Coincidentally, such an approach would also meet the appeal formulated by Auel[20] to focus more on the deliberative, accountability-enforcement functions of national parliaments rather than on their regulatory input in EU context. Yet whereas she above all means the relation between parliament and the national government in EU context, the present study focuses on the accountability of the European Commission to the national parliaments.

5.2.1 The relationship

The *actor* in this accountability relationship is the Commission, although potentially any other initiator of a draft legislative act that is subject to the EWS: a group of Member States, the European Parliament, the Court of Justice, the European Central Bank and the European Investment Bank.[21] Yet typically it is the Commission that takes the initiative to launch EU legislative proposals. A *relationship* with national parliaments and the Commission's *obligation* to justify and to re-justify its proposals in the EWS context exists by virtue of this being provided in the EU Treaty and its Protocols. In addition, the (albeit self-imposed) obligation to justify exists by virtue of the Commission's own commitment to answer letters even though the EWS thresholds have not been reached.

Who exactly is the *forum*? Is it each national parliament individually, since they all review Commission proposals in principle autonomously, or is it the parliaments collectively, since their objections are in the end counted as parts of a larger total? I have argued elsewhere that national parliaments are an agglomeration of domestic bodies whose common bond lies purely in the eye of the beholder. Thus, what makes the national parliaments a community of institutions is, above all, the fact that we *call* them 'the national parliaments' and treat them as a collective in the first place, including even the isolationist ones, for example by counting their votes as part of a total.[22] In the present context, however, the accountability relationship shall be construed in a purely individual manner as between the Commission and any one individual parliament at a time. After all, an actor can have more than one forum.

5.2.2 The object of accountability

In an accountability relationship, the actor is obliged to justify his 'actions',[23] or his 'conduct'.[24] In the case of the EWS, the primary objects of justification are legislative proposals from the Commission. Thus: are proposals already 'conduct' in the sense of the employed definition? It could be argued that Bovens' definition of accountability is at least primarily retrospective, while the EWS envisages the discussion of *draft* measures that have not yet been adopted. One might say, to use American judicial parlance, a case over a mere proposal is not 'ripe' yet. Bovens himself considers consultation procedures and participation by stakeholders as 'proactive inputs into the policy process' but he excludes them from the definition of accountability since justification, judgment and consequences are missing.[25] However, by the time the Commission publishes a proposal, the consultation stage for policy input proper is already over. The proposals themselves *have* already been adopted, even if only as proposals. As such, the decision, or 'action', to publish and introduce a document can very well be the object of accountability. By extension, the contextualisation of an individual proposal in the Commission's overall strategy allows for the accessory evaluation of the Commission's 'conduct' in a broader sense. This corresponds with what has been argued earlier: even the discussion of a domestic bill contains an element of evaluation of the government's behaviour. Arguably, the decision to table a proposal, which ultimately must be adopted by others, may lead to, or would justify, a somewhat lighter accountability compared with accountability for one's autonomous definitive and binding actions.

5.2.3 Asking questions and passing judgment

The EWS envisages the receipt of letters from national parliaments at only one point in the legislative procedure, namely immediately after the publication of a proposal. The letters may, and in practice do, demand a better or more elaborate justification of a proposal or additional information to allow the national parliament to make up its mind. This may safely be considered as 'posing questions'. After the letters are received, the initiator (typically the Commission) might thus have to re-justify the proposal in the form of a rebuttal, but no further rejoinder from national parliaments is provided for. Are letters from national parliaments therefore already 'judgment'? Here we need to introduce a distinction between initial judgment and final judgment. The initial judgment is expressed in the parliament's assessment of a Commission proposal. It extends only to the explanation and justification that the Commission is obliged to include in its proposals anyway. Final judgment would come closer to Bovens' definition, in that judgment is passed not only on the initial action or document but also on the demanded follow-up justification. In the case of the EWS, any follow-up rejoinder on the part of the parliament, barring a second letter, would have to be translated through other means that parliamentarians have at their disposal to influence the EU legislative process. This would be most notably the steering of their own minister in the Council and, where that is applicable, the activation of their fellow political party members or other like-minded politicians in the European

Parliament. Initial judgments may only partly fit the accountability definition employed, and there is no provision for final judgments on the
Commission's supplementary justification. Still, a judgment is passed nevertheless, no matter how it is eventually communicated.

5.2.4 The sanction

The forum's judgment in an accountability process can be either positive or
negative. Should the forum's judgment be negative, the question of consequences for the actor in general, and sanctions against him in particular,
arises. In the context of the EWS, the Commission manifestly does face consequences – positive or negative – as a result of its engaging in the procedure.
However, these consequences are soft and indirect in nature. A positive
reasoned opinion from one or more parliaments can boost the Commission's
weight and constitutes bargaining leverage for the proponents of a particular
proposal in the legislative procedure. Silence on the part of national parliaments could possibly, but not very convincingly, be construed as a sign of
support. Mostly it might indicate permissiveness. The value of a negative
judgment, finally, is where the true nature of the EWS is revealed. The Lisbon
Treaty attaches all manner of legal-sounding consequences to cases where the
Commission chooses to ignore the objections from national parliaments. The
truth remains, however, that after the EWS stage the decision how to proceed
passes to the Commission, the European Parliament and the Council, right
where it always has been.[26]

In reality, for the Commission the possible negative consequences of opposition at the EWS stage are two-fold. First, as an initiator of legislative
proposals, the Commission would need to fear that strong opposition from
many national parliaments, especially lower chambers, will cause, or perhaps
rather correlate with, an unwillingness on the part of the Council, or rather of
many of its members, to approve the measure either. Second, even if the
measure is adopted, as a watchdog of the compliance with European law in
the Member States the Commission would need to fear a higher risk of non-
transposition of such measure in national law. A triggered EWS thus means
an increased risk of non-adoption of, and non-compliance with, a piece of
secondary European law. The latter might be particularly urgent in the case of
objections from senates since they are domestic co-legislators but are typically
more independent from the executive during the adoption stage. Both risks
point towards reputational damage for the Commission, in the sense of
tarnished credibility and authority. In the literature it is contested whether
accountability can exist in the absence of strong and binding sanctions, such
as, in the textbook case of parliamentary no-confidence votes, a dismissal from
office. But arguably, possible embarrassment is a form of available negative
consequences as well – it also lies at the heart of accountability to ombudsmen
or peer accountability. And it is a consequence that can be triggered in the
framework of the EWS.

5.2.5 Summary

The above reasoning shows that the EWS can be considered as a weak form of a procedure for accountability enforcement in Bovens' narrow definition of the term. Some elements of the definition fit entirely: the presence of an institutionalised actor–forum relationship, the Commission being the main actor and national parliaments being forums, and the duty for the Commission to justify, the right for parliaments to ask questions and demand re-justification. Some elements fit only partly: the rudimentary facility for an exchange of opinions which does not allow for a direct final judgment of parliaments on the quality of the re-justification, and the merely indirect nature of the sanctions that national parliaments have at their disposal. Still, this does not stand in the way of the application of accountability theory to the EWS, as long as the caveats are borne in mind.

5.3 The direction of accountability: vertical, diagonal and horizontal

If we apply accountability theory to the EWS, as I suggest we do, then another rather interesting, though perhaps slightly doctrinal question arises. Can we speak here of a principal–agent relationship whereby accountability results from the fact that the forum has delegated power to the actor? In this case, national parliaments would have set up the Commission along with the other EU institutions and delegated legislative powers to the institutions by ratifying the European Union's founding treaties.[27] The alternative view would be that the Commission is held to account by national parliaments simply acting as external stakeholders who are affected by the actor's decision,[28] or as forums who simply have the task to extract accountability without being a principal, like a court does with respect to the executive.

5.3.1 Principal–agent theory

It would appear that the answer to this question very much depends on the discipline within which it is raised, notably law or political science. As a matter of international law, powers have been delegated not by parliaments but by Member States; as a matter of internal constitutional law, the conferral took place either by the people themselves through referendum or, on behalf of the people, by parliaments. Arguably, constitutional law would be ready to view parliament as a permanent institution whose composition is subject to change but whose personality as a legislative assembly is continuous. Of course we should be realistic enough to acknowledge that today's parliament is not the same parliament that had delegated powers years or decades earlier. In that sense, the national parliament of the day is a principal only in a very theoretical sense. Still, firstly any possible repatriation of competences from the Union to the Member States would be effected through Treaty amendment or through withdrawal from the Union, i.e. normally with the approval of the national parliament of the day, even though any one Member State cannot repatriate anything through Treaty amendment without the other Member States' consent, and withdrawal must be negotiated and not abruptly unilateral.[29] Secondly, any such repatriation of competences would benefit the national parliament of the day as the recipient of powers restored as domestic competences. In that sense, the national parliament (of the day) as a principal vis-à-vis the Union, including the Commission, is not as theoretical as it might appear.

And yet, it should be noted that what we are discussing here is the national parliament as a more or less permanent institution with respect to the Commission as an equally permanent institution. What about the members of the Commission of the day? It might after all be argued that, even though the Commission is 'completely independent' and its members 'shall neither seek nor take instructions from any Government or other institution, body, office or entity',[30] at least individually a Commissioner appointed from a particular Member State is a sort of agent of that Member State. For while the Commission as a whole is nominated by the European Council in common accord with the President-elect of the Commission and then approved by the European Parliament,[31] and while after taking office the Commission is subject to dismissal only by the European Parliament,[32] individual Commissioners do depend on their home Member State for at least initial re-nomination.[33]

For the EWS, all this makes little difference, however, for two reasons. First, EU legislative proposals are adopted by the Commission as a collegiate body. Even if a certain individual link to individual home Member States exists, it certainly does not exist with respect to other Member States. If the Commission's size is reduced so that not every Member State will have its own Commissioner, as envisaged by the Lisbon Treaty,[34] these individual links to the Member States will fade even more. Second, the possible sanctions attached to the EWS are very indirect. The real and immediate effect of negative opinions by national parliaments depends on the actions of others, notably the European Parliament and the governments in the Council. In that sense, national parliaments might perhaps be compared with courts of auditors, which cannot make anyone resign by themselves but whose reports may trigger interest on the part of those who can.[35] Or they could be comparable in that sense to media or ombudsmen, with the task to 'generate and process information on agents' decisions and their reasoning' but without having the capacity to sanction the agent like a principal could.[36]

5.3.2 *The multiple directions of accountability*

Taking into consideration that a national parliament can be described as a principal vis-à-vis the Commission in various ways, but that some ways are more plausible than others, we are left with the prospect of conceptualising parliament–Commission accountability relations under the EWS along more than just one dimension. Along four dimensions, to be precise:[37]

- Upwards vertical (hierarchical accountability towards superiors);
- diagonal (judgment by a forum that can trigger a sanction by another forum);
- downwards vertical (as in accountability to consumers); and/or
- horizontal (accountability to peer institutions).

While European institutional law and federalist ideology might easily consider the Commission to be a supranational superior to domestic institutions, the principle of conferral (or perhaps, rather, delegation) of power to the EU which is effected by Treaty ratification, usually in a national parliament, would support the opposite view, namely that national parliaments are the principals and are thus hierarchically superior to the Commission. Thus, the Commission would be accountable to superiors in a vertical manner. This view would also be supported by the fact that subsidiarity review is a means to make sure that the EU institutions, having received delegated powers, do not exceed the terms for the exercise of those powers as laid down in Article 5 TEU, which next to subsidiarity also stipulates proportionality and legality.

Since the sanctions that are available to national parliaments as forums under the EWS are so very indirect, it might equally make sense to rather speak of a diagonal accountability relationship whereby the stick is wielded by more powerful actors. Again, the absence of a convincing, at least of a direct, sanction may call into question the very existence of an accountability regime in the first place. In that case, diagonal accountability would not even be accountability at all. We have seen that the parliaments' sanctions are not all translated via other actors, though, and that they include direct reputational damage as well as the prospect of delayed or incomplete domestic compliance with secondary EU law once it is adopted. Therefore, even if the accountability is partly diagonal, it cannot be exclusively so.

Since the sanctions are so weak overall, one might even be tempted to compare them to consumer accountability as part of a wider consultation procedure. In that sense, the Commission would be accountable to all who are affected by its actions, including national parliaments as an important target audience when it comes to the implementation of directives. Behn proposed to frame something along these lines, but then in public administration, as 360-degree feedback.[38] National parliaments would then be part of the Commission's 'accountability environment' and interact with the Commission as such. This approach is not invalid in itself, however we have also argued that the EWS turns national parliaments into privileged advisory bodies which sufficiently distinguishes them from the rest of stakeholders who might also be consulted.

In a paradigm of 'polycentric constitutionalism', finally, parliament– Commission relations might be considered a matter of horizontal accountability rather than a matter of hierarchy, with neither the Commission nor national parliaments on top.[39] Polycentric constitutionalism, meant to be a more apt term replacing multi-level constitutionalism, is an attempt to leave behind traditional notions of hierarchical and autonomous layers of government in the context of the European Union.[40] Instead, it invites us to embrace the reality of European integration whereby decisions come about through the cooperation of various actors in various European and national capacities, and whereby it is by no means clear at all who is the truly superior authority. Such a horizontal approach would certainly be welcomed by those pro-European national parliamentarians who are reluctant to start competing with the European Parliament for the ultimate representative mandate. Polycentrism would place national parliaments perhaps not in an equal, but at least not in an inferior, position with respect to the other EU institutions, and it would, crucially, turn them into EU institutions themselves. This would be very much in line with a vision of multiple representation points in a transnational multi-level 'parliamentary field' as proposed by Crum and Fossum.[41] It would also be in line with notions of co-actorship in the creation of European law whereby Member States are not just the recipients but also the initiators of European law and active contributors to its creation. It is a notion which is, for example, well-established regarding the interaction between the Court of Justice of the EU and national courts, who are not mere passive recipients of law either.[42] And a horizontal accountability approach would anyway be a default option if we choose not to see any principal–agent relationship between the national parliaments and the Commission of the day, a choice that is legitimate especially in the light of the Treaties' insistence on the Commission's complete independence from the Member States including their domestic parliaments.

Neither choice can truly be dismissed out of hand, and a reliance on each is to some extent justified. What they all have in common, though, is that while they denote different types of accountability, they all presume the existence of accountability in general. Considering the fact that the EWS is not commonly considered an accountability regime, showing that it can be, as has been done in this study, is already an important step towards getting a better grasp of the implications of the EWS. What remains now, as a matter of theoretical consideration, is an attempt to embed EWS accountability in the institutional setting where there is, as seen, more than just one forum but potentially 40 parliaments or individual chambers. Furthermore, we will examine whether the accountability is legal or political in nature, which we shall test empirically.

5.4 The plurality of forums: networks and redundancies

We have established that the EWS can be seen as an accountability regime, even though there is no final answer as to what exact type of regime – vertical, horizontal or diagonal, or a hybrid with elements of more than one type. But what of the fact that the accountability can hardly be one-dimensional considering the potential participation of up to 40 parliaments or chambers in the EWS?

One possible way of reasoning is to insist on the autonomous character of subsidiarity review, in other words on the discretion of each parliament or chamber to conduct scrutiny on its very own terms. This logic seems to underlie the position of those members of COSAC who are reluctant to let that inter-parliamentary conference select EU legislative proposals for collective and coordinated subsidiarity review.[43] However, a purely isolationist viewpoint is hardly satisfactory when it comes to the *results* of EWS review which, whether we like it or not, is based on the weighing and counting of votes as shares of a total of 54. In other words, while national parliaments are not obliged to cooperate with one another and may well see their relation with the Commission in strictly individual terms, it is rather unhelpful to ignore the collective dimension of the EWS as a system that in the end relies on a plurality of forums and that treats them as a collective.

If we accept that the EWS implies the recognition of national parliaments as a collective, which it evidently does, we may proceed to hypothesise about the institutional framework that will result from it. Depending on the degree of inter-parliamentary cohesion observed in reality, two possible models shall be distinguished. The first is *redundancy*, as formulated by Scott.[44] In such a setting, actors are accountable to multiple and mutually overlapping forums, which in turn act as fail-safe mechanisms with respect to one another. Thus, applying redundancy theory to the EWS, this would mean that one parliament's failure to detect and complain about a breach of subsidiarity would be compensated by a reasoned opinion of another parliament. The second model presupposes that national parliaments of different Member States align in an *accountability network* vis-à-vis the Commission. Accountability networks have been posited by Harlow and Rawlings, who made reference to the examples of courts and ombudsmen.[45] A network requires a greater cohesion between forums as compared with otherwise autonomous forums in a redundancy model. In the case of the EWS, it would require national parliaments to share information and to coordinate their priorities and assessment standards.

In each case, we should be aware that a system of multiple forums is not an unambiguously positive thing. Mulgan draws attention to the fact that setups of multiple accountability have their disadvantages as well, including forum-shifting on the part of the actor and an incapacity of those multiple forums to impose effective sanctions.[46] Bovens speaks of the problem of many eyes, as opposed to the problem of many hands that makes it hard to allocate individual responsibility for collective decisions.[47] This in itself does not seem a valid reason for a parliament not to participate in the EWS, though.

5.4.1 Redundancy

Based on what we can derive from the institutional analysis of the EWS and the empirical record of inter-parliamentary cooperation thus far, it is possible to conclude as follows. The EWS itself cannot be a purely redundancy-based accountability regime. The reason for this is that one parliament's failure to spot a subsidiarity breach counts as a positive abstention in the aggregate, and thereby actively weakens the coalition of those parliaments that did spot a breach. A unicameral parliament's abstention means that the thresholds of one-quarter, one-third or an absolute majority of total votes become harder to reach, and must in fact be compensated by the votes of either one other unicameral parliament or of two chambers of bicameral parliaments. This is mitigated, though, to the extent that not just the quantity of objections but also the quality of reasons and the origins of the votes should count for the impact of the EWS in practice.[48]

At the same time, while the EWS *itself* cannot purely be redundancy-based, it may well be part of a larger accountability framework surrounding the Commission which *is* redundancy-based. Thus, the EWS becomes an additional instance of an accountability regime, along with stakeholder accountability in the consultation phase and accountability to the other EU institutions including the Court of Justice of the EU. In that sense, even though the scope of the EWS is narrow and the effects are rather soft, accountability in the EU has been strengthened. Where the EWS fails to generate opposition, such opposition can be generated elsewhere, and if it does not materialise elsewhere, the national parliaments' reasoned opinions may provide useful arguments for the Commission to consider and for others to adopt, also in judicial proceedings.[49] Craig aptly notes that majoritarian single-executive systems in nation-states, supposedly an ideal that the EU cannot hope to live up to, in fact displays an electoral accountability deficit between elections. The EU's complexity, by contrast, provides for a greater number of points, and moments, of entry into the policy process.[50] It is fair to say that with the introduction of the EWS the number of such points has been increased significantly. And this should be welcome: as Flinders argues, informal accountability channels, which no doubt exist, cannot substitute public accountability, where both the questions and the answers are on the record for every citizen to see.[51]

5.4.2 Accountability network

An accountability network is a network of 'agencies specialising in a specific method of accountability'.[52] The existence of a network, as opposed to a mere agglomeration of individuals, presupposes a high degree of solidarity and cooperation, and in theory it can be applied to networks of parliaments. As far as formal cooperation between national parliaments in the context of the EWS is concerned, though, the record is not entirely bleak but still rather mixed. Bengtson observes a 'clear progressive development over time' in the intensity of inter-parliamentary cooperation in the EU, but, due to structural constraints, only up to a point.[53] Raunio does not expect any significant increase of inter-parliamentary cooperation for EWS purposes beyond the existing IPEX database and the usual COSAC meetings.[54] Below the radar, though, informal contacts between the permanent representatives of national parliaments or chambers to the European Parliament seem to be emerging, which help their principals to be aware of what the parliaments of other Member States are working on.[55]

One relatively realistic prospect would be the emergence in practice of a small coalition of active chambers which are most willing to employ the EWS. This would mean the establishment of an *actual* network within a *notional* network. Based on the record of which chambers are the most prolific thus far, it is fair to assume that senates, as opposed to lower chambers, will account for a disproportionate share of overall EWS activity.[56] The problem is that such prolific chambers including senates may not necessarily be the most willing to share information. Especially the UK House of Lords, while accounting for virtually all of the EWS activity of the Westminster Parliament, is not exactly known as a body that is keen to seek cooperation with overseas assemblies.

5.4.3 Summary

Two forms of accountability with multiple forums have been considered: redundancy, where each forum acts as a fail-safe for all other forums, and accountability networks where multiple accountability forums coalesce. What emerged was that the EWS in itself is not a redundancy-based accountability regime because the abstention of any one parliament, i.e. the non-adoption of a reasoned opinion, works to the disadvantage of other national parliaments which try to reach a minimum threshold to trigger at least a yellow card. The EWS can, however, very well be *part* of a larger redundancy-based account-ability regime around the European institutions. Thus, where the EWS fails to extract accountability, judicial review is still available and might even rely on reasoned opinions from the EWS as evidence; where pre-legislative consult-ation processes turned out to be dissatisfactory, the EWS may offer an addi-tional opportunity to articulate dissenting views and to demand a better justification for proposed measures. Regarding networks, it is fair to say that Union-wide inter-parliamentary solidarity is not sufficiently robust to speak of an accountability network, and chances are that it will not increase either. The EWS may well lead to the emergence of a smaller group of prolific opinion-writers, including several senates, but that by itself does not mean that these parliaments or chambers will actually cooperate and see themselves as part of anything resembling a coalition. Here the most promising avenue for coordination between those chambers that are willing to use the EWS actively seems to be the informal contacts between the permanent national parliamentary representatives at the European Parliament. These civil serv-ants can draw each other's attention to proposals that their national parlia-ments find interesting, which would increase the likelihood that a proposal, without Union-wide coordination through COSAC, triggers more than just the usual one, two or three reasoned opinions. And this could very well consti-tute a rudimentary inter-parliamentary accountability network, driven by informal contacts between Brussels-based civil servants representing those national parliaments that, when it comes to the EWS, together form a coalition of the willing.

5.5 The purpose of accountability: democratic or otherwise

There exists an almost universal assumption that the involvement of national parliaments has positive implications for the democratic character of the process or the outcome of EU decision-making.[57] In the same manner, account-ability to parliaments is readily placed in the context of enhancing democratic legitimacy. On the one hand, this is understandable. After all, the degree of democratic accountability, as opposed to other forms of accountability, can be approximated very roughly by comparing systems of accountability towards bodies of which one assumes that they are democratic, in this case parlia-ments. On the other hand, there are purposes for accountability regimes other than the preservation of democratic standards, notably checks and balances and learning.[58] And it is absolutely legitimate to discuss and even measure the success of the EWS in terms of learning potential and checks and balances, without getting into misty debates about democratic legitimacy.

This has also methodological advantages. In contrast to democracy, aspects of learning is measurable quantitatively to some extent based on, for example, how many words are devoted to subsidiarity justification in EU legislative proposals over the years, and how many reasoned opinions still complain of inadequate reasoning. Dutch parliamentary civil servants recount that Commission civil servants who had prepared legislative proposals are some-times very glad to receive fresh input from someone outside their own micro-cosm.[59] Checks and balances can be quantified less easily, but even in purely qualitative terms a case can be made that an additional corrective on supra-national lawmaking is a valuable thing to have.

To be sure, an improvement of democratic legitimacy is a potent normative justification for national parliamentarians and political parties who seek to engage in EU decision-making and for that reason, for example, to call for more frequent debates to confront ministers over Europe or to reserve more funding for administrative support for the European affairs committee secre-tariat or the parliamentary research department. But that does not mean that this is their primary, let alone their only, motive, or that democratic legiti-macy is actually enhanced, or that the side-effects are not far more beneficial. The most pragmatic stance for academia would therefore seem to be to allow for democracy-related arguments to be voiced for purposes of generating publicity, but in the evaluation to concentrate on more tangible effects.

5.6 The EWS as a legal accountability mechanism

'Legal' and 'political' accountability are both commonly distinguished types of accountability. The former tends to be associated with courts, while the latter tends to be associated with parliaments or other 'political institutions'. Harlow points out that lawyers traditionally tend to see judicial review as an instance of the rule of law, rather than as a form of accountability;[60] neverthe-less, the application of accountability theory to courts is accepted in the litera-ture. What the literature does so far not explicitly acknowledge is the possibility of legal accountability unfolding in political forums. It shall be argued that the EWS is such an instance. But what is it that makes accountability 'legal' or 'political' to begin with? In fact, the very use of these terms appears to be intuitive, rather than based on a previously established definition.

5.6.1 *What is political accountability?*

When differentiating between possible types of accountability, Bovens considers four dimensions along which one may categorise regimes. Accountability may be differentiated based on (1) the nature of the forum, (2) the nature of the actor, (3) the nature of the conduct, and (4) the nature of the obligation to render account. Political and legal accountability are, according to his overview, so distinguished because of the nature of the forum: it is owed to political or judicial institutions, respectively.[61] Nevertheless, in reality the distinction between legal and political accountability in the litera-ture is much less sharp. Usually, the distinction is based either on intuition, whereby parliaments are *evidently* political institutions and courts are *evidently* legal forums, or on a mix of different criteria, mostly the nature of the forum and the nature of the evaluation criteria used, e.g. courts are legal forums *and* they apply legal standards.

For example, in his article on accountability relations in the regulatory state, Scott refers to 'legal' and 'political' accountability as two traditional or conventional types of accountability.[62] Legal accountability is the account-ability owed *to* the courts, and *in respect of* certain juridical values. Political accountability is owed to ministers and parliament and thus ultimately to the electorate. All this seems reasonable and straightforward, but it in fact mingles the nature of the forum, the type of evaluation criteria the forum uses, and the nature of the forum's ultimate principle for the purpose of the definition. Similarly, Bovens qualifies the Commission's accountability to the European Parliament as 'political' because the European Parliament 'is a political forum'[63] – although he concedes that different aspects of accountability may come to the fore depending on what aspects of the conduct are at stake. Bovens furthermore distinguishes political from legal accountability as the former is based on a principal–agent relation (voter-parliament or parliament-government) while the latter is not. Finally, he notes that courts are legal forums as they use 'detailed legal standards' in their scrutiny.[64] Meanwhile, Verhey et al., in their in-depth comparative study of political accountability, associate political accountability with government–parliament relations as a matter of course and distinguish it from legal accountability to courts.

Consequently, in their definitions they devote rather more attention to the meaning of the word 'accountability' than to the meaning of the word 'political'.[65] Arnull[66] adopts an approach similar to the one formulated by Oliver,[67] namely contrasting 'legal accountability to the courts' with other forms of accountability, notably accountability to politicians or to the public. In the erudite comparative work by Koopmans on courts versus political institutions, the distinction between the two is largely based on the intuitively self-evident difference between politicians and judges.[68]

Thus, perhaps glossing over some of the nuance found in the literature, it seems fair to say that the intuitive definition of legal and political accountability reads like this: legal accountability is what courts do; political accountability is what parliaments do. The distinction may be so self-evident that it does not seem to require any further explanation. However, it is definitely worth probing deeper. Saying that parliaments enforce political accountability because parliaments are political institutions would be circular reasoning; it is therefore not helpful. A better definition of what is 'political' is needed. In that regard, it is possible to define a body as 'political' not by the way it is constituted, but by the way it works. Mulgan rightly observes that 'political accountability' can be taken to mean the accountability of elected politicians to the public, or the accountability of ministers to parliament, or the accountability of appointed officials to politicians, but also accountability which is based on a 'special type of debate and discussion where judgments and values are contested'.[69] Arnull briefly notes that if accountability is owed to politicians, then scrutiny will be 'politically motivated'.[70] Harlow and Rawlings define accountability networks as a network of 'agencies specialising in a specific method of accountability', and they thus also stress the process of the assessment rather than the character of the forum.[71] Alberti defines 'political accountability' as including assessment criteria of 'appropriateness, convenience or efficacy'.[72]

Meanwhile, saying that courts are legal forums because they use law as their standard for accountability is acceptable, but it says nothing yet of a situation where forums other than courts use the law in such a way. Flinders, for example, helpfully speaks of 'judicial accountability' rather than 'legal accountability' to make clear that he means accountability to courts.[73] This leaves to us the possible application of legal accountability to non-judicial bodies. Romzek and Dubnick, for instance, define legal accountability as a process where law is used as an instrument. This would include not only courts or court-like institutions as forums, but also the legislature.[74]

5.6.2 A new approach: the nature of the assessment criteria

To define what is 'political accountability', let us consider, by way of analogy, the term 'political decision'. When we speak of a 'political decision' that has been taken, often slightly pejoratively as in that someone's appointment must have been a political decision, we do not usually describe the origin of the power for decision-making. Instead, we describe the character of the will-formation process that led to the adoption of the decision. Political decisions are in this sense more or less synonymous with discretionary, to some extent subjective choices. Thus, I suggest the following definition: a political decision is one where different alternatives were lawfully available and the decision-maker opted for one whereas other reasonable people might have opted for another. This would stand in contrast to a non-discretionary decision which could only be taken in one particular way because the law rules out the alternatives. For example: if a court awards a farmer a compensation because he had to give up his land for the construction of a new road whereas he was not allowed a mandatory hearing, such court decision is not political because it merely applies the law (the law on expropriation) to the facts (a public authority expropriates a landowner in breach of the correct procedure). Ideally, any court applying the law in that context would have arrived at the same conclusion; if decisions diverge between jurisdictions, the court of final instance will rule definitively on what the law means. Had the authorities granted a hearing, this would not have been a political decision either. After all, the law requires a hearing and the other alternative – omitting a hearing – is not lawfully available.

The decision to build the road in the first place, by contrast, *is* a political one. It was a political choice to build the road now and not later; to build a new one rather than upgrading an existing one; to connect one destination to the new road system rather than another; to invest in road-building rather than railways; to prioritise infrastructural projects over investments in the hospital system. A different, or differently staffed, legislature or public authority might have chosen differently, but all of these alternatives are by themselves not unlawful. It came down to making a choice of what was most desirable at the time. Of course, different principles feed into political decision-making on the part of the legislature or the public authority wielding discretionary power. Financial soundness is one of them, but so is, for example, the popularity of the decision.

This understanding of what is 'political' – meaning desirability-based – can, as a next step, also be applied to forums rather than actors. A forum that holds an actor to account in order to establish if the actor's conduct was lawful does *not* engage in political accountability. After all, conduct is either lawful or it is not. In the above example, the court will either uphold the expropriation if it was lawful, or otherwise detect and remedy the unlawfulness if it was not. Yet the court will (ideally) refrain from probing deeper into the soundness or desirability of the road-building programme itself, because that was not the question. A municipal council – parliament at local level – meanwhile has at its disposal tools to question the mayor over much more than just whether his civil service crossed the threshold between the lawful and the unlawful in an individual case. For example, it can scrutinise the mayor regarding his choices – why roads rather than hospitals? – which were taken within the realm of legality. This is what political accountability should mean: having to justify decisions based on standards the fulfilment of which depends on validly competing points of view, any possible alternative decisions being equally lawful.

To define an accountability regime as legal or political, I therefore propose to exclusively focus on *the nature of the assessment criteria* used by the accountability forum. Thus, courts would enforce legal accountability because their principal or ideally their only standard, when they review legislative or administrative action, is legality: compliance with the applicable law. I use legality in a broad sense, meaning not just the presence of a legal basis for public action but rather compliance with the entire body of applicable procedural and substantive law. Parliaments, meanwhile, would enforce political accountability not because they are political institutions – whatever that may mean – but because their principal standard, when they review legislative or administrative action, is political desirability: compliance with their own preferences. Such preferences can be contested, as reasonable people can disagree on what is desirable and what is not. In fact, these preferences *should* be contested: this is the essence of democratic pluralism. This leads us to two underlying definitions, one observation from constitutional law resulting from the definition, and one working hypothesis for the present study, namely:

- Political accountability is based on the *desirability* of the action assessed;
- Legal accountability is based on the *legality* of the action assessed;
- Courts ideally employ legal accountability only;
- Parliaments typically, but not necessarily exclusively, employ political accountability.

Evidently, the picture is not as black-and-white in reality. Courts, especially constitutional courts, are frequently exposed to criticism, or simply the observation, that their rulings took into account political considerations. When the Court of Justice of the EU, the European Court for Human Rights, or a domestic constitutional court, for example, formulate their judgments in a particular way – bold and activist, or cautious and minimalist – commentators are ready to ascribe this to 'ulterior' or at least not purely law-based motives. Stone Sweet refers to 'constitutional politics' where courts rule on the constitutionality of legislation;[75] Sadurski contests the very notion that law, especially constitutional human-rights provisions which are necessarily vague, can have a single orthodox meaning which only judges can correctly identify.[76] Conversely, not all decisions by public authorities are political in the sense of being discretionary. As regards parliaments, it may be said that certain types of parliamentary procedures at least resemble judicial procedures for the establishment of facts and the allocation of guilt. These include parliamentary impeachment procedures against office-holders; parliamentary investigation or inquiry; or the procedure for the lifting of a member's parliamentary immunity for the purpose of allowing criminal investigation to proceed. Compared with the day-to-day scrutiny of the government, these procedures are, however, atypical in parliamentary practice, and enquiry is usually understood as fact-finding for the purpose of final political assessment.[77] It therefore remains a valid observation that parliaments *typically* focus on political desirability, and are perhaps even tailored to do so.

Thus, in spite of the need to observe certain nuances, the above definition will hold. It allows us to characterise any given accountability relation as political or legal, not based on intuitive understanding but on a pre-established criterion: essentially, is the forum judging on legality or desirability? If it employs the former, legal accountability obtains; if it employs the latter, then this is a case of political accountability. Ideally, a court only uses legality as a criterion. A parliament usually focuses on desirability. It may take considerations of legality into account in its judgment; but even then a censure against the cabinet for unlawful conduct, for example, is not a sanction for the specific conduct itself but a political repercussion of the conduct resulting in a loss of confidence in the cabinet altogether. And trustworthiness is still a political criterion.

Having defined 'political' and 'legal' accountability based on the nature of the assessment criteria employed by the forum, rather than the nature of the forum itself, we should now take the next decisive step and ask: can then a parliament employ purely legal accountability by exclusively employing standards of legality in its judgment?

5.6.3 *Legal accountability to a national parliament: the EWS in practice*

Are national parliaments, empirically speaking, willing to concentrate on the application of legal criteria in participating in the EWS? That is, do they at least partly phrase their letters in terms of subsidiarity compliance, perhaps coupled with observations on proportionality and legality in the sense of the presence of a legal basis for EU action? Or are they submitting replies that are not only politically motivated but also politically phrased, meaning that Commission proposals are either endorsed or rejected based on preferences irrespective of aspects of their compliance with legal principles such as subsidiarity or proportionality?

It is true that both Working Groups of the European Convention which originally drafted the EWS for the Constitutional Treaty had envisaged it to be a 'political' dialogue.[78] Nevertheless in several national parliaments it may be observed that actually a distinction is made between (political) desirability review and (legal) admissibility review of Commission proposals, and that there is a readiness to remain faithful to the prescribed EWS standards and procedures. The most compelling *prima facie* evidence of such readiness is the structuring of parliamentary opinions under the headings of subsidiarity assessment and other principles, such as legality proper and proportionality. Chambers thereby distinguish, at least seek or purport to distinguish, the various review criteria and to phrase their arguments accordingly.

Based on the letters published by the Commission regarding proposals launched in 2009 (letters on proposals launched earlier are being added but the archive is not yet complete),[79] indeed the following picture emerges. Several parliaments or chambers explicitly include subsidiarity as a heading in the structure of their opinions and formulate (part of) their opinion under that heading. This includes those parliaments or chambers which only issued reasoned opinions on legislative proposals in the context of a COSAC-coordinated subsidiarity check, but not of their own motion, namely the Belgian House of Representatives and Senate, the German Bundestag, the French National Assembly, the Czech Chamber of Deputies, the two chambers of the Irish parliament jointly, the lower chamber of the parliament of Slovenia and the unicameral parliaments of Bulgaria, Latvia, Hungary and Malta. These chambers in other words, over the observed period, do not reply to EU legislative proposals unless triggered by COSAC, but they stick to subsidiarity considerations when they do. Some of these chambers do also reply to other items such as consultation documents, however that is not covered by the EWS and would rather fall under properly 'political dialogue'.

Furthermore, there are parliaments or chambers that also issued reasoned opinions on legislative proposals outside the context of COSAC-coordinated subsidiarity checks, and that even then adhere, at least partly, to subsidiarity-based reasoning. This group includes the two chambers of the Italian parliament (although since then their choice of phrasing has become less consistent), the two chambers of the Dutch parliament acting separately or jointly, the French Senate, the Greek parliament and the Austrian Bundesrat. The Portuguese parliament phrases its opinions in EWS terms some of the time – it had been mentioned in a 2008 report by the Commission alongside the Dutch parliament and the French Senate as a parliament that did stick to subsidiarity considerations instead of political issues[80] – but that is not always the case in the examined period.

An excellent example of a concentration on legal review, and its separation from political review, is provided by the opinion of the Hungarian parliament on the 2006 postal services directive:

> The individual elements of the [postal services directive] proposal (such as the abolition of the reserved area [which is exempt from liberalisation]) have not been found to be disproportionate in a legal sense either. As to their practicability, the Committee will form its opinion in the course of a scrutiny procedure.

To draw a stark contrast, the German Bundesrat has the habit of providing highly detailed amendments to virtually each article of a draft directive or regulation it replies to, in the style of a co-legislative chamber, while the UK House of Lords keeps producing its usual in-depth reports on selected legislative projects. Both chambers seem to draw up their opinions or reports for their own purposes – of communicating with their own government or the public

– and not for the primary purpose of the EWS. The Commission is merely put in 'Cc', as it were. Over the examined period the Luxembourgish parliament responded to COSAC-selected proposals only, but discussed subsidiarity only marginally and did not even attempt to phrase its opinion in such terms. The Lithuanian parliament responded only to one non-COSAC item, namely a proposal concerning the security of gas supply, and voiced purely political opinions rather than views on subsidiarity. In its opinion on the COSAC-selected items it did observe the EWS review criteria, however. The Czech Senate, meanwhile, did not refer to subsidiarity even while participating in COSAC subsidiarity checks, let alone while responding to other proposals, and instead discussed the political desirability of the proposed measures.

Nevertheless, it is fair to say that while some parliaments or chambers choose to carry out autonomous and openly, one might say unabashedly, political scrutiny in communicating with the Commission, most parliaments or chambers that do participate in the EWS are willing to adapt their reasoning to the review criteria stipulated in Protocol No. 2 TEU/TFEU, or, if they go beyond subsidiarity, proper, still stick to more or less objectifiable criteria.

5.7 Conclusion

Is the EWS an accountability regime between the national parliaments and (mainly) the Commission, and if so, what kind of accountability regime is it? We have argued that even participation in a legislative process, such as through the EWS, carries an accountability aspect in that the initiator's justification for proposing a measure can and does become contested and additional justification may be demanded. The EWS is an imperfect example of an accountability regime, of course, mainly because it is meant to cover only the quality of the initiator's *initial* justification of a draft legislative act, not its re-justification of the same draft legislative act or the content of amended draft legislative acts, and the sanctions that national parliaments have at their disposal are very indirect: national parliamentary opposition may herald opposition in the Council and less-than-smooth implementation of EU legislation after its adoption. Still, at least partly the EWS does display the elements of accountability as a relation between an actor and a forum. What is the nature of the accountability relation, then? It is highly debatable whether the Commission can be considered an agent to national parliaments as principals in any meaningful sense, even though such notion is not entirely absurd and can be justified under a particular reading of concepts of constitutional law. And apart from a principal–agent relationship, resulting in upwards vertical accountability of the Commission to its national superiors, cases can also be made to argue that in the EWS the Commission is accountable to national parliaments as it is accountable to any stakeholder (downward vertical accountability), as it is accountable to auditors which may sound an alarm but cannot adopt a sanction themselves (diagonal account-ability), and as it is accountable to any other fellow participant in EU decision-making within a polycentric transnational landscape (horizontal accountability).

In any case, the national parliaments themselves cannot use the EWS in order to insure one another as if each parliament is the backup for all others: if one parliament does not object to a proposal, the others will have a harder time reaching the EWS thresholds. A redundancy model therefore does not apply to the EWS, although the EWS as a whole can well be part of an even larger redundancy-based accountability regime in and around Brussels. Does the notion of accountability networks, i.e. coalitions between multiple forums, offer a better conceptualisation of the EWS? In reality the emergence of a Union-wide inter-parliamentary network, beyond what takes place within COSAC, does not look very likely, although the selection of proposals by COSAC for collective EWS review is certainly not bad and it would be a shame if they were to be discontinued. Apart from that, some promise lies in the informal contacts between national parliamentary representatives, i.e. Brussels-based civil servants answering to their home national parliaments, who can tip each other off if a proposal attracts the interest of the national parliament that they represent. Finally, is accountability under the EWS a political or a legal form of accountability? This study has shown that under the EWS several national parliaments are willing to at least partly include legal considerations in addressing the Commission over proposed pieces of European legislation. Assuming that the EWS can be qualified as a weak form of accountability enforcement, this in turn shows that 'legal accountability', which is typically associated with courts rather than parliaments, can take place inside a parliament. Considering that parliaments are often written off as impotent to pose any meaningful counterweight against the executive, these findings show that parliaments can nevertheless be flexible in finding new roles to keep enforcing accountability via techniques that are not traditionally parliamentary in nature. The findings also contribute to the next stage of international research into the role of national parliaments in the EU: research is to move beyond the stocktaking of domestic rules and procedures and towards deeper analysis of actual behaviour on the part of parliamentarians. And even more research lies ahead. A deeper analysis must be carried out to what extent legal accountability can *substitute* political accountability, and how parliamentarians *themselves* see their role as enforcers of legal accountability. More pertinently, we need to remember that legal accountability is not necessarily democratic in nature: it is traditionally wielded by unelected courts, and it is geared towards calm objectivity rather than polarisation and choice. We thus must consider whether an activity that is not meant to be democratic automatically *becomes* more democratic if it is enforced by an elected institution like parliament; or whether democracy plays any role at all in this. We have argued that democratic accountability is not the only type of accountability, and that in the EWS other purposes probably outweigh the democratic aspect: the EWS is useful to improve learning on the part of the initiator of EU legislation, and to complement a system of checks and balances in the Union's institutional architecture. Both grounds are legitimate in their own right, and there is no need to conflate subsidiarity review under the EWS with the notion of democratic legitimacy.

6 The early warning system as legal review

National parliaments as councils of state

The bulk of the argument contained in this chapter has been first published in Ph. Kiiver, 'The Early Warning System for the Principle of Subsidiarity: The National Parliament as a Conseil d'Etat for Europe', *European Law Review* 36, 2011, 98–108 and has been reprinted in issue 6/2011 of *European Current Law*, pp. ix–xvii. Thanks to Thomson Reuters for the permission to reprint it as a chapter adapted to this book.

6.1 Introduction

Joseph Weiler once suggested the setting up of an EU institution that would check draft EU legislation to make sure that the EU had competence to legislate as intended, and to verify that the legislation in question complies with the principle of subsidiarity. Such a French-style *Conseil Constitutionnel* would be meant to help with 'restoring faith in the inviolability of the boundaries between Community and Member State competences'.[1] In the present chapter I shall argue that while the EU Constitutional Treaty and the Treaty of Lisbon did not establish a *Conseil Constitutionnel* for the EU, the Early Warning System (EWS) for the principle of subsidiarity that they introduced did bring about the emergence of a sort of *Conseil d'Etat* in the form of national parliaments exercising an advisory role in the EU legislative process. Several EU Member States have such a council of state that checks domestic bills before they are introduced in parliament, and this could well become a recognisable role model for national parliaments that are still struggling to define their proper role in the EU. Of course, national parliamentarians may not particularly like the idea that they, as democratic lawmakers, should be reduced to issuing non-binding advice on rather formal aspects of bills in the fashion of a council of state. However, both the procedural setup and the empirical reality of the use of the EWS thus far do merit such an analogy. For a host of national parliaments in the EU, the alternative to playing *Conseil d'Etat* in this way is that they are sidelined altogether, the European legislative game simply being played without them. In such a case, being a diligent watchdog sifting EU bills could in fact be quite an attractive scenario.

6.2 National parliaments as councils of state

The main argument of the present chapter is that both the procedural setup of the EWS and its empirical use justify an analogy to be drawn with consultation on bills in Member States that feature a council of state. What is meant by council of state here is not a monarchical privy council, cabinet or presidential advisory body, but specifically the French-style *Conseil d'Etat* as a consultative body to which the government submits its bills before it submits them to parliament. The capacity of councils of state as supreme courts of administrative jurisdiction is not relevant here either, only their advisory function. Apart from France,[2] consultative councils of state also exist in a roughly comparable form in Belgium,[3] the Netherlands,[4] Luxembourg,[5] Italy[6] and Spain.[7]

The argument is based on the following analogies: (1) the EWS can be seen as an institutionalised advice procedure, and (2) the empirical use of the EWS by a number of national parliaments to issue opinions on the *lawfulness*, rather than the political desirability, of legislation is comparable to a typical consultative task of a council of state. In other words, the EWS is designed as a relatively narrow advice procedure, similar to the advice procedure applicable to councils of state regarding bills, and empirical analysis reveals that several national parliaments in fact do use the EWS in such a manner. There is of course a certain paradox to this view. The EWS, with its involvement of national parliaments, had been hailed as a much more democratic mechanism compared with more 'technocratic' devices that had been considered but rejected by the European Convention.[8] Our assessment here would, paradoxically but convincingly, place the emphasis on the technocratic nature of the EWS *even though* it is carried out by parliaments.

6.2.1 *The EWS as an advice procedure*

In principle, in the ordinary legislative procedure the involvement of national parliaments under the EWS is simply a step in the process between the publication of a Commission proposal and its filing on the agenda of the Council and the European Parliament. This would call for a qualification of the EWS as a part of co-decision. The Commission is in fact intending to include its correspondence with national parliaments in its Pre-Lex database of legislative dossiers. At the same time, we should note that the EWS is not laid down in Article 294 TFEU, where it would logically belong, but in a Protocol (No. 2) on subsidiarity and proportionality. The Protocol has the same rank and binding effect as the Treaties proper; still, national parliaments are optically uncoupled from co-decision. Their function under the Protocol is chiefly referred to in Article 5 (3) TEU (subsidiarity) and Article 12 TEU (the role of national parliaments), the latter being placed in the Title on democratic principles.

Not just optically, also substantively it would be an exaggeration to speak of the EWS as a form of co-legislation. First, as noted, national parliamentary reasoned opinions are not binding, even though Article 7 (3) of Protocol No. 2 TEU/TFEU sounds impressive. The Commission may have the right to withdraw proposals, and the Council and the European Parliament may have the right to reject them, but it is up to the European institutions whether to make use of that right. The Commission is never forced to amend or withdraw proposals, and the Council and the European Parliament can *always* reject or shelve legislation, even without a yellow or orange card.[9] The Commission in fact notes that '[r]elations with national parliaments have been intensified whilst fully respecting the respective prerogatives of the EU institutions and, more generally, ensuring the balance of the "institutional triangle"'.[10] Secondly, the Treaty of Lisbon is actually the first European integration treaty to introduce the term 'Union legislator' to describe the Council and the European Parliament together, even though the term is somewhat hidden.[11] With such a dogmatically clear definition, there is little space left for other European co-legislators, such as national parliaments.

And yet the EWS is beyond any doubt more than a loose consultation. It is, in spite of the earlier qualifications, highly formalised. The most crucial elements are:

- the obligation to send proposals to national parliaments;[12]
- the obligation to wait for a certain period for reasoned opinions to arrive;[13]
- the counting and weighing of reasoned opinions;[14] and
- the obligation to re-justify when enough negative opinions are issued.[15]

This goes beyond the mere listening to informal input from random stake-holders. It resembles, as I argue, formalised advice procedures as they exist for national legislation with respect to councils of state. For, typically, the consultation of a council of state on domestic bills, at least on government bills as opposed to private member's bills, is not optional but mandatory as well. In fact, the EWS is in one sense even a bit weightier than the typical consultation of a council of state since, in the national legislative process, governments are usually under no obligation to justify their deviation from an opinion of the council of state whereas the EU initiator, if the EWS is triggered, is obliged to review its proposal and to justify the proposal's retention.

Another parallel between the EWS and domestic consultations of councils of state is that the EWS is worded negatively. Parliaments may issue objections but are not expected to give their positive approval: silence means tacit consent, a reasoned opinion under Article 6 of Protocol No. 2 TEU/TFEU is an objection, 'stating why [the parliament] considers that the draft in question does *not* comply with the principle of subsidiarity [emphasis added]'. Similarly, the Dutch Council of State, for instance, is expected to either have an objection or to have no objections to a bill's transmission to parliament. It is not expected, for example, actively to endorse the government's political priorities or urge it to boldly go further. Even the most positive advice formula reads that the Council of State sees 'no reason to make any substantive comments'.[16] While such restraint may not be found in all councils of state, the review of whether a bill is in compliance with the national constitution and the state's international obligations – a typical consultative task for councils of state, as we shall see below – is also, by definition, a closed question to which the answer is either 'negative' or 'not negative'.

The negative formulation of the EWS has, incidentally, not prevented several national parliaments from actually submitting positive reasoned opinions to the Commission. Such positive opinions confirm that the parliament in question has no objections, or agrees with the Commission that the relevant principles have been observed. An example of a proposal triggering positive opinions (one from the Dutch parliament and one from each chamber of the Italian parliament) was the reduced VAT directive.[17] When national parliaments participate in subsidiarity checks coordinated by COSAC, many parliaments also confirm that they detect no breach of law,[18] which again boils down to positive advice in the sense of a motion of no-objection.

6.2.2 Focus on legality, not desirability

The Dutch Council of State has formulated a task for itself routinely to review bills in the light of their compliance with, among other things, higher norms: the constitution, general principles of law, European Union law and other international obligations of the state.[19] The same applies to its Luxembourgish counterpart,[20] while the Belgian Council of State even stresses the technical and apolitical nature of its opinions on bills, and of its consideration of the bills' compatibility with the constitution and international treaties.[21]

The review of the constitutionality of bills, for instance, is a review of their legality: an assessment based on legal criteria. Meanwhile, activities such as policy analysis of the necessity or effectiveness of law are much more closely related to the *desirability* of legislation. After all, legislation that is superfluous or hard to enforce is not immediately unlawful, it is first and foremost undesirable. Legality review, by contrast, implies an assessment of the *admissibility* of legislation and its compliance with certain norms, irrespective of whether the law's adoption is opportune or not. And also as regards the EWS, we should note that compliance with the principle of subsidiarity is not merely a question of how desirable a certain piece of EU legislation is or would be. What is at stake is the question whether the EU may (lawfully) legislate at all.

The above observations are not merely academically intriguing, they are empirically realistic. As we have seen in the previous chapter, several national parliaments distinguish between (political) desirability review and (legal) admissibility review of Commission proposals, and in many of them there is a readiness to remain faithful to the prescribed EWS standards and procedures. Even if a parliament goes beyond subsidiarity proper, it still is likely to phrase its concerns as objectively as possible, such as under the neat heading of proportionality or legality. For example, apart from the many parliaments and chambers that only use the EWS if COSAC invites them to, the Dutch parliament, the French Senate, the Greek parliament, the Austrian Bundesrat and, at least partly, the Italian chambers and the Portuguese parliament, tend to stick to objective wording even when writing reasoned opinions on their own motion. The German Bundesrat, the UK Lords and the Czech Senate, by contrast, do not.

Four Dutch examples may illustrate the point. In a joint opinion of the two chambers of the Dutch parliament on the proposed framework decision on the fight against terrorism,[22] the States-General argued that subsidiarity and proportionality had been complied with only in a 'strict sense' whereas they had further questions on which they wished the Commission to elaborate. In other words, legally, the adoption of the proposal would not lead to a breach of EU law, but other than that there is room for debate: the definition of 'public provocation' of terrorist offences, for instance, seemed rather broad. Regarding a proposal on cross-border healthcare,[23] the Dutch parliament raised the question whether it was compatible with Article 152 (5) TEC (now Article 168 TFEU), which stipulates that 'Union action shall respect the responsibilities of the Member States for the definition of their health policy and for the organisation and delivery of health services and medical care.' The Dutch parliament argued that the scope of the proposed measure was not entirely clear and that therefore no clearance under the EWS could be given. The proposed equal treatment directive[24] was also criticised as, again, it was not clear what the impact on domestic law would be, so a positive reply under the EWS could not be given either. Perhaps the finest empirical example of the Dutch parliament's distinguishing between legal and political review was its response to a proposal on minimum standards for the protection of stateless persons in the field of asylum law:[25] the two chambers jointly sent a positive letter, stating that together they had no objections under the EWS, but the senatorial First Chamber sent a separate letter – a sort of concurring opinion – asking more general critical questions on EU asylum policy. Evidently, the parliament did not wish to mix up political considerations with the EWS and opted for separate replies.

6.3 Implications for the EWS

The drawing of an analogy between national parliaments in the EWS and councils of state in domestic lawmaking has a number of practical consequences. One such consequence is that national parliaments that are willing to embrace such an analogy may actually be performing a function that is more consistent with their domestic role. In the debate on the role of national parliaments in the EU, one frequently gets the impression that parliamentarians are expected to play a role in a European context that they do not even play in the domestic context. A realistic assessment of what we can expect of national parliaments would have to take into account, among other things, that, domestically, parliamentarians are typically not there to *develop* policies but to ask critical questions to the government (the opposition more so than coalition parties), to demand proper justification of policies and, finally, to *legitimise* these policies through majority consent.[26] Bringing European activity under the EWS in line with traditional domestic patterns of parliamentary behaviour might generate expectations that are realistic.

The second consequence is that the diligence with which EWS activity is carried out becomes more relevant than the question whether democratic legitimacy is conveyed in the process. After all, an unelected council of state is not respected for its democratic credentials but rather for its intellectual rigour. One probable reason why the Dutch parliament sticks so relatively faithfully to the letter and spirit of the EWS is that its participation in the EWS was, at least originally, a joint project between the Second (lower) Chamber and the senatorial First Chamber. In the domestic lawmaking process, the First Chamber, even though it has an absolute veto on all bills, is used to limiting its review of bills to the consideration of their constitutionality, leaving the political assessment to the directly elected parliamentarians in the lower chamber. This habit coincides with the First Chamber's more general willingness to invest time into European affairs: as senators are indirectly elected, they have less need to cater to the more immediate preoccupations of voters and have more time to consider policy issues that do not promise electoral reward. Both phenomena may have left an imprint on Dutch EWS practice.

We can also observe disproportionate participation by upper chambers in other systems: all 11 British letters on EU proposals launched in 2009 originated in the House of Lords, not a single one from the Commons; seven out of eight French letters came from the Senate; the Czech Senate was the one to respond to 22 out of the 23 EU proposals that triggered a Czech parliamentary response; six out of ten Austrian letters came from the federal-senatorial Bundesrat; and even though the German Bundesrat is a federal inter-executive chamber rather than a proper senate, let alone a parliament in the strict sense, one should also point out that this German Bundesrat authored 15 out of 17 German letters over the examined period.

While senates are usually subordinate to lower chambers – their veto can in most systems be overruled, the government normally relies on the confidence of the lower chamber and not the senate – one should readily agree that, in the EWS, reasoned opinions from senates are not necessarily of an inferior value to opinions from lower chambers. Formally, the two votes are equally weighty. Substantively, senates seem to have more energy to invest in the process. In fact, as senates are typically more independent from the executive of the day, their opinion should even have a greater *added* value than opinions approved by a majority in the lower chamber, which is usually the same majority that keeps the government in office. The senates themselves seem to embrace a stronger European role and welcome in particular that the EWS accords them co-equal status with the lower chambers.[27]

Of course we should not forget that the democratic legitimacy of senates, if they are indirectly elected, partially elected, elected on corporatist grounds or, like the Lords, entirely unelected, is weaker than that of lower chambers.[28] In that light, it would appear misguided to place Article 12 TEU, which refers to the EWS in which senates are co-equal to lower chambers, in the 'Democratic Principles' Title of the EU Treaty. Again, logically, the EWS belongs in the chapter on the ordinary EU legislative process.

The relative formality, perhaps even formalism, of EWS review standards could furthermore solve a frequently cited concern that there does not seem to be a uniform definition of the term 'subsidiarity'.[29] Perhaps it truly is difficult to separate it from proportionality and sheer desirability.[30] However, we should recall that Protocol No. 2 TEU/TFEU places an obligation on the Commission or other initiator of legislation to justify its proposals in the light of subsidiarity (and proportionality). If this justification is found wanting, Protocol No. 2 is breached by default. The case can even be made, as we have done in the preceding chapter, that the EWS is thereby an accountability mechanism vis-à-vis the Commission, in that national parliaments as forums ask questions to the Commission as an actor and the Commission has to justify; and, since the dialogue is designed to revolve around the legality, not political desirability of proposals, one could even speak of legal rather than political accountability.[31]

The final practical consequence of the present analysis is that COSAC should by all means continue to select potentially controversial proposals for collective scrutiny under the EWS. Without coordination between national parliaments, Commission proposals trigger usually a maximum of three to four opinions each; proposals subjected to coordinated review are processed by around 30 parliaments or chambers.[32] For parliaments that are still seeking to define their role, such coordination would seem crucial. Unfortunately, rotating COSAC presidencies have lately omitted to select proposals for collective review, as more and more chambers seem to argue that the EWS is established enough, that scrutiny should cover broadly political issues and that subsidiarity control, now that the pilot projects have been completed, should be an autonomous task for parliaments without interference from COSAC.[33] This is a shame, considering that COSAC coordination has triggered EWS activity where otherwise, in all likelihood, there would have been none and that EWS review may act as a concrete catalyst for further political scrutiny.

6.4 Conclusion

In the run-up to the entry into force of the EWS, not everybody was confident that national parliaments would embrace a mechanism that is both relatively narrow and relatively weak. Raunio noted: 'Giving parliaments the power of veto ("the red card") would thus have provided national MPs with a considerably stronger incentive for taking the early warning system seriously'.[34] Peters specified: 'Parliaments are not at their best in exercising routine mechanisms of a technical nature. They are not suited to play this kind of inspectorial role'.[35] It turns out, however, that several national parliaments do take the EWS seriously, and that they in fact adhere to a review format that can indeed be described as 'technical', or perhaps rather as 'legal'. At least the arguments put forward by them, while they are no doubt politically motivated in the sense that without political incentives parliamentarians are unlikely to even invest time and energy in EWS participation, are phrased narrowly and legally. In other words: they are strikingly similar to advisory opinions of councils of state. In that light, one should hope that, even though COSAC is scaling back its coordination activities, a coalition of active national parliaments or chambers will nevertheless emerge to continue to take the EWS seriously. It is quite possible, in fact probable and absolutely legitimate, that national senates, as opposed to lower chambers, will be well-represented in such a coalition of active chambers. In the context of the EWS, a realistic model to adopt would then be the scrutiny of EU legislative proposals in the fashion of a council of state as it is, in several Member States, consulted on domestic bills before they are submitted to the domestic legislature. Such council of state-type activity is advisory, not co-legislative, but that does not mean it is irrelevant. Scrutiny under the EWS should then focus on the lawfulness, on the admissibility of legislation, rather than its political desirability. Political considerations may still be triggered in the wake of EWS review, although it is probably too late at the EWS stage to make much of a substantive difference. Instead, EWS review may well focus on the quality of the justification of proposals in the light of subsidiarity (and other principles), which should keep the Commission and other initiators on their toes. Perhaps the yellow or orange cards of the EWS will never be triggered, but that should not automatically be considered a sign of the system's weakness. If the Commission and the other initiators of EU legislation stay within the limits of conferred competences and of the principles of the exercise of these competences, and if national parliaments or chambers call them to account for their choices and reasoning in proposing new EU measures, then there will simply be no need for any yellow or orange cards to be raised.

7 National parliaments in the constitutional reality of the early warning system

7.1 Introduction

Having considered the procedural details of the European Union's early warning system for subsidiarity (EWS), the choices that underlie its setup, the way national parliaments can and do use it in reality, and the various ways in which we can conceptualise it as a legal accountability and legislative advice procedure, what broader conclusions can we draw from what we have seen? The following paragraphs shall, by way of summary and broader outlook, offer considerations about the EWS's complexity, about the typology of national parliaments that emerge from its use, about its place in the debate about democracy, transparency and accountability in the EU, and about possible ways to strengthen the EWS.

7.2 The legal setting of the EWS: greater complexity than meets the eye

The EWS, it turns out, is not as easy to summarise and explain as one might think. For example, it is not simply a review mechanism taking place during the first eight weeks after the introduction of an EU legislative proposal. The eight-week period under Protocol No. 2 TEU/TFEU can be effectively shorter since the corresponding eight-week scrutiny delay from Protocol No. 1 TEU/TFEU is subject to an urgency override. The period can also be longer than eight weeks. That is if national parliaments happen to receive their language version of a proposal before other parliaments do, since the clock starts ticking only when the last language version has been transmitted, but also if national parliaments are willing to consult language versions other than their own, and if they make use of information sources earlier on in the legislative process, notably during the consultation stage. The month of August is not counted for EWS purposes by the Commission, but this exclusion applies neither to the other initiators of EU draft legislative acts, such as groups of Member States, nor to other periods when one or more national parliaments happen not to be in session and are therefore unable to cast a reasoned opinion.

And what is a reasoned opinion? Reasoned opinions are not subject to any mandatory format, and need not necessarily be called 'reasoned opinions'. It appears from the practice of both the Commission and the COSAC secretariat, though, that opinions are not likely to be counted as votes unless the parliament or chamber issuing them explicitly alleges a breach of subsidiarity. However, parliamentarians apparently feel more comfortable adopting a more cautious phrasing. Practitioners from the Dutch parliament point out that their reasoned opinions try to incorporate a cross-party consensus as much as possible, leading to formulations such as 'on the one hand, on the other hand'.[1] But it is submitted here that an allegation of a breach and a nuanced opinion do not have to be mutually exclusive. A letter may well contain an allegation of a breach of subsidiarity as a standard formula, which can then be followed by more elaborate reasoning.

Reasoned opinions must be considered to have been adopted by a national parliament or chamber. What exactly is a 'national parliament' for EU purposes is defined nowhere in the Treaties. It is submitted that it should be considered an autonomous concept of Union law, or at least a national concept interpreted with due regard to EU law: governments cannot be free to label any body they like as their national parliament, and the EU institutions and other Member States cannot be compelled to accept everything. One possible formula is that a 'national parliament' is a Union concept rooted in common constitutional traditions of the Member States in defining the 'legislature' for purposes of the European Convention on Human Rights, except where EU law itself clearly excludes certain bodies from the definition even though they might be ECHR 'legislatures', for example heads of state.[2] Such a borrow-then-subtract approach has the advantage that it can trace its origin in domestic law while providing clarity and predictability: the Treaties and Protocols are, for example, perfectly able to distinguish national from regional parliaments and whole parliaments from individual chambers. A more flexible but more casuistic and thus less predictable approach would be to allow for national autonomy in defining the term but subject it to EU constraints, notably where unfair advantages or disadvantages arise from Member States' creativity. This is not a trivial matter, by the way: the definition of a 'national parliament' for the purposes of the EWS has implications for the scope of the term in other instances, such as the national parliaments' binding veto against the application of the general passerelle.

Either way, issues such as internal voting and quorum thresholds for the adoption of a parliamentary opinion should remain firmly a matter of internal procedural autonomy. That includes the question of how big a majority of component members, of members present, or of votes cast, needs to be in order to issue a reasoned opinion. The adoption of the opinion can furthermore take place by a plenary vote, or by the resolution of a committee acting on behalf of the plenary, or even, theoretically, by the vote of a parliamentary minority if domestic law provides that the parliament or chamber as a whole is obliged or considered to act upon a minority initiative.

What about the distribution of votes under the EWS? The principle whereby two EWS votes are allocated with each national parliament over-represents small Member States' parliaments and sits uncomfortably with majoritarian principles, but could be justified as a follow-up control on the Treaty-based conferral of competences to the EU which took place by unanimity as well. The principle whereby each chamber in a bicameral parliament must have one vote over-represents the senates and sits uncomfortably with domestic constitutional law and practice, but could be justified as a pragmatic solution that, incidentally, encourages senates, which are often far more active and prolific than their lower chambers, to provide valuable input to the EU policy process.

As we can see, the procedural aspect of the EWS alone is more complex than what might have been expected, and probably than what the Convention members have been expecting when they first proposed the EWS in 2004. There surely must have been a feeling, though, that some aspects of the EWS must yet crystallise in practice; this study made a number of proposals to help that crystallisation process along.

7.3 A new typology of national parliaments

Our empirical analysis of the national parliaments' use of the EWS produces findings which can be translated into a new categorisation of national parliaments in the EU according to how they behave under the EWS. As noted earlier, from the mid-1990s onwards attempts have been made to place national parliaments within a typological framework based on comparative assessments of their role or performance in EU scrutiny. When we now focus on the parliaments' attitude in the EWS, a new sort of typology emerges which I propose to frame as follows:

- Literalists;
- Pseudo-Colegislators;
- Pre-empters; and
- Absentees.

Interestingly, this EWS-based typology only partly coincides with other, more general categorisations such as 'strong', 'moderate' or 'weak'.

7.3.1 *Literalists*

A literalist parliament or chamber is defined as one that, based on the character of the reasoned opinions it issues, takes the system of Protocol No. 2 TEU/TFEU relatively literally in that it faithfully formulates its opinions according to the format of a relatively narrow check. This means that the reasoning is actually related to subsidiarity or, if a broader reasoning is applied, an attempt is made to phrase it in terms of related and more or less objective principles, notably proportionality and legality. Worded negatively, literalist parliaments or chambers do *not* see the EWS as an invitation to discuss consultation documents (the EWS only targets draft legislative acts) or to discuss the political merits of proposals in great detail, let alone to put forward specific amendments to their text or concrete recommendations for their improvement. This group would include most notably the two chambers of the Dutch parliament acting separately or jointly, the French Senate, the Greek parliament and the Austrian Bundesrat, as well as partly the two chambers of the Italian parliament and the Portuguese parliament. These chambers phrase their objections in formal terms not only when they participate in COSAC subsidiarity reviews, but also when they adopt letters of their own motion. The Portuguese parliament, the Dutch parliament and the French Senate have in fact even been mentioned, almost commended, in a 2008 report by the Commission as parliaments or chambers that did stick to subsidiarity considerations instead of political issues.[3]

The obvious question is what causes a parliament or chamber to embrace a literal approach to the EWS. One plausible explanation might be that the EWS stimulates scrutiny of European legislative proposals and a dialogue with the Commission where otherwise there would have been none, so the terms of the EWS are a readily acceptable starting point. Furthermore, the focus of the EWS on subsidiarity, or at least on relatively formal review criteria adjacent to subsidiarity, allows national parliamentarians who are in principle not Eurosceptic to engage in the process without risking to come across as trying to compete with the European Parliament. After all, they are merely doing what Article 12 (b) TEU envisages them to do: see to it that the subsidiarity principle gets respected. Yet another explanation is more utilitarian. Upon enquiry, Dutch parliamentary civil servants noted that an important reason for Dutch parliamentarians to relate their opinions to subsidiarity, and for the staff to formulate the written letters accordingly, is the concern that otherwise these opinions will at some point not be counted as reasoned opinions and therefore as votes under the EWS.[4]

7.3.2 Pseudo-colegislators

A pseudo-colegislator is a parliament or chamber whose participation in the EWS indicates that it is willing to contribute to the EU legislative process appearing as if it were a co-legislative body itself. The routine submission of detailed reports and elaborate amendments on EU proposals, without any particular regard to the format envisaged by the EWS and the limitations to its scope, indicates such an attitude. Positively, this may be interpreted as self-assuredness, as determination to convey messages not just to the Commission but to the national government for subsequent Council negotiations, and as a refusal to be unduly constrained in the breadth of national parliamentary input. Negatively, this attitude may reveal path-dependence in the treatment of EU proposals as if they were domestic bills, or a failure to realise that the EWS is meant as a check, not as policy consultation. However, a look at the membership of that category might reveal another possibility. The group of pseudo-colegislators includes the German Bundesrat, the UK House of Lords and the Czech Senate, as well as the Luxembourgish parliament. It could therefore be that particularly upper chambers are liable to use and in fact overuse the EWS in order to compensate their relative weakness vis-à-vis the national government, which is accountable only to the lower chamber and not to them. Probably, the senators, Lords and Länder simply seek to get their message across, and if the EWS presents itself as an additional opportunity to express their opinion, they will seize it.

7.3.3 Pre-empters

Pre-empters would comprise those parliaments or chambers which have decided not to participate in the EWS in the first place, except for the occasional participation in collective COSAC checks, and instead to use the EWS, or rather the political dialogue, as a means to provide input on consultation documents – communications, white and green papers – rather than draft legislative acts. The admittedly quite realistic premise is that last-minute objections, to be formulated within a mere eight weeks and on rather narrow grounds, to proposals that have already been finalised by the Commission, stand little hope of changing anything. Exercising influence on their own government in the Council might be the more promising route to take at that stage. The corollary is, of course, that since the EWS does not target consultation documents and the other parliaments do not usually respond to consultation documents, pre-empters are effectively bailing out of the community of national parliaments as foreseen by the EWS. Since they respond to consultation documents rather than draft legislative acts, they abstain from casting reasoned opinions against draft legislative acts, which in turn means that the likelihood of reaching the relevant thresholds to actually trigger the EWS is decreased. The most prominent pre-empters are the parliaments of Denmark, Sweden and Finland.

Raunio[5] hypothesised that 'those parliaments which are either already more strongly involved in EU politics or that represent more Eurosceptical electorates will make more active use of the [EWS] mechanism.' Interestingly, this hypothesis turns out to be only partially true. The Nordic parliaments, who indeed enjoy a reputation of occupying the 'strong' category in comparative rankings, do engage in a direct dialogue with the Commission, but they do so outside the EWS proper. Instead, they use the political dialogue to discuss early consultation documents and shun the EWS for actual legislative proposals. As far as chambers with a Eurosceptic record are concerned, remarkable activism can indeed be found in the Czech Senate and the UK Lords, but again it is not entirely clear whether this has to do with Euroscepticism or rather with the fact that these are both upper chambers who either have more time and freedom to engage in scrutiny that does not promise much electoral reward, or who are in this way compensating for their constitutional inferiority to the lower chambers and the government. Quite possibly all of these factors play a role.

7.3.4 *Absentees*

Absentees are, finally, those parliaments or chambers which do not participate in the EWS at all, or only if encouraged to do so by collective exercises coordinated by COSAC, and which are not known to reply to early consultation documents either. These EWS absentees typically coincide with 'weak players' or 'informal influencers' in other rankings and categorisations, most of them tend to be found in the South and East of Europe, and in fact they make up the largest group of parliaments and chambers. Perhaps optimistically they might be described as 'slow starters', and it is for them that practical advice on how to use the EWS might bring the greatest added value.

7.3.5 *The issue of convergence*

One interesting line of empirical research concerns the question whether EU integration leads to a process of convergence of national parliamentary law and practice around common standards.[6] Here we need to differentiate between a possible convergence of general behaviour and attitude towards, in this case, the EWS; a possible convergence of internal institutional adaptation to the EWS procedure at a micro-level; and a possible convergence of interest around particular types of proposals for consideration under the EWS.

Regarding general attitude, the above typology on the parliaments' approach to the EWS reveals not so much convergence as a confirmation of other patterns of behaviour: Nordic parliaments charging ahead, other parliaments lagging behind, some parliaments in the middle taking a narrow approach to the EWS and some considering it as an open invitation to joint policymaking. Regarding internal institutional adaptation, an interesting object of research could be whether the plenary, the European affairs committees or sectoral committees are in charge of or involved in the EWS, even though so far not much convergence can be observed here.[7] Incrementalism and path-dependence, it should be recalled, are familiar features of national parliamentary behaviour.

What about the convergence of interest around EU proposals considered salient enough to merit attention? The empirical evidence of the EWS shows that, without coordination efforts in COSAC, national parliaments do not actually share a lot of interest. Few of the Commission's individual proposals receive more than three responses. The exception is, indeed, where COSAC selects certain proposals to be reviewed by all participating parliaments and chambers, when usually around 30 and up to almost 40 parliaments or chambers join in the exercise. It could hypothetically be that COSAC already itself identifies the most salient proposals, so that the rest of the proposals in a given year almost by definition attract a weak response. However, it should also be noted that even though the participation rate in COSAC exercises is high, most responses are either positive or neutral, in that parliaments or chambers do not actually find any breach of subsidiarity or adjacent principles. This indicates that at least there is a realistic possibility that the item would not have been selected for scrutiny if it had not been for COSAC steering. In some parliaments, this possibility is in fact a near-certainty, namely in those inside the 'absentee' category who normally never send any letters to the Commission.

Where a COSAC exercise has taken place, though, opinions do seem to converge around a number of sensitive issues, meaning that many national parliaments find them problematic. These are EU proposals having little or no cross-border dimension, proposals which regulate what is or could be regulated by an international convention outside the EU framework, and proposals which threaten to exceed the Union's competence to regulate in the first place.[8] Yet again, it could be that COSAC has selected these items for review precisely because its members are likely to be concerned about these aspects.

7.4 The impact of reasoned opinions: observations and hypotheses

What is the purpose of the EWS? Some authors argue that it is all about the national parliaments' right to block EU legislation,[9] while others point out that it merely relies on the EU institutions themselves to do the actual blocking.[10] At the other end of the spectrum it is argued that the EWS is merely symbolic,[11] a 'dignified' rather than 'efficient' part of the EU constitution in Bagehot's terms,[12] and that it should not distract parliamentarians from the much more promising regular political scrutiny of their own national governments.[13] Somewhere in the middle it is argued that the EWS is not just symbolic, but that it is not a co-legislative veto mechanism either, and that instead the true meaning of the EWS simply lies in the added motivation for EU institutions to give better reasons for their actions.[14] The setup is one of constructive argument rather than one of typical legislative bargaining.[15]

Still, even if deliberation rather than veto rights lies at the heart of the EWS, we cannot completely ignore the tendency of observers and participants of the EWS to perceive it as a means to stop undesired projects from being adopted. The Dutch lower chamber, which has just been described as literalist in its faithful adherence to the EWS as a relatively narrow review mechanism, still cannot resist framing its participation in terms of influence and the quest to assemble enough votes to trigger orange and yellow cards.[16] Practitioners also note that subsidiarity review is seen as a small part of overall national parliamentary participation in the EU, and that academics are far more interested in the EWS than the politicians themselves.[17] It is therefore only fair to devote attention to the practical effect, or impact, of reasoned opinions, including its use and usefulness as a veto tool.

7.4.1 National parliaments as a 'veto cloud' with a suspensive veto

The problem with the conceptualisation of national parliaments under the EWS as anything resembling a veto point in a conventional sense is that the system does not lend itself to such a clear-cut labelling. First, the component parts of the 'point', i.e. the parliaments and chambers, are relatively diverse, acting under different procedures and normally without much coordination. Second, the EWS does at no point actually envisage a veto, in the sense that it would be legally impossible to adopt a decision against the will of the veto player. The EWS might well approach what we could call a suspensive veto, meaning that an additional effort must be made to carry on with the legislative process, in this case the formulation of additional justification for maintaining a proposal contested by a yellow or orange card. This could be compared with a veto that delays but does not stop decision-making because it is subject to an override. Still, in reality it is much more relevant to what extent the legislator proper, the European Parliament and the Council, are willing to adopt, reject or amend the proposal. This, in turn, will no doubt be determined by many factors, and it is not likely that purely the number of reasoned opinions in the EWS will in itself produce much effect. It will be equally if not much more decisive, for example, where the reasoned opinions came from, as shall be elaborated in subsequent paragraphs. If the terminology of vetoes must be employed, it is suggested that the term 'veto cloud' is much more fitting than the term 'veto point'. The point is nebulous and fuzzy around the edges, its effect is not binary but a matter of degree.

Of course, the analogy with the role of a council of state, a consultative body that is asked to express its advisory opinion on bills before they are submitted to the legislature,[18] captures the logic of the EWS much better than veto points and even better than veto clouds. But even advisory opinions can be negative, and the body that issued them will be legitimately curious about what happens to the proposal in the end.

7.4.2 Hypotheses on individual dossiers

Do reasoned opinions matter? It is crucial to have a follow-up review to establish whether the national parliamentary effort to use the EWS actually makes a difference in the consideration of EU legislative proposals, irrespective of voting thresholds. This is not to say that the number of reasoned opinions or blocked proposals is a measure, let alone the sole measure of the success of the EWS. But no-one is likely to participate in such a system if nothing tangible can be claimed as a result. As Barrett put it:[19]

It may be (and indeed, it is to be hoped) that the consciousness on the part of national parliamentarians that there will now be a system under which the input of national parliaments may make a difference at European level may motivate and stimulate national parliaments and their governments alike into better equipping and resourcing national legislatures to take seriously the role they occupy in relation to the European legislative process.

The greatest methodological challenge in assessing how big the difference exactly is, in cases where the EWS is employed, is to disentangle causality from correlation and coincidence. Let us assume that the Council rejects a Commission proposal that had attracted a great number of reasoned opinions from national parliaments. That may well be because the Council actually took these opinions seriously and agreed with them. But it may also be because certain national governments complied with the majority opinions in their own lower chambers. Or because the governments' opinion was identical to the opinion of their supportive parliamentary party groups in their own lower chambers to begin with. Or because government party groups in the lower chambers were even encouraged or instructed by the government itself to pass a negative reasoned opinion. Or because there was a combination of the above. It is very likely that national parliaments' reasoned opinions are anyway not the only source of negative feedback to a given proposal in that they express criticism that is also expressed by lobby groups, by otherwise unrelated individuals of comparable political colour including members of the European Parliament, or by the Committee of the Regions and the Economic and Social Committee. But these expressions may equally be linked by coincidence, or by causation where coordination has taken place, as well as correlation where certain ideas and constituencies are simply represented in several national and European bodies at the same time.

Probably the only way to identify coincidence, correlation and causation between the EWS in the fate of individual proposals is empirical research in the form of in-depth case studies on the entire track of selected legislative dossiers from consultation and adoption to national implementation and compliance. Qualitative findings gathered from interviews would be crucial to distinguish between initial opinions and opinions held after the conduct of national parliamentary discussions and the adoption of reasoned opinions, and to identify to what extent reasoned opinions are used in discussions in the EU legislative process.

For example, the proposal for a freight rail services regulation as part of the 2004 Third Railway Package had been subjected to coordinated subsidiarity review in COSAC,[20] and has attracted the highest number of negative votes of any of the proposals in that package, for various reasons. Subsequently, the European Parliament rejected the proposal, and the Council did not take the matter further, letting the proposal lapse. The European Parliament's rejection was not based on subsidiarity grounds, though, but rather on the ground that the proposal would have increased the cost of rail transportation as opposed to haulage by road.[21] A senior practitioner from the European Parliament's transport committee cannot recall either that the COSAC experiment played much of a role in the transport committee's deliberations.[22] Perhaps national parliamentary opinions are listened to like the opinions from other committees, namely more or less attentively depending on whether the actor holding the opinion is important or not.

Future field research in this area will become increasingly feasible as more and more proposals are not only subjected to the EWS but actually reach the implementation stage and judicial review. And in that research, it would be worth considering and testing at least the following set of hypotheses regarding the possible impact, positive or negative, of the EWS on the outcome of an EU legislative process. Impact would broadly describe the effect of an opinion on the ease with which an EU proposal gets endorsed in the legislative process, but it would have to be defined more concretely. For example, one may consider the classification of a proposal in the Council as an A item (ready for approval without debate) or B item (scheduled for debate), the amount and nature of amendments introduced, or the size of the eventually supportive Council majority if many EWS votes had been triggered. And again, means must be found to control for the possibility that some proposals are sensitive or controversial by themselves, and that this is then reflected in the EWS, rather than that a triggered EWS all of a sudden makes an otherwise mundane proposal salient.

Hypothesis 1: The effect of the total amount of reasoned opinions as a curve gradually increases with the number of reasoned opinions, even before the EWS thresholds are reached, but it jumps at the yellow card threshold and increases exponentially around the orange card threshold.

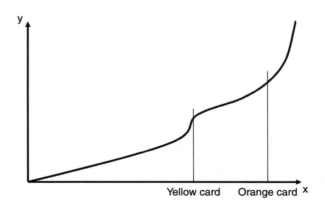

Figure 7.1 The relative impact of reasoned opinions (hypothesis)

x = number of EWS votes cast, y = impact on EU legislative process

At lower numbers of reasoned opinions, a linear relation with their impact would reflect the expectation that the less criticism a proposal attracts in the EWS, the easier it will sail through the legislative process. The curve's jump at the yellow card threshold of one-quarter or one-third of the votes of national parliaments would reflect the expectation that a formal triggering of the yellow card generates news value for the media. The reaching of numbers approximately around the orange card threshold, i.e. more than half of the votes of national parliaments, is likely to correlate with a critical mass of opposition against the proposal in the Council. This also means that the maximum impact, i.e. the absolute impossibility of an adoption of the act, is reached well before unanimity of EWS votes, but rather at a point where EWS votes correlate with solid blocking minorities or hostile majorities against proposals in the Council.

Hypothesis 2: The effect of individual reasoned opinions on Council negotiations correlates with the size of the Member State where the reasoned opinion originates, but the correlation is stronger or weaker depending on whether the opinion originates in an upper or lower chamber, whether it originates in a chamber where the government has a majority, and whether the opinion coincides with the government's preferences or not.

Since in most bicameral Member States the senates are constitutionally inferior to the lower chambers, opinions from such lower chambers are, all else being equal, likely to carry more weight when compared with senatorial opinions. It is likely that the effect of a negative opinion in support of the government from the lower chamber is strong in that it heralds objections from the respective government in the Council. In other words, the chamber is against the proposal and so is the government. This we should see as a correlation, rather than as causation: parliaments do not usually *cause* their governments to object to EU proposals, it is rather that the opinion of a lower chamber majority and that of the cabinet do tend to coincide for endogenous reasons. It could be, of course, that the senate in a bicameral system is controlled by a majority that is hostile to the incumbent government, or that the government is a minority government facing an opposition majority even in the lower chamber. Where in such a situation an opposition-controlled parliament or chamber adopts a negative reasoned opinion in line with the government's preferences, a strong impact on Council negotiations may be expected in that this strengthens the government's hand as a manifestation of national consensus against a proposal.

A similarly interesting scenario concerns the adoption of a negative reasoned opinion against the government's preferences. In other words, the chamber is against a proposal but the government is not. Again, the disruptive effect of such an opinion is likely to be stronger if it originates in a unicameral parliament or lower chamber of a bicameral parliament, where the government either has a majority or faces the opposition as a minority cabinet, than when it originates in a senate to which the government is not accountable and which it can more easily ignore. Potentially, such a moderate form of domestic constraint could be sold as a moderately convincing instance of hand-tying, where the government might bargain for slightly better terms in the Council by referring to domestic unrest.

A final consideration concerns positive reasoned opinions, where a parliament or chamber indicates to have no objections to a proposal under the EWS. As a rule, the positive effect of a positive opinion on an act's adoption is likely to be weaker than the negative effect of a negative opinion. And again, a positive opinion from an opposition-controlled chamber in line with the government's preferences will be more impressive than a conveniently positive opinion from a majority that is loyal to the government anyway.

7.5 The constitutional context of the EWS: democracy, accountability, transparency

So far we have avoided as far as possible any claims, or even references, to notions of democracy in our discussion of subsidiarity review. This avoidance was deliberate. Following Majone, who persuasively advocated greater sobriety when discussing the questions whether the EU is a federation or a proto-state,[23] it is proposed to apply similar restraint when discussing the implications of the EWS for the European Union's democratic credentials. For to presume or imply that the operation of the EWS enhances the democratic character of EU decision-making as a whole, in whosoever's eyes, one would have to accept a number of premises which are largely a matter of opinion and make assertions that are hard to verify empirically. It is however, not necessary to overburden the discourse with such sweeping notions as democracy in the first place. Nor is it necessary to be distracted by the fact that Article 12 TEU, which lists (some) instances in which national parliaments contribute to the good functioning of the Union, including the EWS, is placed within Title II of the Treaty which is devoted to 'Democratic Principles'. There is sufficient reason to embrace the EWS, the principles underlying it and the spillovers it can generate, based on far less ambitious but equally important considerations.

If we view the EWS as an accountability mechanism,[24] we should recall that accountability as an actor–forum relationship does not necessarily have to be democratic in nature. Neither the actor nor the forum has to be democratic, although at least the forum would have to be democratic in order to qualify a regime as *democratic* accountability. Still, accountability can serve more purposes than merely democracy. Bovens formulates two other purposes, namely learning, i.e. the improvement of action through feedback, and constitutional checks and balances.[25] Neither of these two dimensions contains any claim to a democratic character, but both are valuable in their own right.

A similar thing can be said about the implications of the EWS for the notion of transparency. Weiler once made a number of proposals for 'enhancing transnational democracy'.[26] One is the introduction of a Constitutional Council to check EU legislation ex ante, and we have argued that the EWS at least did introduce a sort of Council of State: national parliaments issuing advisory opinions on legislative proposals.[27] Another was to introduce a database where documentation on the steps in the EU decision-making process would be put online.[28] The Commission's work to include reasoned opinions from national parliaments on Pre-Lex arguably goes some way in that direction, the main added value being that now also the opinions, or at least priorities or concerns, of opposition parties and dissenting upper chambers are made public if they are reflected in reasoned opinions. We should probably not overestimate the appeal of such online services to the general public; but it may well be useful to ministries and parliamentary support staff, sectoral interest groups monitoring only specific types of legislation, as well as law firms and government authorities who might mount challenges to EU legislation in force and cite reasoned opinions as evidence or use them as a source of inspiration for their own reasoning.

Of course, there are limits to what enhanced transparency can achieve, notably if available information is not actually picked up. Transparency and participation alone cannot guarantee public accountability which might mitigate a legitimacy crisis.[29] Furthermore, there are not only costs but also benefits to secrecy, notably in Council deliberations.[30] Still, Timmermans convincingly referred to subsidiarity and transparency as twin concepts in the quest to enhance the Union's legitimacy.[31] In fact, for what it is worth, subsidiarity enforcement can directly bring about enhanced transparency, at least regarding the justification, rationale and added value of EU legislation.

7.6 Strengthening the EWS

There will not be many observers who would argue that the EWS goes too far and should be abolished or reduced in its intrusiveness. If anything, as seen, a case can be made that the EWS is worth expanding. This, in turn, can theoretically be done in two ways. Either the system is formally beefed up via a Treaty amendment, or the actors involved try to make the most of the current setup.

Regarding formal amendments, the most obvious and at the same time most radical reform that comes to mind would be to assign a binding veto power to the EWS: the elusive 'red card'. That, however, is neither very realistic nor is it the only way to upgrade the system. There are plenty of possibilities between the current system and the extreme option. One such possibility is to lower the yellow card threshold to one-quarter of total EWS votes, thus applying the reduced threshold for the area of freedom, security and justice across the board. It could be lowered even more, for instance to correspond with the vote value of the mandatory minimum blocking minority in the Council, which is four Member States,[32] or, translated into EWS terms, eight votes, cast by e.g. three unicameral parliaments and two chambers of bicameral parliaments. Or the vote value of reasoned opinions from chambers of bicameral parliaments could be increased, notably by allowing such chambers to cast two votes just like a unicameral parliament can, instead of penalising them for having another chamber next door that is perhaps idle. Another possibility is to explicitly include all grounds from Article 5 TEU in the EWS, i.e. add legality and proportionality to subsidiarity as an official review criterion. And one could extend the EWS period beyond the current eight weeks to slow down the process even more and give even resources-strapped national parliaments a better chance to engage in the system.

Yet another possibility is to assign somewhat stronger legal effects to the EWS if it is triggered. An example could be to automatically elevate the voting thresholds in the European Parliament and/or the Council of Ministers if the EWS is triggered so that a proposal that has met with national parliamentary resistance becomes harder to adopt in Brussels. Another example could be to automatically refer such controversial proposals up to the European Council in the fashion of the emergency brake procedure that exists for sensitive matters.[33] In such cases, however, it would be appropriate to assume a negative correlation between the impact and the breadth of the EWS. In other words, an EWS that produces only mild results should not be construed too narrowly, and reasoned opinions should be deemed valid and admissible even if they seem to go a bit beyond the terms of the EWS proper. If the EWS becomes legally more binding, though, it is only fair to expect that national parliaments stick more literally to the scope of the EWS, e.g. by leaving out arguments about proportionality and discussing subsidiarity only. Strictly speaking, of course, even though the EWS is elaborated in a Protocol on the application of the principles of proportionality and subsidiarity, reasoned opinions may concern only subsidiarity, and questions of competence allocation are not even mentioned in that Protocol. Still, it appears from both the literature that these other principles do matter to subsidiarity, and it appears from practice that national parliaments do have a need for sufficient scope to bring forward arguments that are at least related to these other principles.[34] And as long as the EWS does not produce any terribly intrusive legal effects, a more creative approach to its practical application is surely justified, without violating the letter of the law.

This study has proposed to make the most of the current setup by arguing that it is very well possible to feed not only subsidiarity-based complaints but also related arguments into the EWS. National parliaments are entitled to establish a breach of subsidiarity, for example, where a proposed EU measure has no or little cross-border implications. They are also entitled to complain in a reasoned opinion that a proposal would go beyond the scope of EU competences. Not only would such a proposal violate the principle of conferral making the subsidiarity test redundant and a positive verdict impossible. It would also make the act's adoption impossible to justify under subsidiarity if the test *were* conducted, since a subject-matter cannot be 'better' regulated at Union level if the Union has no competence to regulate in the first place. National parliaments are also entitled to complain in a reasoned opinion that there is no *necessity* for the Union to act because an international convention outside the EU framework is already in place, or that a proposal goes too far, which are types of complaints that should not be dismissed as falling under proportionality instead of subsidiarity. After all, proportionality is not the only principle that contains an element of gradation: there may for instance be enough subsidiarity to justify a framework directive but it may run out if it comes to a regulation. In that sense, subsidiarity can be seen as federal proportionality, and the countervailing interest to be protected is the integrity of domestic competences. Finally, national parliaments are entitled in their reasoned opinions to establish a breach of subsidiarity due to an inadequate justification or too summary a reasoning on the part of the initiator. First, inadequate justification breaches the procedural aspect of subsidiarity laid down in Article 5 of Protocol No. 2 TEU/TFEU. Second, on the substance, it is justified to make a rebuttable assumption that if even the initiator such as the Commission cannot justify its own proposals, chances are they cannot be justified at all. As a result, we arrive at an application of the EWS that suits national parliaments' needs and makes it more effective in a way that is still defensible in the light of the current black-letter law.

7.7 Conclusion

The EWS may not be the most radical or most transformative institutional innovation in the history of the European Union. But it is not entirely meaningless and, in fact, it prompted interesting developments of both a legal and an empirical nature. The legal framework of the EWS itself, as it is laid down in Protocol No. 2 TEU/TFEU, is not entirely watertight and does leave some scope for legal interpretation and empirical experimentation. But what exactly is the point? The purpose of the EWS cannot be to block as many proposals as possible, this cannot be a measure of its success. Yet at the very least, sharper scrutiny of the reasons for EU legislative proposals might conceivably make the Commission, and the other initiators of EU legislation, refrain from launching measures which they feel they cannot plausibly justify. The Commission and the other initiators might conceivably try harder to argue why a certain proposal is necessary, and surely if convincing arguments exist then there is no need to hide them. It may well be that, as a policy-maker, one sometimes feels the need to take action even if one cannot provide exact data on how big the problem is and how it would be remedied in quantitative terms. Policy discretion unfolds where decisions need to be taken under time pressure with limited information. But if the Member States truly wanted the initiators of EU legislation to behave in such way, they could have omitted or repealed all the additional checks on legislative initiative that exist in the Treaties. They could have set up a system of generous competence allocation where not each and every piece of legislation must be so elaborately justified. But they did not opt for such a system. Thus, we must remind ourselves that the EU legislator is not authorised to legislate in a cavalier manner, on the basis of general competences like a legislature in a unitary state might. We must presume that subsidiarity review is there for a reason. And there are valid grounds for believing that this subsidiarity review is worth making it work.

Notes

1 Introduction

1 Treaty of Lisbon amending the Treaty on European Union and the Treaty establishing the European Community, signed at Lisbon, 13 December 2007, OJ 2007/C 306/01. After consolidation, the crucial provisions regarding the principle of subsidiarity and the Early Warning System are Articles 5 (3) and 12 (b) TEU as well as Protocol No. 2 which, pursuant to the Lisbon Treaty, is attached to both the TEU and the TFEU, hence Protocol No. 2 TEU/TFEU.

2 Article G (5) TEU regarding the insertion of a new Article 3b TEC, the second clause of which read: 'In areas which do not fall within its exclusive competence, the Community shall take action, in accordance with the principle of subsidiarity, only if and in so far as the objectives of the proposed action cannot be sufficiently achieved by the Member States and can therefore, by reason of the scale or effects of the proposed action, be better achieved by the Community.'

3 Declarations 13 and 14 of the Maastricht Final Act annexed to the TEU, OJ C 191, 29 July 1992.

4 Treaty of Amsterdam, OJ C 340, 10 November 1997. The two relevant Protocols received a consolidated numbering, before being superseded by the Lisbon Treaty, as Protocol No. 9 on the role of national parliaments in the European Union and Protocol No. 30 on the application of the principles of subsidiarity and proportionality.

5 The EWS as included in the Draft Treaty establishing a Constitution for Europe proposed by the European Convention, CONV 850/03, differed slightly from the version as eventually adopted by the IGC, OJ 2004/C 310/01; the version of the EWS adopted by the Lisbon IGC in turn differed slightly from the one included in the Treaty establishing a Constitution for Europe. The differences are discussed in greater detail in par. 3.2 below.

6 See T. Raunio, 'National Legislatures in the EU Constitutional Treaty', in J. O'Brennan and T. Raunio, eds, *National Parliaments within the Enlarged European Union: From 'Victims' of Integration to Competitive Actors?*, London: Routledge, 2007; S. Hölscheidt, 'Formale Aufwertung – geringe Schubkraft: die Rolle der nationalen Parlamente gemäß dem Lissabonner Vertrag', *integration* 31, 2008, 254–65.

7 Article 7 (3) of Protocol No. 2 TEU/TFEU, see also par. 3.4.2 below.

8 See Ph. Kiiver, 'The European Constitution and the Role of National Parliaments: Hard Law Language, Soft Content', in A. Albi and J. Ziller, eds, *The European Constitution and National Constitutions: Ratification and Beyond*, The Hague: Kluwer Law International, 2007.

9 R. Schütze, 'Subsidiarity After Lisbon: Reinforcing the Safeguards of Federalism?', *Cambridge Law Journal* 68, 2009, 525–36.

10 A. Dashwood, 'The Relationship between the Member States and the European Union/European Community', *Common Market Law Review* 41, 2004, 355–81, p. 369.

11 S. Weatherill, 'Using National Parliaments to improve Scrutiny of the Limits of EU Action', *European Law Review* 28, 2003, 909–12, pp. 909–10; J. Kokott and A. Rüth, 'The European Convention and its Draft Treaty Establishing a Constitution for Europe: Appropriate Answers to the Laeken Questions?', *Common Market Law Review* 40, 2003, 1315–45, p. 1335.

12 See par. 3.5.4 below.

13 Article 7 (2) of Protocol No. 2 TEU/TFEU.

14 See also the table in par. 3.4 below.

15 See Chapter 4 below.

16 T. Raunio, *Destined for Irrelevance? Subsidiarity Control by National Parliaments*, Real Instituto Elcano Working Paper WP 36/2010.

17 Ph. Kiiver, *The National Parliaments in the European Union – A Critical View on EU Constitution-Building*, The Hague: Kluwer Law International, 2006, p. 161.

18 See also the second part of Article 5 (3) TEU: 'The institutions of the Union shall apply the principle of subsidiarity as laid down in the Protocol on the application of the principles of subsidiarity and proportionality. National Parliaments ensure compliance with the principle of subsidiarity in accordance with the procedure set out in that Protocol.'

19 See Chapter 4 below.

20 Not all commentaries on the EWS were negative, of course. A rather positive assessment has been provided by I. Cooper, 'The Watchdogs of Subsidiarity: National Parliaments and the Logic of Arguing in the EU', *Journal of Common Market Studies* 44, 2006, 281–304.

21 See the Conclusions of the XXXII COSAC, The Hague, 22–23 November 2004, item 5.

22 'A citizens' agenda – Delivering results for Europe', COM (2006) 211 final, p. 9.

23 The Commission uploads the incoming letters and its replies to an archive that is available online at ec.europa.eu/dgs/secretariat_general/relations/relations_other/npo/index_en.htm.

24 See Ph. Kiiver, 'The Treaty of Lisbon, the National Parliaments and the Principle of Subsidiarity', *Maastricht Journal of European and Comparative Law* 15, 2008, 77–83.

2 National parliaments in the European Union

1 D. Judge, 'The Failure of National Parliaments?', *West European Politics* 18, 1995, 79–100.

2 M. Niblock, *The EEC: National Parliaments in Community Decision-Making*, London: Chatham House, 1971, p. 98; Chr. Sasse, *Regierungen, Parlamente Ministerrat – Entscheidungsprozesse in der Europäischen Gemeinschaft*, Bonn: Europa Union, 1975, p. 101.

3 Unlike most other Member States, Denmark features a tradition of minority cabinets combined with a relatively Eurosceptic public opinion; the centralisation of scrutiny in the European affairs committee tends to marginalise sectoral committees; and even then negotiating mandates are not imposed by the committee, they are rather proposed by the minister for tacit consent.

4 See for a more detailed overview of the historical developments: Ph. Kiiver, *The National Parliaments in the European Union – A Critical View on EU Constitution-Building*, The Hague: Kluwer Law International, 2006, pp. 9–18 and 43–69.

5 O. Tans, C. Zoethout and J. Peters, eds, *National Parliaments and European Democracy; A Bottom-up Approach to European Constitutionalism*, Groningen: Europa Law Publishing, 2007.

6 Article 3 of the Protocol on the role of national parliaments in the European Union, replaced by Protocol No. 1 TEU/TFEU as inserted by the Treaty of Lisbon.

7 House of Lords, *European Union – Tenth Report*, 2008. This issue only seems to be relevant in the English language, though, where the word 'shall' is used to indicate a mandatory prescription in legislation. In languages such as German and French, legislation is typically drafted in a declaratory present-tense manner anyway ('Die nationalen Parlamente tragen aktiv bei', 'Les parlements nationaux contribuent activement'), which in both cases can still imply either a description or a prescription.

8 G. Barrett, ed., *National Parliaments and the European Union: The Constitutional Challenge for the Oireachtas and Other Member State Legislatures*, Dublin: Clarus, 2008, p. xxiii.

9 Article 48 (2) to (5) TEU.

10 Article 48 (3) TEU, second clause.

11 Article 48 (6) TEU.

12 Article 49 TEU.

13 L. Besselink, 'The Netherlands', in G.C. Rodriguez Iglesias and L. Ortiz Blanco, eds, *The Role of National Parliaments in the European Union – Proceedings of the XXIV FIDE Congress, Madrid 2010, Vol. 1*, Madrid: Servicio de publicaciones de la Facultad de Derecho Universidad Complutense, 2010.

14 For discussions of this ruling see, inter alia, D. Thym, 'In the Name of Sovereign Statehood: A Critical Introduction to the Lisbon Judgment of the German Constitutional Court', *Common Market Law Review* 46, 2009, 1795–822; D. Doukas, 'The Verdict of the German Federal Constitutional Court on the Lisbon Treaty: Not guilty, but don't do it again!', *European Law Review* 34, 2009, 866–88; Ph. Kiiver, 'The Lisbon Judgment of the German Constitutional Court: A Court-Ordered Strengthening of the National Legislature in the European Union', *European Law Journal* 16, 2010, 578–88.

15 See e.g. Ph. Norton, ed., *National Parliaments and the European Union*, London: Routledge, 1996; E. Smith, ed., *National Parliaments as Cornerstones of European Integration*, London: Kluwer Law International, 1996; F. Laursen and S. Pappas, eds, *The Changing Role of Parliaments in the European Union*, Maastricht: EIPA, 1995; A. Maurer and W. Wessels, eds, *National Parliaments on their Ways to Europe: Losers or Latecomers?*, Baden-Baden: Nomos, 2001.

16 T. Raunio, 'Always One Step Behind? National Legislatures and the European Union', *Government and Opposition* 34, 1999, 180–202.

17 T. Bergman, 'National Parliaments and EU Affairs Committees: notes on empirical variation and competing explanations', *Journal of European Public Policy* 4, 1997, 373–87.

18 Norton, op. cit.

19 Bergman, op. cit.

20 Maurer and Wessels, op. cit.

21 See A. Fraga, 'The Parliament of Portugal: Loyal Scrutiny and Informal Influence', in Maurer and Wessels, op. cit.

22 Kiiver, *National Parliaments*, pp. 43–69.

23 G. Majone, 'Europe's "Democratic Deficit": The Question of Standards', *European Law Journal* 4, 1998, 5–28.

24 See e.g. A. Jyränki, ed., *National Constitutions in the Era of Integration*, The Hague: Kluwer Law International, 1999; Z. Bankowski and A. Scott, eds, *The European Union and its Order*, Oxford: Blackwell, 2000; N. Walker, ed., *Sovereignty in Transition*, Oxford: Hart, 2003; J. Weiler and M. Wind, eds, *European Constitutionalism Beyond the State*, Cambridge: Cambridge University Press, 2003; P. Magnette, *What is the European Union?*, Basingstoke: Palgrave 2005; N. Tsagourias, ed., *Transnational Constitutionalism: International and European Perspectives*, Cambridge:

Cambridge University Press, 2007; P. Dobner and M. Loughlin, eds, *The Twilight of Constitutionalism?*, Oxford: Oxford University Press, 2010. For a refreshing bit of philosopher-bashing see J. Nergelius, *The Constitutional Dilemma of the European Union*, Groningen: Europa Law Publishing, 2009.

25 M. Burgess, 'Federalism', in A. Wiener and Th. Diez, eds, *European Integration Theory*, 2nd edn., Oxford: Oxford University Press, 2009.

26 G. Mancini, *Democracy and Constitutionalism in the European Union*, Oxford: Hart, 2000, p. 254.

27 Ibid., p. 34 et seq.

28 Ph. Norton, 'National Parliaments and the European Union: Where to from here?', in P. Craig and C. Harlow, eds, *Lawmaking in the European Union*, London: Kluwer Law International, 1998, p. 213.

29 C. Janowski, *Die nationalen Parlamente und ihre Europa-Gremien: Legitimationsgarant der EU?*, Baden-Baden: Nomos, 2005, pp. 234–9.

30 A. von Bogdandy and J. Bast, eds, *Principles of European Constitutional Law*, Oxford: Hart, 2005; K. Lenaerts and P. Van Nuffel, *Constitutional Law of the European Union*, London: Sweet & Maxwell, 2011.

31 See, e.g., on the notion of constitutional tolerance: J. Weiler, 'In Defence of the Status Quo: Europe's constitutional *Sonderweg*', in Weiler and Wind, op. cit. See further, on the relationship between pluralist constitutionalism and the EU principle of loyalty: A. Verhoeven, *The European Union in Search of a Democratic and Constitutional Theory*, The Hague: Kluwer Law International, 2002.

32 M. Poiares Maduro, 'Contrapunctual Law: Europe's Constitutional Pluralism in Action', in Walker, op. cit.

33 I. Pernice, 'Multilevel Constitutionalism and the Treaty of Amsterdam: European Constitution-Making Revisited', *Common Market Law Review* 36, 1999, 703–50; L. Besselink, 'National Parliaments in the EU's Composite Constitution: A plea for a Shift in Paradigm', in Ph. Kiiver, ed., *National and Regional Parliaments in the European Constitutional Order*, Groningen: Europa Law Publishing, 2006.

34 Besselink, 'Composite Constitution'.

35 Ph. Dann, *Parlamente im Exekutivföderalismus*, Berlin: Springer, 2004.

36 W. Van Gerven, *The European Union: A Polity of States and Peoples*, Oxford: Hart, 2005, p. 364 et seq.

37 G. Majone, *Dilemmas of European Integration: The Ambiguities and Pitfalls of Integration by Stealth*, Oxford: Oxford University Press, 2005; C. Harlow, *Accountability in the European Union*, Oxford: Oxford University Press, 2002.

38 Ph. Weber-Panariello, *Nationale Parlamente in der Europäischen Union*, Baden-Baden: Nomos, 1995, p. 317.

39 J. Weiler, *The Constitution of Europe: 'Do the New Clothes Have an Emperor?' and Other Essays on European Integration*, Cambridge: Cambridge University Press, 1999, p. 264 et seq.

40 Th. Saalfeld, 'Deliberate Delegation or Abdication? Government Backbenchers, Ministers and European Union Legislation', *The Journal of Legislative Studies* 11, 2005, 343–71.

41 D. Curtin, *Executive Power of the European Union: Law, Practices, and the Living Constitution*, Oxford: Oxford University Press, 2009, p. 249.

42 C. Harlow, *Accountability in the European Union*, Oxford: Oxford University Press, 2002, p. 192.

43 A. Menon and S. Weatherill, 'Legitimacy, Accountability, and Delegation in the European Union', in A. Arnull and D. Wincott, eds, *Accountability and Legitimacy in the European Union*, Oxford: Oxford University Press, 2002.

44 K. Auel, 'Democratic Accountability and National Parliaments: Redefining the Impact of Parliamentary Scrutiny in EU Affairs', *European Law Journal* 13, 2007, 487–504.

3 The institutional and procedural logic of the early warning system

1 See Chapter 4 below.
2 European Convention, Final Report of Working Group IV of 22 October 2002, CONV 353/02, WG IV 17.
3 T. Raunio, *Destined for Irrelevance? Subsidiarity Control by National Parliaments*, Real Instituto Elcano Working Paper WP 36/2010; see also Ph. Kiiver, 'The Composite Case for National Parliaments in the European Union: Who Profits from Enhanced Involvement?', *European Constitutional Law Review* 2, 2006, 227–52.
4 Proposed amendment by Poul Schlüter, available at european-convention.eu.int/Docs/Treaty/pdf/20000/20000_ProtSub%20Schlüter%20EN.pdf.
5 Proposed amendment by E. Brok and others, available at european-convention.eu.int/Docs/Treaty/pdf/20000/Sub-6BrokEN.pdf.
6 See paras 3.4, 3.8 and 3.9 below.
7 See par. 3.5.1 below.
8 See par. 3.4.2 below.
9 Article 5 (3) TEU.
10 The Amsterdam Protocol referred to subsidiarity, the area of freedom, security and justice and fundamental rights as possibly interesting topics for contributions from COSAC as an interparliamentary forum.
11 See par. 3.4.2 below.
12 Chr. Pennera, 'Les parlements nationaux dans le système de l'Union européenne', in G. C. Rodriguez Iglesias and L. Ortiz Blanco, eds, *The Role of National Parliaments in the European Union – Proceedings of the XXIV FIDE Congress, Madrid 2010, Vol. 1*, Madrid: Servicio de publicaciones de la Facultad de Derecho Universidad Complutense, 2010, p. 105.
13 See par. 7.3.3 below.
14 See par. 3.3.4 below.
15 Article 2 Protocol No. 2 TEU/TFEU.
16 Article 4 Protocol No. 1 TEU/TFEU.
17 Article 5 Protocol No. 2 TEU/TFEU.
18 Article 7 Protocol No. 2 TEU/TFEU.
19 M. Wyrzykowski, R. Puchta and M. Ziolkowski, 'The Role of National Parliaments in the European Union (General Report)', in Rodriguez Iglesias and Ortiz Blanco, *The Role of National Parliaments in the European Union – Proceedings of the XXIV FIDE Congress, Madrid 2010, Vol. 1*, Madrid: Servicio de publicacones de la Facultad de Derecho Universidad Complutense, 2010, p. 20; Pennera, op. cit., p. 105.
20 See par. 4.3.5 below.
21 See Chapter 4 below.
22 See e.g. J.-V. Louis, 'National Parliaments and the Principle of Subsidiarity: Legal Options and Practical Limits', *European Constitutional Law Review* 4, 2008, 429–52.
23 J. Rivers, 'Proportionality and Discretion in International and European Law', in N. Tsagourias, ed., *Transnational Constitutionalism: International and European Perspectives*, Cambridge: Cambridge University Press, 2007, p. 109.
24 COM (2008) 428 final.
25 See Chapter 6 below.
26 See Chapter 5 below.
27 See par. 3.8 below.
28 See par. 4.7 below.
29 See par. 3.7.2 below.
30 European Commission, *Practical arrangements for the operation of the subsidiarity control mechanism under protocol no 2 of the Treaty of Lisbon*, letter of President Barroso and Vice-president Wallström of 1 December 2009, Annex, available at ec.europa.eu/dgs/secretariat_general/relations/relations_other/npo/docs/letter_en.pdf.

31 Article 93 (1) (2a) and 93 (2) Basic Law.
32 Th. Giegerich, *Europäische Verfassung und deutsche Verfassung im transnationalen Konstitutionalisierungsprozeß*, Berlin: Springer, 2003, p. 813, referring to the opinion of Hans Hugo Klein who argued, in the *Maunz/Dürig* commentary to the Basic Law, that the majority requirements as normally apply under State law for the adoption of decisions will have to apply and that States are not free to turn this procedure into a minority right by analogy to the right of a defined Bundestag minority to launch abstract review proceedings.
33 Article 28 (1) Basic Law.
34 German Federal Constitutional Court, judgment of 16 July 1998, 2 BvR 1953/95.
35 See R. Holzhacker, 'National Parliamentary Scrutiny over EU Issues', *European Union Politics* 3, 2002, 459–79.
36 Article 5 Protocol No. 2 TEU/TFEU.
37 See par. 3.3.2 above.
38 Article 294 (7) (b) TFEU.
39 Wyrzykowski et al., op. cit., p. 23.
40 Also, the question has been raised and discussed in some detail by Barrett in G. Barrett, ed., *National Parliaments and the European Union: The Constitutional Challenge for the Oireachtas and Other Member State Legislatures* (Dublin: Clarus 2008), pp. xxx–xxxi.
41 P. Conlan et al., 'Ireland', in Rodriguez Iglesias and Ortiz Blanco, op. cit., p. 318, and A. Juhász-Tóth and A. Mohay, 'Hungary', ibid., p. 285.
42 N. Angelides, 'Cyprus', ibid., p. 141.
43 G. Gramaxo Roseira, 'Portugal', ibid., p. 393.
44 Y. Carl, 'Luxembourg', ibid., p. 353.
45 Chr. Mellein, 'Germany', ibid., p. 254.
46 M. Cerar, 'Slovenia', ibid., p. 422.
47 J. Suchman, 'Czech Republic', ibid., p. 160.
48 See par. 4.5.8 below.
49 See par. 4.5.2 below.
50 P. Hardy, 'United Kingdom', in Rodriguez Iglesias and Ortiz Blanco, op. cit., p. 548.
51 Article 7 (2) Protocol No. 2 TEU/TFEU.
52 European Commission, *Practical Arrangements*.
53 Article 3 Protocol No. 2 TEU/TFEU.
54 European Commission, *Practical Arrangements*.
55 Article 6 Protocol No. 2 TCE.
56 Contribution of the XXXIV COSAC in London, October 2005.
57 See par. 4.5.1 below.
58 Article 3 Protocol No. 2 TEU/TFEU.
59 Article 6 Protocol No. 2 TEU/TFEU, first sentence.
60 European Commission, *Practical Arrangements*, p. 4.
61 E-mail correspondence with the cabinet of Commission Vice-President Šefčovič between 9 and 22 March 2011.
62 European Commission, *Practical Arrangements*, p. 4.
63 Ibid., p. 3.
64 E-mail correspondence with the cabinet of Commission Vice-President Šefčovič between 9 and 22 March 2011.
65 Article 6 Protocol No. 2 TEU/TFEU.
66 E-mail correspondence with the cabinet of Commission Vice-President Šefčovič between 9 and 22 March 2011.
67 Wyrzykowski, op. cit., p. 22.

68 See par. 3.7.2 below.
69 See par. 4.5.4 below.
70 European Commission, *Practical Arrangements*, p. 4.
71 See also Pennera, op. cit., p. 167.
72 Article 3 Protocol No. 2 TEU/TFEU.
73 See par. 4.5.6 below.
74 Article 8, second clause of Protocol No. 2 TEU/TFEU.
75 See par. 3.8 below.
76 J. Laso Pérez, 'Spain', in Rodriguez Iglesias and Ortiz Blanco, op. cit., pp. 464–6.
77 G. Vara Arribas and D. Bourdin, *The Role of Regional Parliaments in the Process of Subsidiarity Analysis within the Early Warning System of the Lisbon Treaty*, Brussels: Committee of the Regions, 2011.
78 Article 8 Protocol No. 2 TEU/TFEU.
79 M. Claes, *The National Courts' Mandate in the European Constitution*, Oxford: Hart, 2005, pp. 535–8.
80 COSAC Secretariat, Report on the Results of the Subsidiarity Check on the Commission Proposal for a Regulation of the European Parliament and of the Council on jurisdiction, applicable law, recognition and enforcement of decisions and authentic instruments in matters of succession and the creation of a European Certificate of Succession, Madrid, May 2010.
81 See Chapter 6 below.
82 W. Sadurski, *Rights Before Courts: A Study of Constitutional Courts in Postcommunist States of Central and Eastern Europe*, New York: Springer, 2005.
83 See e.g. R. Schütze, 'Subsidiarity After Lisbon: Reinforcing the Safeguards of Federalism?', *Cambridge Law Journal* 68, 2009, 525–36, p. 531 et seq., see also Louis, op. cit., pp. 429–52.
84 Wyrzykowski, op. cit., p. 24.
85 J. Kokott and A. Rüth, 'The European Convention and its Draft Treaty Establishing a Constitution for Europe: Appropriate Answers to the Laeken Questions?', *Common Market Law Review* 40, 2003, 1315–45, p. 1335; S. Weatherill, 'Better Competence Monitoring', *European Law Review* 30, 2005, 23–41.
86 *Kamerstukken* I, 2009–2010, 30953, no. L.
87 § 93d of the Bundestag Rules of Procedure.
88 Wyrzykowski et al., op. cit., p. 24.
89 See also Mellein, op. cit.
90 Ibid., see also Article 45 of the German Basic Law.
91 Article 61 of the French Constitution.
92 Articles 151-9 and 151-11 of the Rules of Procedure of the National Assembly.
93 Mellein, op. cit., p. 258.
94 Agreement of 19 December 2005, available at www.lachambre.be/kvvcr/showpage. cfm?language=nl&section=/pri/europe&story=sub.xml&rightmenu=right_pri.
95 M. Hailbronner, 'Die Justiziabilität des Subsidiaritätsprinzips im Lichte der Subsidiaritätsprotokolle', in I. Pernice, ed., *Der Vertrag von Lissabon: Reform der EU ohne Verfassung?*, Baden-Baden: Nomos, 2008, pp. 142–3.
96 § 12 (4) of the Integrationsverantwortungsgesetz; § 93d of the Bundestag Rules of Procedure; Mellein, op. cit., p. 258.
97 Protocol No. 3 TEU/TFEU.
98 Proposed amendment by Mme Palacio, available at http://european-convention. eu.int/Docs/Treaty/pdf/20000/Protsub%20Palacio%20FR.pdf.
99 Proposed amendment by Teija Tiilikainen, Antti Peltomäki, Kimmo Kiljunen, Jari Vilén, Hannu Takkula and Esko Helle, available at european-convention. eu.int/Docs/Treaty/pdf/20000/Protsub%20Tiilikainen%20EN.pdf. See also the amendment proposed by the Earl of Stockton MEP to the same effect.

100   A. Estella, *The EU Principle of Subsidiarity and its Critique*, Oxford: Oxford University Press, 2002.

101   D. Keyaerts, 'Ex ante Evaluation of EU Legislation Intertwined with Judicial Review? Comment on Vodafone Ltd v Secretary of State for Business, Enterprise and Regulatory Reform (C–58/08)', *European Law Review* 35, 2010, 869–84.

102   See also P. Craig, 'Legal Control of Regulatory Bodies: Principle, Policy, and Teleology', in P. Birkinshaw and M. Varney, eds, *The European Union Legal Order after Lisbon*, Alphen: Kluwer Law International, 2010, pp. 106–8.

103   Estella, op. cit.

104   Hailbronner, op. cit., p. 144.

105   For an overview, see par. 2.1 above.

106   Treaty establishing a Constitution for Europe, Final Act, Declaration (No. 49) by the Kingdom of Belgium on national parliaments.

107   Treaty of Lisbon, Final Act, Declaration (No. 51) by the Kingdom of Belgium on national parliaments.

108   Agreement of 19 December 2005.

109   E-mail correspondence with the cabinet of European Commission Vice President Ševčovič between 10 and 21 December 2010.

110   W. Pas, 'The Belgian "National Parliament" from the Perspective of the EU Constitutional Treaty', in Ph. Kiiver, ed., *National and Regional Parliaments in the European Constitutional Order*, Groningen: Europa Law Publishing, 2006.

111   Article 88–7 of the French Constitution, Article 151-12 of the Rules of Procedure of the National Assembly.

112   Article 24, second clause, of the French Constitution.

113   § 10 of the Integrationsverantwortungsgesetz (IntVG), the Assumption of Responsibility for Integration by the Bundestag and the Bundesrat in Matters of the European Union Act.

114   § 4 IntVG.

115   See par. 3.7.2 above.

116   Wyrzykowski et al., op. cit., p. 13.

117   European Court of Justice, Case C-369/90, *Mario Vincente Micheletti and others* v. *Delegacion del Gobierno en Cantabria* ECR [1992] I-4258; Case C-200/02 *Zhu and Chen* v. *Secretary of State for the Home Department*. My thanks to Nikos Skoutaris for this remark.

118   R. Barents, *The Autonomy of Community Law*, The Hague: Kluwer Law International, 2004.

119   European Court of Justice, Case 61/65 *Vaassen* v. *Beambtenfonds voor het Mijnbedrijf* [1966] ECR 272; Case 246/80 *Broeckmeulen* v. *Huisarts Registratie Commissie* [1981] ECR 2311.

120   E-mail correspondence with the European Department of the Belgian House of Representatives between 10 and 17 December 2010.

121   S. Fish and M. Kroenig, *The Handbook of National Legislatures: A Global Survey*, Cambridge: Cambridge University Press, 2009, p. 1.

122   Ph. Norton, 'Introduction: The Institution of Parliaments', in Ph. Norton, ed., *Parliaments and Governments in Western Europe*, London: Frank Cass, 1998.

123   Article 16 (2) TEU does not stipulate that the Council comprises national ministers but that it comprises 'a representative of each Member State at ministerial level' in order to accommodate Belgian, but also German preferences to allow a regional minister to represent the Member State in matters that domestically would fall under exclusive regional competences.

124   See Chapter 5 below.

125   H.-G. Kamann, *Die Mitwirkung der Parlamente der Mitgliedstaaten an der europäischen Gesetzgebung*, Frankfurt: Peter Lang, 1997, pp. 91–3.

126   See Chapters 4 and 7 below.

127 *Santoro* v. *Italy*, ECtHR, 1 July 2004, no. 36681/97.
128 *Matthews* v. *UK*, ECtHR, 18 February 1999, no. 24833/94.
129 *Guliyev* v. *Azerbaijan* (admissibility), ECtHR, 27 May 2004, no. 35584/02; *Boskoski* v. *Macedonia* (admissibility), ECtHR, 2 September 2004, no. 11676/04.
130 Article 7 (1) Protocol No. 2 TEU/TFEU.
131 Article 14 (2) TEU.
132 Article 16 (4) TEU.
133 See Chapter 6 below.
134 See S. Patterson and A. Mughan, eds, *Senates: Bicameralism in the Contemporary World*, Columbus: Ohio State University Press, 1999.
135 Article 6 Protocol No. 2 to the Draft Treaty establishing a Constitution for Europe, CONV 850/03.
136 Article 7 Protocol No. 2 to the Treaty establishing a Constitution for Europe, OJ 2004/C 310/01.
137 Article 6 of Protocol No. 2 to the Treaty of Lisbon amending the Treaty on European Union and the Treaty establishing the European Community, OJ 2007/C 306/01.
138 See par. 3.8 above.
139 Article 16 (4) TEU.
140 I say technically because the senate does at times insist on additional amendments, even though a bill has already been submitted to it, as a precondition for its approval of the bill as a whole. This practice, called 'novelle', is considered controversial in academic circles and is probably unconstitutional.
141 See the Joint Statement of the 6th meeting of the Association of European Senates, Warsaw, 25 May 2004, available at www.senateurope.org.
142 See Chapter 7 below.
143 See Chapter 4 below.

4 The material scope of the EWS: subsidiarity and other criteria

1 See R. Schütze, 'Subsidiarity After Lisbon: Reinforcing the Safeguards of Federalism?', *Cambridge Law Journal* 68, 2009, 525–36.
2 A. Dashwood, 'The Relationship Between the Member States and the European Union/European Community', *Common Market Law Review* 41, 2004, 355–81, p. 368.
3 K. Van Kersbergen and B. Verbeek, 'The Politics of Subsidiarity in the European Union', *Journal of Common Market Studies* 32, 1994, 215–36.
4 See also R. von Borries and M. Hauschild, 'Implementing the Subsidiarity Principle', *Columbia Journal of European Law* 5, 1999, 369–88, p. 375.
5 G. De Búrca, 'The Principle of Subsidiarity and the Court of Justice as an Institutional Actor', *Journal of Common Market Studies* 36, 1998, 217–35, p. 220. See also T. Koopmans, 'Subsidiarity, Politics and the Judiciary', *European Constitutional Law Review* 1, 2005, 112–16, who, in the context of judicial review of subsidiarity, speaks of a 'growing "judicialization" of political problems', p. 115.
6 European Convention, Final Report of Working Group I of 23 September 2002, CONV 286/02 WG I 15, p. 2; Final Report of Working Group IV of 22 October 2002, CONV 353/02, WG IV 17, p. 10.
7 European Commission, *Practical arrangements for the operation of the subsidiarity control mechanism under protocol no 2 of the Treaty of Lisbon*, letter of President Barroso and Vice-president Wallström of 1 December 2009, Annex, available at ec.europa.eu/dgs/secretariat_general/relations/relations_other/npo/docs/letter_en.pdf.
8 See par. 4.5.8 below.
9 Schütze, op. cit., p. 532.

10 G. De Búrca, op. cit., p. 220.
11 Chr. Calliess, *Subsidiaritäts- und Solidaritätsprinzip in der Europäischen Union*, 2nd edn, Baden-Baden: Nomos, 1999.
12 Schütze, op. cit., p. 533 et seq.
13 P. Hardy, 'United Kingdom', in G. C. Rodriguez Iglesias and L. Ortiz Blanco, eds, *The Role of National Parliaments in the European Union – Proceedings of the XXIV FIDE Congress, Madrid 2010, Vol. 1*, Madrid: Servicio de publicaciones de la Facultad de Derecho Universidad Complutense, 2010, p. 545.
14 G. De Búrca, op. cit., p. 219.
15 A. Estella, *The EU Principle of Subsidiarity and its Critique*, Oxford: Oxford University Press, 2002, p. 95.
16 N. Emiliou, *The Principle of Proportionality in European Law: A Comparative Study*, The Hague: Kluwer Law International, 1996, p. 185.
17 Estella, op. cit., p. 109.
18 See par. 4.5.3 below.
19 Ibid.
20 Estella, op. cit., p. 159 et seq.
21 I. Cooper, 'The Watchdogs of Subsidiarity: National Parliaments and the Logic of Arguing in the EU', *Journal of Common Market Studies* 44, 2006, 281–304.
22 R. Behn, *Rethinking Democratic Accountability*, Washington, DC: Brookings Institution Press, 2001, p. 63.
23 Article 17 TEU.
24 Article 5 TEU.
25 Article 3 TEU.
26 Estella, op. cit., p. 137 et seq, confirmed by Chr. Pennera, 'Les parlements nationaux dans le système de l'Union européenne', in G. C. Rodriguez Iglesias and L. Ortiz Blanco, eds, *The Role of National Parliaments in the European Union – Proceedings of the XXIV FIDE Congress, Madrid 2010, Vol. 1*, Madrid: Servicio de publicaciones de la Facultad de Derecho Universidad Complutense, 2010, op. cit., p. 112.
27 See the discussion of the Court's ruling on the Working Time Directive in De Búrca, op. cit., see also Estella, op. cit.
28 Estella, op. cit., p. 159 et seq.
29 See A. Føllesdal, 'Survey Article: Subsidiarity', *Journal of Political Philosophy* 6, 1998, 190–218, p. 197.
30 T. Raunio and M. Wiberg, 'Does Support Lead to Ignorance? National Parliaments and the Legitimacy of EU Governance', *Acta Politica* 35, 2000, 146–68.
31 See Chapters 5 and 6 below.
32 See COSAC Secretariat, Report on the results of COSAC's Pilot project on the 3rd Railway Package to test the 'Subsidiarity early warning mechanism', Luxembourg, 17–18 May 2005.
33 COM (2004) 139 final.
34 COM (2004) 142 final.
35 COM (2004) 143 final.
36 COM (2004) 144 final.
37 COM (2006) 399 final.
38 See COSAC Secretariat, Report on the results of COSAC's subsidiarity and proportionality check on the Commission proposal for a Regulation on the applicable law and jurisdiction in divorce matters, Helsinki, 19–21 November 2006.
39 COM (2006) 594 final.
40 COSAC Secretariat, Report on the results of the subsidiarity and proportionality check coordinated by COSAC on the Commission proposal for a Directive concerning the full accomplishment of the internal market of Community postal services, Berlin, 12 February 2007.

41 COM (2007) 650 final.
42 COSAC Secretariat, Report on the results of the Test on the subsidiarity check mechanism of the Lisbon Treaty coordinated by COSAC on the Commission proposal for a Framework Decision on Combating Terrorism.
43 COM (2008) 426 final.
44 COSAC Secretariat, Report on the Results of the Subsidiarity Check on the Proposal for a Council Directive on Implementing the Principle of Equal Treatment between Persons Irrespective of Religion or Belief, Disability, Age or Sexual Orientation, Paris, 3–4 November 2008.
45 COM (2008) 818 final.
46 COSAC Secretariat, Report on the Results of the Subsidiarity Check on the Proposal for a Directive of the European Parliament and of the Council on Standards of Quality and Safety of Human Organs Intended for Transplantation, Prague, 10–12 May 2009.
47 Impact assessment, Brussels, 8 December 2008, SEC (2008) 2957, p. 3.
48 Another case is the Bundestag's reasoning on the Succession Certificate, see par. 4.5.8 below.
49 COM (2009) 338 final.
50 COSAC Secretariat: Report on the Results of the Subsidiarity Check on the Proposal for a Council Framework Decision on the Right to Interpretation and to Translation in Criminal Proceedings, October 2009.
51 COM (2009) 338 final, par. 24.
52 COM (2009) 154 final.
53 COSAC Secretariat, Report on the Results of the Subsidiarity Check on the Commission Proposal for a Regulation of the European Parliament and of the Council on jurisdiction, applicable law, recognition and enforcement of decisions and authentic instruments in matters of succession and the creation of a European Certificate of Succession, Madrid, May 2010.
54 The Bundestag's opinion is not included in the annex to the COSAC secretariat's report but is archived on the Commission's website.
55 Estella, op. cit., p. 109.
56 See also M. Hailbronner, 'Die Justiziabilität des Subsidiaritätsprinzips im Lichte der Subsidiaritätsprotokolle', in I. Pernice, ed., *Der Vertrag von Lissabon: Reform der EU ohne Verfassung?*, Baden-Baden: Nomos, 2008, p. 143.
57 Article 352 (2) TFEU.
58 Schütze, op. cit.
59 A. Meuwese, *Impact Assessment in EU Lawmaking*, Leiden: E.M. Meijers Instituut, 2008.
60 G. Majone, *Dilemmas of European Integration: The Ambiguities and Pitfalls of Integration by Stealth*, Oxford: Oxford University Press, 2005, p. x.

5 The early warning system as an accountability mechanism

1 R. Mulgan, 'Accountability: An Ever-Expanding Concept?', *Public Administration* 78, 2000, 555–73.
2 M. Bovens, 'Analysing and Assessing Accountability: A Conceptual Framework', *European Law Journal* 13, 2007, 447–68.
3 M. Maccarthaigh, 'Accountability Through National Parliaments: Practice and Problems', in J. O'Brennan and T. Raunio, eds, *National Parliaments within the Enlarged European Union: From 'Victims' of Integration to Competitive Actors?*, London: Routledge, 2007.
4 C. Harlow, *Accountability in the European Union*, Oxford: Oxford University Press, 2002.

5 S. Gustavsson, Chr. Karlsson and Th. Persson, eds, *The Illusion of Accountability in the European Union*, London: Routledge, 2009. For a partly more positive view see M. Bovens, D. Curtin and P. 't Hart, eds, *The Real World of EU Accountability: What Deficit?* Oxford: Oxford University Press, 2010.

6 H. Agné, 'Irretrievable Powers and Democratic Accountability', in Gustavsson et al., op. cit.

7 Th. Larue, 'Delegation to the Permanent Representation and Mechanisms of Accountability', in Gustavsson et al., op. cit.

8 A. Menon and S. Weatherill, 'Legitimacy, Accountability, and Delegation in the European Union', in A. Arnull and D. Wincott, eds, *Accountability and Legitimacy in the European Union*, Oxford: Oxford University Press, 2002.

9 For an exception, which considers the EWS as a 'check' on the Commission, see M. Tsakatika, *Political Responsibility and the European Union*, Manchester: Manchester University Press, 2008, pp. 68–9.

10 See par. 3.3.2 above.

11 See F. Amtenbrink, 'On the Legitimacy and Democratic Accountability of the European Central Bank', in Arnull and Wincott, op. cit.; D. Naurin, 'The European Central Bank – Independent and Accountable?', in Gustavsson et al., op. cit.

12 D. Curtin, *Executive Power of the European Union: Law, Practices, and the Living Constitution*, Oxford: Oxford University Press, 2009.

13 P. Craig, 'The Nature of the Community: Integration, Democracy, and Legitimacy', in P. Craig and G. de Búrca, eds, *The Evolution of EU Law*, Oxford: Oxford University Press, 1999, pp. 72–4.

14 See B. de Witte, 'Executive Accountability under the European Constitution and the Lisbon Treaty; Nihil Novi sub Sole?', in L. Verhey, Ph. Kiiver and S. Loeffen, eds, *Political Accountability and European Integration*, Groningen: Europa Law Publishing, 2009.

15 P. Craig, 'The Locus and Accountability of the Executive in the European Union', in P. Craig and A. Tomkins, eds, *The Executive and Public Law: Power and Accountability in Comparative Perspective*, Oxford: Oxford University Press, 2006, p. 318.

16 D.G. Dimitrakopoulos, 'Incrementalism and Path Dependence: European Integration and Institutional Change in National Parliaments', *Journal of Common Market Studies* 39, 2001, 405–22.

17 European Convention, Final Report of Working Group IV of 22 October 2002, CONV 353/02, WG IV 17.

18 See e.g. Ph. Norton, ed., *Parliaments and Citizens in Western Europe*, London: Frank Cass, 2002.

19 See Chapter 6 below.

20 K. Auel, 'Democratic Accountability and National Parliaments: Redefining the Impact of Parliamentary Scrutiny in EU Affairs', *European Law Journal* 13, 2007, 487–504.

21 Article 3 Protocol No. 2 TEU/TFEU.

22 See Ph. Kiiver, 'European Scrutiny in National Parliaments: Individual Efforts in the Collective Interest?', in O'Brennan and Raunio, op. cit.

23 C. Scott, 'Accountability in the Regulatory State', *Journal of Law and Society* 27, 2000, 38–60.

24 Bovens, op. cit.

25 Ibid., p. 453.

26 See par. 3.4.2 above.

27 Th. Saalfeld, 'Deliberate Delegation or Abdication? Government Backbenchers, Ministers and European Union Legislation', *The Journal of Legislative Studies* 11, 2005, 343–71.

28 R. Keohane, 'Accountability in World Politics', in Gustavsson et al., op. cit., p. 13.

29 Article 50 TEU.
30 Article 17 (3) TEU.
31 Article 17 (7) TEU.
32 Article 17 (8) TEU.
33 See also D. Spence, 'The President, the College and the Cabinets', in D. Spence, ed., *The European Commission*, London: John Harper, 2006, pp. 42–6.
34 Article 17 (5) TEU.
35 See Scott, op. cit. and Bovens, op. cit., p. 460.
36 A. Benz, C. Harlow and Y. Papadopoulos, 'Introduction', *European Law Journal* 13, 2007, 441–6, p. 444.
37 The dimensions are derived from Scott, op. cit. and Bovens, op. cit.
38 Behn, op. cit., p. 198.
39 L. Besselink, 'National Parliaments in the EU's Composite Constitution: A Plea for a Shift in Paradigm', in Ph. Kiiver, ed., *National and Regional Parliaments in the European Constitutional Order*, Groningen: Europa Law Publishing, 2006.
40 See also par. 2.3 above.
41 B. Crum and E. Fossum, 'The Multilevel Parliamentary Field: A Framework for Theorizing Representative Democracy in the EU', *European Political Science Review* 1, 2009, 249–71.
42 E. Hirsch Ballin and L. Senden, *Co-actorship in the Development of European Law-Making: The Quality of European Legislation and its Implementation and Application in the National Legal Order*, The Hague: Asser Press, 2005.
43 M. Knudsen and Y. Carl, 'COSAC – Its Role to Date and its Potential in the Future', in G. Barrett, ed., *National Parliaments and the European Union: The Constitutional Challenge for the Oireachtas and Other Member State Legislatures*, Dublin: Clarus, 2008.
44 Scott, op. cit.
45 C. Harlow and R. Rawlings, 'Promoting Accountability in Multilevel Governance: A Network Approach', *European Law Journal* 13, 2007, 447–68.
46 R. Mulgan, *Holding Power to Account: Accountability in Modern Democracies*, Basingstoke: Palgrave Macmillan, 2003.
47 Bovens, op. cit.
48 See the hypotheses in par. 7.4.2 below.
49 See par. 3.7 above.
50 Craig, *Nature of the Community*.
51 M. Flinders, *The Politics of Accountability in the Modern State*, Aldershot: Ashgate, 2001.
52 Harlow and Rawlings, op. cit.
53 Chr. Bengtson, 'Interparliamentary Cooperation Within Europe', in O'Brennan and Raunio, op. cit.
54 T. Raunio, *Destined for Irrelevance? Subsidiarity Control by National Parliaments*, Real Instituto Elcano Working Paper WP 36/2010.
55 Chr. Neuhold, *Late wake-up call or early warning? Parliamentary participation and cooperation in light of the Lisbon Treaty*, UACES Conference paper, January 2011, available at www.uaces.org/pdf/papers/1102/Neuhold.pdf.
56 See Chapters 4 above and 7 below.
57 For example, Article 12 TEU on national parliaments is placed in the Treaty title on democratic principles.
58 Bovens, op. cit.
59 Discussion on 3 December 2010 in The Hague.
60 Harlow, op. cit., p. 144.
61 Bovens, op. cit., p. 461.
62 Scott, op. cit.
63 Bovens, op. cit., p. 461.

64 Ibid., pp. 455–6.
65 L. Verhey, H. Broeksteeg and I. Van den Driessche, eds, *Political Accountability in Europe: Which Way Forward? A Traditional Concept of Parliamentary Democracy in an EU Context*, Groningen: Europa Law Publishing, 2008.
66 A. Arnull, 'Introduction: the European Union's Accountability Deficit', in Arnull and Wincott, eds, *Accountability and Legitimacy in the European Union*, Oxford: Oxford University Press, 2002, p. 3.
67 D. Oliver, *Government in the United Kingdom: the Search for Accountability, Effectiveness and Citizenship*, Milton Keynes: Open University Press, 1991, p. 22.
68 T. Koopmans, *Courts and Political Institutions: A Comparative View*, Cambridge: Cambridge University Press, 2003.
69 R. Mulgan, *Holding Power to Account: Accountability in Modern Democracies*, Basingstoke: Palgrave Macmillan, 2003, pp. 32–3.
70 Arnull, op. cit., p. 3.
71 Harlow and Rawlings, op. cit., p. 546.
72 E. Alberti, 'Political Accountability in Spain', in Verhey et al., op. cit., p. 213.
73 Flinders, op. cit.
74 B. Romzek and M. Dubnick, 'Accountability in the Public Sector: Lessons from the Challenger Tragedy', *Public Administration Review* 47, 1987, 227–38, cited by R. Mulgan, op. cit., p. 33.
75 A. Stone Sweet, *Governing with Judges: Constitutional Politics in Europe*, Oxford: Oxford University Press, 2000.
76 W. Sadurski, *Rights Before Courts: A Study of Constitutional Courts in Postcommunist States of Central and Eastern Europe*, Dordrecht: Springer, 2005.
77 While the present study is devoted to the lawfulness of legislative proposals, the legal-accountability implications of an assessment by parliament of the lawfulness of conduct in the context of impeachment, enquiry and immunity-lifting procedures certainly merits further research.
78 See the Final Report of Convention WG I (Subsidiarity), CONV 286/02, p. 2 and of WG IV (National Parliaments), CONV 353/02, p. 10, respectively.
79 The archive is available online at ec.europa.eu/dgs/secretariat_general/relations/relations_other/npo/index_en.htm.
80 Annual Report 2008 on relations between the European Commission and national parliaments, Brussels, 7 July 2009, COM (2009) 343 final, p. 5.

6 The EWS as legal review: national parliaments as councils of state

1 J. Weiler, *The Constitution of Europe: 'Do the New Clothes Have an Emperor?' and Other Essays on European Integration*, Cambridge: Cambridge University Press, 1999, p. 354.
2 Article 39 of the French Constitution.
3 Article 160 of the Belgian Constitution.
4 Article 73 of the Dutch Constitution.
5 Article 83bis of the Luxembourgish Constitution.
6 Article 100 of the Italian Constitution.
7 Article 107 of the Spanish Constitution.
8 I. Cooper, 'The Watchdogs of Subsidiarity: National Parliaments and the Logic of Arguing in the EU', *Journal of Common Market Studies* 44, 2006, 281–304.
9 See par. 3.4 above.
10 Annual Report 2008 on relations between the European Commission and national parliaments, Brussels, 7 July 2009, COM (2009) 343 final, p. 3.
11 Protocol No. 2 TEU/TFEU: Article 4, first sentence, and Article 7 (3), fourth sentence and sub-paragraphs a and b.

12 Article 2 Protocol No. 1 and Article 4 Protocol No. 2 TEU/TFEU.
13 Article 4 Protocol No. 1 and Article 6 Protocol No. 2 TEU/TFEU.
14 Article 7 (1) Protocol No. 2 TEU/TFEU.
15 Article 7 (2) and (3) Protocol No. 2 TEU/TFEU.
16 G.J. Veerman, *Over wetgeving: principes, paradoxen en praktische beschouwingen*, The Hague: Sdu, 2007, p. 75.
17 COM (2008) 428. The Commission is uploading incoming letters and its own replies to national parliaments at ec.europa.eu/dgs/secretariat_general/relations/relations_other/npo/index_en.htm.
18 See Chapter 4 above.
19 This the Councils of State indicate themselves in their presentations; see, for the Netherlands, www.raadvanstate.nl/adviezen.
20 www.conseil-etat.public.lu/fr/attributions/index.html.
21 www.raadvst-consetat.be/?page=proc_consult_page4andlang=en.
22 COM (2007) 650.
23 COM (2008) 414.
24 COM (2008) 426.
25 COM (2009) 554.
26 See K. Auel, 'Democratic Accountability and National Parliaments: Redefining the Impact of Parliamentary Scrutiny in EU Affairs', *European Law Journal* 13, 2007, 487–504.
27 See the Joint Statement of the 6th meeting of the Association of European Senates, Warsaw, 25 May 2004, available at www.senateurope.org.
28 See for a comparative overview: S. Patterson and A. Mughan, eds, *Senates: Bicameralism in the Contemporary World*, Columbus: Ohio State University Press, 1999.
29 COSAC, 'Report on the Results of the Subsidiarity Check on the Proposal for a Council Directive on Implementing the Principle of Equal Treatment between Persons Irrespective of Religion or Belief, Disability, Age or Sexual Orientation', November 2008, p. 12.
30 See Chapter 4 above.
31 See Chapter 5 above.
32 Reports on the COSAC subsidiarity checks are available at www.cosac.eu/en/info/earlywarning.
33 The possibility of such a turn of events had in fact already been anticipated even at a time when COSAC envisaged making collective subsidiarity checks a regular feature of its work, see M. Knudsen and Y. Carl, 'COSAC – Its Role to Date and its Potential in the Future', in G. Barrett, ed., *National Parliaments and the European Union: The Constitutional Challenge for the Oireachtas and Other Member State Legislatures*, Dublin: Clarus, 2008.
34 T. Raunio, *Destined for Irrelevance? Subsidiarity Control by National Parliaments*, Real Instituto Elcano Working Paper WP 36/2010.
35 J. Peters, 'The Role of National Parliaments, Checks and Balances between EU and the Member States', in L. Verhey, Ph. Kiiver and S. Loeffen, eds, *Political Accountability and European Integration*, Groningen: Europa Law Publishing, 2009, p. 42.

7 National parliaments in the constitutional reality of the early warning system

1 Discussion on 3 December 2010 in The Hague.
2 See par. 3.8 above.
3 Annual Report 2008 on relations between the European Commission and national parliaments, Brussels, 7 July 2009, COM (2009) 343 final, p. 5.
4 Discussion on 3 December 2010 in The Hague.

5 T. Raunio, *Destined for Irrelevance? Subsidiarity Control by National Parliaments*, Real Instituto Elcano Working Paper WP 36/2010.

6 B. Crum and E. Fossum, 'The Multilevel Parliamentary Field: A Framework for Theorizing Representative Democracy in the EU', *European Political Science Review* 1, 2009, 249–71; B. Wessels, 'Roles and Orientations of Members of Parliament in the EU Context: Congruence or Difference? Europeanisation or Not?' in K. Auel and A. Benz, eds, *The Europeanisation of Parliamentary Democracy*, London: Routledge, 2006.

7 Chr. Neuhold, *Late wake-up call or early warning? Parliamentary participation and cooperation in light of the Lisbon Treaty*, UACES Conference paper, January 2011, available at www.uaces.org/pdf/papers/1102/Neuhold.pdf.

8 See Chapter 4 above.

9 D. Kornobis-Romanowska, 'Poland', in G. C. Rodriguez Iglesias and L. Ortiz Blanco, eds, *The Role of National Parliaments in the European Union – Proceedings of the XXIV FIDE Congress, Madrid 2010, Vol. 1*, Madrid: Servicio de publicaciones de la Facultad de Derecho Universidad Complutense, 2010, p. 375.

10 G. Gramaxo Roseira, 'Portugal', ibid., p. 394. See also par. 3.4 above.

11 R. Laffranque and O. Aarma, 'Estonia', ibid., p. 198.

12 Duff MEP quoted by P. Hardy, 'United Kingdom', ibid., p. 546.

13 P. Helander, 'Finland', ibid., p. 211.

14 J. Suchman, 'Czech Republic', ibid., p. 161.

15 I. Cooper, 'The Watchdogs of Subsidiarity: National Parliaments and the Logic of Arguing in the EU', *Journal of Common Market Studies* 44, 2006, 281–304.

16 *Bovenop Europa, Evaluatie van de versterkte EU-ondersteuning van de Tweede Kamer 2007-2011*, The Hague: Tweede Kamer, 2011.

17 Ibid., p. 7.

18 See Chapter 6 above.

19 G. Barrett, 'Introduction', in G. Barrett, ed., *National Parliaments and the European Union*, Dublin: Clarus, 2008, p. xli.

20 See Chapter 4 above.

21 http://www.europolitics.info/rail-transport-european-parliament-buries-proposal-on-quality-of-rail-freight-artr173371-20.html.

22 E-mail correspondence between 13 and 19 May 2011.

23 G. Majone, 'Europe's "Democratic Deficit": The Question of Standards', *European Law Journal* 4, 1998, 5–28.

24 See Chapter 5 above.

25 M. Bovens, 'Analysing and Assessing Accountability: A Conceptual Framework', *European Law Journal* 13, 2007, 447–68.

26 J. Weiler, *The Constitution of Europe: 'Do the New Clothes Have an Emperor?' and Other Essays on European Integration*, Cambridge: Cambridge University Press, 1999.

27 See Chapter 6 above.

28 Weiler, op. cit., p. 352.

29 Chr. Harrington and U. Turem, 'Accounting for Accountability in Neoliberal Regulatory Regimes', in M. Dowdle, ed., *Public Accountability: Designs, Dilemmas and Experiences*, Cambridge: Cambridge University Press, 2006.

30 D. Stasavage, 'Does Transparency make a Difference?', in Chr. Hood and D. Heald, eds, *Transparency: The Key to Better Governance?*, Oxford: Oxford University Press, 2006.

31 Chr. Timmermans, 'Subsidiarity and Transparency', *Fordham International Law Journal* 22, 1998–1999, S106–27.

32 Article 16 (4) TEU.

33 Articles 48, 82 and 83 TFEU.

34 See Chapter 4 above.

Bibliography

Agné, H., 'Irretrievable Powers and Democratic Accountability', in S. Gustavsson, Chr. Karlsson and Th. Persson, eds, *The Illusion of Accountability in the European Union*, London: Routledge, 2009.

Alberti, E., 'Political Accountability in Spain', in L. Verhey, H. Broeksteeg and I. Van den Driessche, eds, *Political Accountability in Europe: Which Way Forward? A Traditional Concept of Parliamentary Democracy in an EU Context*, Groningen: Europa Law Publishing, 2008.

Albi, A. and Ziller, J., eds, *The European Constitution and National Constitutions: Ratification and Beyond*, The Hague: Kluwer Law International, 2007.

Amtenbrink, F., 'On the Legitimacy and Democratic Accountability of the European Central Bank', in A. Arnull and D. Wincott, eds, *Accountability and Legitimacy in the European Union*, Oxford: Oxford University Press, 2002.

Angelides, N., 'Cyprus', in G. C. Rodriguez Iglesias and L. Ortiz Blanco, eds, *The Role of National Parliaments in the European Union – Proceedings of the XXIV FIDE Congress, Madrid 2010, Vol. 1*, Madrid: Servicio de publicaciones de la Facultad de Derecho Universidad Complutense, 2010.

Arnull, A. and Wincott, D., eds, *Accountability and Legitimacy in the European Union*, Oxford: Oxford University Press, 2002.

Auel, K., 'Democratic Accountability and National Parliaments: Redefining the Impact of Parliamentary Scrutiny in EU Affairs', *European Law Journal* 13, 2007, 487–504.

Bankowski, Z. and Scott, A., eds, *The European Union and its Order*, Oxford: Blackwell, 2000.

Barents, R., *The Autonomy of Community Law*, The Hague: Kluwer Law International, 2004.

Barrett, G., ed., *National Parliaments and the European Union: The Constitutional Challenge for the Oireachtas and Other Member State Legislatures*, Dublin: Clarus, 2008.

Behn, R., *Rethinking Democratic Accountability*, Washington, DC: Brookings Institution Press, 2001.

Bengtson, Chr., 'Interparliamentary Cooperation Within Europe', in J. O'Brennan and T. Raunio, eds, *National Parliaments within the Enlarged European Union: From 'Victims' of Integration to Competitive Actors?*, London: Routledge, 2007.

Benz, A., Harlow, C. and Papadopoulos, Y., 'Introduction', *European Law Journal* 13, 2007, 441–6.

Bergman, T., 'National Parliaments and EU Affairs Committees: notes on empirical variation and competing explanations', *Journal of European Public Policy* 4, 1997, 373–87.

Besselink, L., 'National Parliaments in the EU's Composite Constitution: A Plea for a Shift in Paradigm', in Ph. Kiiver, ed., *National and Regional Parliaments in the European Constitutional Order*, Groningen: Europa Law Publishing, 2006.

Besselink, L., 'The Netherlands', in G. C. Rodriguez Iglesias and L. Ortiz Blanco, eds, *The Role of National Parliaments in the European Union – Proceedings of the XXIV FIDE Congress, Madrid 2010, Vol. 1*, Madrid: Servicio de publicaciones de la Facultad de Derecho Universidad Complutense, 2010.

Birkinshaw, P. and Varney, M., eds, *The European Union Legal Order after Lisbon*, Alphen: Kluwer Law International, 2010.

Bovens, M., 'Analysing and Assessing Accountability: A Conceptual Framework', *European Law Journal* 13, 2007, 447–68.

Bovens, M., Curtin, D. and 't Hart, P., eds, *The Real world of EU Accountability: What Deficit?* Oxford: Oxford University Press, 2010.

Burgess, M., 'Federalism', in A. Wiener and Th. Diez, eds, *European Integration Theory*, 2nd edn., Oxford: Oxford University Press, 2009.

Calliess, Chr., *Subsidiaritäts- und Solidaritätsprinzip in der Europäischen Union*, 2nd edn., Baden-Baden: Nomos, 1999.

Carl, Y., 'Luxembourg', in G. C. Rodriguez Iglesias and L. Ortiz Blanco, eds, *The Role of National Parliaments in the European Union – Proceedings of the XXIV FIDE Congress, Madrid 2010, Vol. 1*, Madrid: Servicio de publicaciones de la Facultad de Derecho Universidad Complutense, 2010.

Cerar, M., 'Slovenia', in G. C. Rodriguez Iglesias and L. Ortiz Blanco, eds, *The Role of National Parliaments in the European Union – Proceedings of the XXIV FIDE Congress, Madrid 2010, Vol. 1*, Madrid: Servicio de publicaciones de la Facultad de Derecho Universidad Complutense, 2010.

Claes, M., *The National Courts' Mandate in the European Constitution*, Oxford: Hart, 2005.

Conlan, P., Fahey, E., Donnelly, C. and Biggins, J., 'Ireland', in G. C. Rodriguez Iglesias and L. Ortiz Blanco, eds, *The Role of National Parliaments in the European Union – Proceedings of the XXIV FIDE Congress, Madrid 2010, Vol. 1*, Madrid: Servicio de publicaciones de la Facultad de Derecho Universidad Complutense, 2010.

Cooper, I., 'The Watchdogs of Subsidiarity: National Parliaments and the Logic of Arguing in the EU', *Journal of Common Market Studies* 44, 2006, 281–304.

Craig, P., 'The Nature of the Community: Integration, Democracy, and Legitimacy', in P. Craig and G. de Búrca, eds, *The Evolution of EU Law*, Oxford: Oxford University Press, 1999.

Craig, P., 'The Locus and Accountability of the Executive in the European Union', in P. Craig and A. Tomkins, eds, *The Executive and Public Law: Power and Accountability in Comparative Perspective*, Oxford: Oxford University Press, 2006.

Craig, P., 'Legal Control of Regulatory Bodies: Principle, Policy, and Teleology', in P. Birkinshaw and M. Varney, eds, *The European Union Legal Order after Lisbon*, Alphen: Kluwer Law International, 2010.

Craig, P. and De Búrca, G., eds, *The Evolution of EU Law*, Oxford: Oxford University Press, 1999.

Craig, P. and Harlow, C., eds, *Lawmaking in the European Union*, London: Kluwer Law International, 1998.

Craig, P. and Tomkins, A., eds, *The Executive and Public Law: Power and Accountability in Comparative Perspective*, Oxford: Oxford University Press, 2006.

Crum, B. and Fossum, E., 'The Multilevel Parliamentary Field: A Framework for Theorizing Representative Democracy in the EU', *European Political Science Review* 1, 2009, 249–71.

Curtin, D., *Executive Power of the European Union: Law, Practices, and the Living Constitution*, Oxford: Oxford University Press, 2009.

Dann, Ph., *Parlamente im Exekutivföderalismus*, Berlin: Springer, 2004.

Dashwood, A., 'The Relationship between the Member States and the European Union/European Community', *Common Market Law Review* 41, 2004, 355–81.

De Búrca, G., 'The Principle of Subsidiarity and the Court of Justice as an Institutional Actor', *Journal of Common Market Studies* 36, 1998, 217–35.

De Witte, B., 'Executive Accountability under the European Constitution and the Lisbon Treaty; Nihil Novi sub Sole?', in L. Verhey, Ph. Kiiver and S. Loeffen, eds, *Political Accountability and European Integration*, Groningen: Europa Law Publishing, 2009.

Dimitrakopoulos, D. G., 'Incrementalism and Path Dependence: European Integration and Institutional Change in National Parliaments', *Journal of Common Market Studies* 39, 2001, 405–22.

Dobner, P. and Loughlin, M., eds, *The Twilight of Constitutionalism?*, Oxford: Oxford University Press, 2010.

Doukas, D., 'The Verdict of the German Federal Constitutional Court on the Lisbon Treaty: Not guilty, but don't do it again!', *European Law Review* 34, 2009, 866–88.

Dowdle, M., ed., *Public Accountability: Designs, Dilemmas and Experiences*, Cambridge: Cambridge University Press, 2006.

Emiliou, N., *The Principle of Proportionality in European law: A Comparative Study*, The Hague: Kluwer Law International, 1996.

Estella, A., *The EU Principle of Subsidiarity and its Critique*, Oxford: Oxford University Press, 2002.

Fish, S. and Kroenig, M., *The Handbook of National Legislatures: A Global Survey*, Cambridge: Cambridge University Press, 2009.

Flinders, M., *The Politics of Accountability in the Modern State*, Aldershot: Ashgate, 2001.

Føllesdal, A., 'Survey Article: Subsidiarity', *Journal of Political Philosophy* 6, 1998, 190–218.

Fraga, A., 'The Parliament of Portugal: Loyal Scrutiny and Informal Influence', in A. Maurer and W. Wessels, eds, *National Parliaments on their Ways to Europe: Losers or Latecomers?*, Baden-Baden: Nomos, 2001.

Giegerich, Th., *Europäische Verfassung und deutsche Verfassung im transnationalen Konstitutionalisierungsprozeß*, Berlin: Springer, 2003.

Gramaxo Roseira, G., 'Portugal', in G. C. Rodriguez Iglesias and L. Ortiz Blanco, eds, *The Role of National Parliaments in the European Union – Proceedings of the XXIV FIDE Congress, Madrid 2010, Vol. 1*, Madrid: Servicio de publicaciones de la Facultad de Derecho Universidad Complutense, 2010.

Gustavsson, S., Karlsson, Chr. and Persson, Th., eds, *The Illusion of Accountability in the European Union*, London: Routledge, 2009.

Hailbronner, M., 'Die Justiziabilität des Subsidiaritätsprinzips im Lichte der Subsidiaritätsprotokolle', in I. Pernice, ed., *Der Vertrag von Lissabon: Reform der EU ohne Verfassung?*, Baden-Baden: Nomos, 2008.

Hardy, P., 'United Kingdom', in G. C. Rodriguez Iglesias and L. Ortiz Blanco, eds, *The Role of National Parliaments in the European Union – Proceedings of the XXIV FIDE Congress, Madrid 2010, Vol. 1*, Madrid: Servicio de publicaciones de la Facultad de Derecho Universidad Complutense, 2010.

Harlow, C., *Accountability in the European Union*, Oxford: Oxford University Press, 2002.

Harlow, C. and Rawlings, R., 'Promoting Accountability in Multilevel Governance: A Network Approach', *European Law Journal* 13, 2007, 447–68.

Harrington, Chr. and Turem, U., 'Accounting for Accountability in Neoliberal Regulatory Regimes', in M. Dowdle, ed., *Public Accountability: Designs, Dilemmas and Experiences*, Cambridge: Cambridge University Press, 2006.

Helander, P., 'Finland', in G. C. Rodriguez Iglesias and L. Ortiz Blanco, eds, *The Role of National Parliaments in the European Union – Proceedings of the XXIV FIDE Congress, Madrid 2010, Vol. 1*, Madrid: Servicio de publicaciones de la Facultad de Derecho Universidad Complutense, 2010.

Hirsch Ballin, E. and Senden, L., *Co-actorship in the Development of European Law-Making: The Quality of European Legislation and its Implementation and Application in the National Legal Order*, The Hague: Asser Press, 2005.

Hölscheidt, S., 'Formale Aufwertung – geringe Schubkraft: die Rolle der nationalen Parlamente gemäß dem Lissabonner Vertrag', *integration* 31, 2008, 254–65.

Holzhacker, R., 'National Parliamentary Scrutiny over EU Issues', *European Union Politics* 3, 2002, 459–79.

Hood, Chr. and Heald, D., eds, *Transparency: The Key to Better Governance?*, Oxford: Oxford University Press, 2006.

Janowski, C., *Die nationalen Parlamente und ihre Europa-Gremien: Legitimationsgarant der EU?*, Baden-Baden: Nomos, 2005.

Judge, D., 'The Failure of National Parliaments?', *West European Politics* 18, 1995, 79–100.

Juhász-Tóth, A. and Mohay, A., 'Hungary', in G. C. Rodriguez Iglesias and L. Ortiz Blanco, eds, *The Role of National Parliaments in the European Union – Proceedings of the XXIV FIDE Congress, Madrid 2010, Vol. 1*, Madrid: Servicio de publicaciones de la Facultad de Derecho Universidad Complutense, 2010.

Jyränki, A., ed., *National Constitutions in the Era of Integration*, The Hague: Kluwer Law International, 1999.

Kamann, H.-G., *Die Mitwirkung der Parlamente der Mitgliedstaaten an der europäischen Gesetzgebung*, Frankfurt: Peter Lang, 1997.

Keohane, R., 'Accountability in World Politics', in S. Gustavsson, Chr. Karlsson and Th. Persson, eds, *The Illusion of Accountability in the European Union*, London: Routledge, 2009.

Keyaerts, D., 'Ex ante Evaluation of EU Legislation Intertwined with Judicial Review? Comment on Vodafone Ltd v Secretary of State for Business, Enterprise and Regulatory Reform (C–58/08)', *European Law Review* 35, 2010, 869–84.

Kiiver, Ph., *The National Parliaments in the European Union – A Critical View on EU Constitution-Building*, The Hague: Kluwer Law International, 2006.

Kiiver, Ph., ed., *National and Regional Parliaments in the European Constitutional Order*, Groningen: Europa Law Publishing, 2006.

Kiiver, Ph., 'The Composite Case for National Parliaments in the European Union: Who Profits from Enhanced Involvement?', *European Constitutional Law Review* 2, 2006, 227–52.

Kiiver, Ph., 'The European Constitution and the Role of National Parliaments: Hard Law Language, Soft Content', in A. Albi and J. Ziller, eds, *The European Constitution and National Constitutions: Ratification and Beyond*, The Hague: Kluwer Law International, 2007.

Kiiver, Ph., 'European Scrutiny in National Parliaments: Individual Efforts in the Collective Interest?', in J. O'Brennan and T. Raunio, eds, *National Parliaments within the Enlarged European Union: From 'Victims' of Integration to Competitive Actors?*, London: Routledge, 2007.

Kiiver, Ph., 'The Treaty of Lisbon, the National Parliaments and the Principle of Subsidiarity', *Maastricht Journal of European and Comparative Law* 15, 2008, 77–83.

Kiiver, Ph., 'The Lisbon Judgment of the German Constitutional Court: A Court-Ordered Strengthening of the National Legislature in the European Union', *European Law Journal* 16, 2010, 578–88.

Kiiver, P., 'The Early Warning System for the Principle of Subsidiarity: The National Parliament as a Conseil d'Etat for Europe', *European Law Review* 36, 2011, 98–108.

Knudsen, M. and Carl, Y., 'COSAC – Its Role to Date and its Potential in the Future', in G. Barrett, ed., *National Parliaments and the European Union: The Constitutional Challenge for the Oireachtas and Other Member State Legislatures*, Dublin: Clarus, 2008.

Kokott, J. and Rüth, A., 'The European Convention and its Draft Treaty Establishing a Constitution for Europe: Appropriate Answers to the Laeken Questions?', *Common Market Law Review* 40, 2003, 1315–45.

Koopmans, T., *Courts and Political Institutions: A Comparative View*, Cambridge: Cambridge University Press 2003.

Koopmans, T., 'Subsidiarity, Politics and the Judiciary', *European Constitutional Law Review* 1, 2005, 112–16.

Kornobis-Romanowska, D., 'Poland', in G. C. Rodriguez Iglesias and L. Ortiz Blanco, eds, *The Role of National Parliaments in the European Union – Proceedings of the XXIV FIDE Congress, Madrid 2010, Vol. 1*, Madrid: Servicio de publicaciones de la Facultad de Derecho Universidad Complutense, 2010.

Laffranque, R. and Aarma, O., 'Estonia', in G. C. Rodriguez Iglesias and L. Ortiz Blanco, eds, *The Role of National Parliaments in the European Union – Proceedings of the XXIV FIDE Congress, Madrid 2010, Vol. 1*, Madrid: Servicio de publicaciones de la Facultad de Derecho Universidad Complutense, 2010.

Larue, Th., 'Delegation to the Permanent Representation and Mechanisms of Accountability', in S. Gustavsson, Chr. Karlsson and Th. Persson, eds, *The Illusion of Accountability in the European Union*, London: Routledge, 2009.

Laso Pérez, J., 'Spain', in G. C. Rodriguez Iglesias and L. Ortiz Blanco, eds, *The Role of National Parliaments in the European Union – Proceedings of the XXIV FIDE Congress, Madrid 2010, Vol. 1*, Madrid: Servicio de publicaciones de la Facultad de Derecho Universidad Complutense, 2010.

Laursen, F. and Pappas, S., eds, *The Changing Role of Parliaments in the European Union*, Maastricht: EIPA, 1995.

Lenaerts, K. and Van Nuffel, P., *Constitutional Law of the European Union*, London: Sweet & Maxwell, 2011.

Louis, J.-V., 'National Parliaments and the Principle of Subsidiarity: Legal Options and Practical Limits', *European Constitutional Law Review* 4, 2008, 429–52.

Maccarthaigh, M., 'Accountability Through National Parliaments: Practice and Problems', in J. O'Brennan and T. Raunio, eds, *National Parliaments within the*

Enlarged European Union: From 'Victims' of Integration to Competitive Actors?, London: Routledge, 2007.

Magnette, P., *What is the European Union?*, Basingstoke: Palgrave, 2005.

Majone, G., 'Europe's "Democratic Deficit": The Question of Standards', *European Law Journal* 4, 1998, 5–28.

Majone, G., *Dilemmas of European Integration: The Ambiguities and Pitfalls of Integration by Stealth*, Oxford: Oxford University Press, 2005.

Mancini, G., *Democracy and Constitutionalism in the European Union*, Oxford: Hart, 2000.

Maurer, A. and Wessels, W., eds, *National Parliaments on their Ways to Europe: Losers or Latecomers?*, Baden-Baden: Nomos, 2001.

Mellein, Chr., 'Germany', in G. C. Rodriguez Iglesias and L. Ortiz Blanco, eds, *The Role of National Parliaments in the European Union – Proceedings of the XXIV FIDE Congress, Madrid 2010, Vol. 1*, Madrid: Servicio de publicaciones de la Facultad de Derecho Universidad Complutense, 2010.

Menon, A. and Weatherill, S., 'Legitimacy, Accountability, and Delegation in the European Union', in A. Arnull and D. Wincott, eds, *Accountability and Legitimacy in the European Union*, Oxford: Oxford University Press, 2002.

Meuwese, A., *Impact Assessment in EU Lawmaking*, Leiden: E.M. Meijers Instituut, 2008.

Mulgan, R., 'Accountability: An Ever-Expanding Concept?', *Public Administration* 78, 2000, 555–73.

Mulgan, R., *Holding Power to Account: Accountability in Modern Democracies*, Basingstoke: Palgrave Macmillan, 2003.

Naurin, D., 'The European Central Bank – Independent and Accountable?', in S. Gustavsson, Chr. Karlsson and Th. Persson, eds, *The Illusion of Accountability in the European Union*, London: Routledge, 2009.

Nergelius, J., *The Constitutional Dilemma of the European Union*, Groningen: Europa Law Publishing, 2009.

Neuhold, Chr., *Late wake-up call or early warning? Parliamentary participation and cooperation in light of the Lisbon Treaty*, UACES Conference paper, January 2011, available at www.uaces.org/pdf/papers/1102/Neuhold.pdf.

Niblock, M., *The EEC: National Parliaments in Community Decision-Making*, London: Chatham House, 1971.

Norton, Ph., ed., *National Parliaments and the European Union*, London: Routledge, 1996.

Norton, Ph., ed., *Parliaments and Governments in Western Europe*, London: Frank Cass, 1998.

Norton, Ph., 'National Parliaments and the European Union: Where to from here?', in P. Craig and C. Harlow, eds, *Lawmaking in the European Union*, London: Kluwer Law International, 1998.

Norton, Ph., ed., *Parliaments and Citizens in Western Europe*, London: Frank Cass, 2002.

O'Brennan, J. and Raunio, T., eds, *National Parliaments within the Enlarged European Union: From 'Victims' of Integration to Competitive Actors?*, London: Routledge, 2007.

Oliver, D., *Government in the United Kingdom: the Search for Accountability, Effectiveness and Citizenship*, Milton Keynes: Open University Press, 1991.

Pas, W., 'The Belgian "National Parliament" from the Perspective of the EU Constitutional Treaty', in Ph. Kiiver, ed., *National and Regional Parliaments in the European Constitutional Order*, Groningen: Europa Law Publishing, 2006.

Patterson, S. and Mughan, A., eds, *Senates: Bicameralism in the Contemporary World*, Columbus: Ohio State University Press, 1999.

Pennera, Chr., 'Les parlements nationaux dans le système de l'Union européenne', in G. C. Rodriguez Iglesias and L. Ortiz Blanco, eds, *The Role of National Parliaments in the European Union – Proceedings of the XXIV FIDE Congress, Madrid 2010, Vol. 1*, Madrid: Servicio de publicaciones de la Facultad de Derecho Universidad Complutense, 2010.

Pernice, I., 'Multilevel Constitutionalism and the Treaty of Amsterdam: European Constitution-Making Revisited', *Common Market Law Review* 36, 1999, 703–50.

Pernice, I., ed., *Der Vertrag von Lissabon: Reform der EU ohne Verfassung?*, Baden-Baden: Nomos, 2008.

Peters, J., 'The Role of National Parliaments, Checks and Balances between EU and the Member States', in L. Verhey, Ph. Kiiver and S. Loeffen, eds, *Political Accountability and European Integration*, Groningen: Europa Law Publishing, 2009.

Poiares Maduro, M., 'Contrapunctual Law: Europe's Constitutional Pluralism in Action', in N. Walker, ed., *Sovereignty in Transition*, Oxford: Hart, 2003.

Raunio, T., 'Always One Step Behind? National Legislatures and the European Union', *Government and Opposition* 34, 1999, 180–202.

Raunio, T., 'National Legislatures in the EU Constitutional Treaty', in J. O'Brennan and T. Raunio, eds, *National Parliaments within the Enlarged European Union: From 'Victims' of Integration to Competitive Actors?*, London: Routledge, 2007.

Raunio, T., *Destined for Irrelevance? Subsidiarity Control by National Parliaments*, Real Instituto Elcano Working Paper WP 36/2010.

Raunio, T. and Wiberg, M., 'Does Support Lead to Ignorance? National Parliaments and the Legitimacy of EU Governance', *Acta Politica* 35, 2000, 146–68.

Rivers, J., 'Proportionality and Discretion in International and European Law', in N. Tsagourias, ed., *Transnational Constitutionalism: International and European Perspectives*, Cambridge: Cambridge University Press, 2007.

Rodriguez Iglesias, G. C. and Ortiz Blanco, L., eds, *The Role of National Parliaments in the European Union – Proceedings of the XXIV FIDE Congress, Madrid 2010, Vol. 1*, Madrid: Servicio de publicaciones de la Facultad de Derecho Universidad Complutense, 2010.

Romzek, B. and Dubnick, M., 'Accountability in the Public Sector: Lessons from the Challenger Tragedy', *Public Administration Review* 47, 1987, 227–38.

Saalfeld, Th., 'Deliberate Delegation or Abdication? Government Backbenchers, Ministers and European Union Legislation', *The Journal of Legislative Studies* 11, 2005, 343–71.

Sadurski, W., *Rights Before Courts: A Study of Constitutional Courts in Postcommunist States of Central and Eastern Europe*, Dordrecht: Springer, 2005.

Sasse, Chr., *Regierungen, Parlamente Ministerrat – Entscheidungsprozesse in der Europäischen Gemeinschaft*, Bonn: Europa Union, 1975.

Schütze, R., 'Subsidiarity After Lisbon: Reinforcing the Safeguards of Federalism?', *Cambridge Law Journal* 68, 2009, 525–36.

Scott, C., 'Accountability in the Regulatory State', *Journal of Law and Society* 27, 2000, 38–60.

Smith, E., ed., *National Parliaments as Cornerstones of European Integration*, London: Kluwer Law International, 1996.

Spence, D., 'The President, the College and the Cabinets', in D. Spence, ed., *The European Commission*, London: John Harper, 2006, pp. 42–6.

Stasavage, D., 'Does Transparency make a Difference?', in Chr. Hood and D. Heald, eds, *Transparency: The Key to Better Governance?*, Oxford: Oxford University Press, 2006.

Stone Sweet, A., *Governing with Judges: Constitutional Politics in Europe*, Oxford: Oxford University Press, 2000.

Suchman, J., 'Czech Republic', in G. C. Rodriguez Iglesias and L. Ortiz Blanco, eds, *The Role of National Parliaments in the European Union – Proceedings of the XXIV FIDE Congress, Madrid 2010, Vol. 1*, Madrid: Servicio de publicaciones de la Facultad de Derecho Universidad Complutense, 2010.

Tans, O., Zoethout, C. and Peters, J., eds, *National Parliaments and European Democracy; A Bottom-up Approach to European Constitutionalism*, Groningen: Europa Law Publishing, 2007.

Thym, D., 'In the Name of Sovereign Statehood: A Critical Introduction to the Lisbon Judgment of the German Constitutional Court', *Common Market Law Review* 46, 2009, 1795–822.

Timmermans, Chr., 'Subsidiarity and Transparency', *Fordham International Law Journal* 22, 1998–1999, S106–27.

Tsagourias, N., ed., *Transnational Constitutionalism: International and European Perspectives*, Cambridge: Cambridge University Press, 2007.

Tsakatika, M., *Political Responsibility and the European Union*, Manchester: Manchester University Press, 2008.

Van Gerven, M., *The European Union: A Polity of States and Peoples*, Oxford: Hart, 2005.

Van Kersbergen, K. and Verbeek, B., 'The Politics of Subsidiarity in the European Union', *Journal of Common Market Studies* 32, 1994, 215–36.

Vara Arribas, G. and Bourdin, D., *The Role of Regional Parliaments in the Process of Subsidiarity Analysis within the Early Warning System of the Lisbon Treaty*, Brussels: Committee of the Regions, 2011.

Veerman, G. J., *Over wetgeving: principes, paradoxen en praktische beschouwingen*, The Hague: Sdu, 2007.

Verhey, L., Broeksteeg, H. and Van den Driessche, I., eds, *Political Accountability in Europe: Which Way Forward? A Traditional Concept of Parliamentary Democracy in an EU Context*, Groningen: Europa Law Publishing, 2008.

Verhey, L., Kiiver, Ph. and Loeffen, S., eds, *Political Accountability and European Integration*, Groningen: Europa Law Publishing, 2009.

Verhoeven, A., *The European Union in Search of a Democratic and Constitutional Theory*, The Hague: Kluwer Law International, 2002.

von Bogdandy, A. and Bast, J., eds, *Principles of European Constitutional Law*, Oxford: Hart, 2005.

von Borries, R. and Hauschild, M., 'Implementing the Subsidiarity Principle', *Columbia Journal of European Law* 5, 1999, 369–88, p. 375.

Walker, N., ed., *Sovereignty in Transition*, Oxford: Hart, 2003.

Weatherill, S., 'Using National Parliaments to Improve Scrutiny of the Limits of EU Action', *European Law Review* 28, 2003, 909–12.

Weatherill, S., 'Better Competence Monitoring', *European Law Review* 30, 2005, 23–41.

Weber-Panariello, Ph., *Nationale Parlamente in der Europäischen Union*, Baden-Baden: Nomos, 1995.

Weiler, J., *The Constitution of Europe: 'Do the New Clothes Have an Emperor?' and Other Essays on European Integration*, Cambridge: Cambridge University Press, 1999.

Weiler, J., 'In Defence of the Status Quo: Europe's Constitutional *Sonderweg*', in J. Weiler and M. Wind, eds, *European Constitutionalism Beyond the State*, Cambridge: Cambridge University Press, 2003.

Weiler, J. and Wind, M., eds, *European Constitutionalism Beyond the State*, Cambridge: Cambridge University Press, 2003.

Wessels, B., 'Roles and Orientations of Members of Parliament in the EU Context: Congruence or Difference? Europeanisation or Not?' in K. Auel and A. Benz, eds, *The Europeanisation of Parliamentary Democracy*, London: Routledge, 2006.

Wiener, A. and Diez, Th., eds, *European Integration Theory*, 2nd edn., Oxford: Oxford University Press, 2009.

Wyrzykowski, M., Puchta, R. and Ziolkowski, M., 'The Role of National Parliaments in the European Union (General Report)', in G. C. Rodriguez Iglesias and L. Ortiz Blanco, eds, *The Role of National Parliaments in the European Union – Proceedings of the XXIV FIDE Congress, Madrid 2010, Vol. 1*, Madrid: Servicio de publicaciones de la Facultad de Derecho Universidad Complutense, 2010.

Index

Numbers in bold represent where a term is discussed in greater depth.

accountability 3–4, 9, 11, 14, 15, 17, 24, 56–57, 75, **103–25**, 145–6
amended draft legislative act 7, **22**, 67, 124
Amsterdam, Treaty of – 1, 6, 9, 34, 40, 71
annulment procedure 8, 11, 25, 39, 41, 42, **43–8**, 52
Austria 56, 64, 66, 83, 85, 88, 90, 123, 130, 131, 137
autonomous concept of Union law **48–62**, 135

Belgium 41, 46, **50–62**, 64, 74, 78, 79, 80, 81, 82, 83, 89, 90, 123, 127, 129
bicameralism 1, 20, 33, 50, 53, 57, 60, 62, **63–6**, 68, 115, 136, 144, 146
Bulgaria 35, 64, 86, 87, 88, 89, 123

common constitutional traditions 49, **58–62**, 135
constitutional identity 51, 53, 62
Convention, European – 2, 5, 8, 10, **19–20**, 26, 27, 34, 46–7, 55, 62, 64–5, 72, 106, 122, 127, 136
COSAC 3, 9, 19, 24, 34, 36, 40, **55–6**, 62, 72, 74, **77–96**, **114–16**, 123–5, 129–30, **132–5**, 137, 138, 139–40, 142–3
Council of Europe 83
Council of Ministers 2, 5, 6, 7, 8, 9, 11, 12, 14, 15–16, 18, 21, 22, 26, 27, **28–33**, 35, 37, 38, 40, 41, 47, 49, 56, 57, 63, 65, 90, 99, **104**, 108, 109, 111, 124, 127, 128, 138, 141, 142, 143, 144, 145, 146, 147

Court of Justice of the EU 7, 8, 11, 21, 25, 27, 31, 34, 36, 39, 40, 41, 42, **43–8**, 49, 50, 52, 58–9, 61–2, 71, 74–6, 101, 107, 113, 115, 121
Cyprus 11, 32, 36, 56, 64, 80, 89, 90
Czech Republic 32, 35, 36, 64, 66, 77, 78, 79, 80, 82, 84, 88, 123, 124, 130, 131, 138, 139

democracy 4, 9, **13–17**, 56, 57, 104, 105, 106, 117, 121, 125, 126, 127, 131–2, 134, 145–6
Denmark 5, 11, 26, 64, 89, 138

emergency brake procedure 147
Estonia 64, 79, 87, 89
European Convention on Human Rights 49, **58–61**, 88, 135
European Council 9, 10, 11, 14, 19, 49, 52, 56, 59, 111, 147
European Parliament 1, 2, 3, 6, 7, 9, 13, 14, 16, 18, 19, 21, 22, 27, **28–33**, 34, 36, 37, 38, 40, 41, 47, 49, 59, 62, 63, 104, 107, 109, 111, 113, 115, 116, 118, 127–8, 137, 141, 142–3, 147

Finland 2, 64, 78–9, 80, 87, 89, 138
flexibility clause 7, 11, 49, 99
France 4, 22, 35, 39, 44, 45, 52, 56, 57, 64, 65, 66, 77, 80, 82, 84, 86, 89, 90, 106, 123, 126, 127, 130, 131, 137

Germany 11, 14, 16, 25, 26, 32, 35, 44–7, 51, 52, 57, 60, 64, 66, 77, 80, 82, 83, 85, 88, 89, 90, 91, 98, 123, 130, 131, 138

Greece 64, 83, 87, 90, 123, 130, 137

Hungary 31, 33, 64, 74, 75, 77, 80, 83, 86, 89, 90, 100, 123

impact assessments 39, 47–8, 79, 83, 86, 89, 90, 95–6, 101
Ireland 5, 31, 64, 72, 74, 77, 78, 80, 83, 84, 86, 88, 90, 95, 123
Italy 24, 35, 57, 59, 64, 65, 77, 85, 89, 90, 123, 127, 129, 130, 137

Laeken Declaration 19, 20
Latvia 64, 82, 89, 123
Lisbon judgment 14, 16
Lithuania 39, 42, 64, 80, 82, 89, 96, 124
Luxembourg 32, 53, 57, 64, 77, 78–9, 82, 87, 89, 124, 127, 129, 138

Maastricht judgment 14
Maastricht, Treaty of – 1, 5, 71
Malta 64, 88, 123

Netherlands, The – 11, 24, 35, 44, 56, 64, 65, 78, 79, 80, 81, 83, 84, 85, 89, 117, 123, 127, 128, 129, 130, 131, 135, 137, 140

passerelle 7, 9, 10, 11, 49–50, 51, 52, 53, 54, 56, 58, 60, 61, 135–6

Poland 64, 79, 89
political dialogue (Barroso initiative) 18, 22, 23, 39, 96–7, 98, 100, 122, 123, 138
Portugal 32, 35, 64, 82, 89, 90, 123, 130, 137
preliminary reference procedure 42–3, 47, 55

qualified majority voting 10, 30, 31, 49, 94

regional parliaments 10, 18, 40–1, 50, 48–62
Romania 35, 64, 89, 90

Slovakia 64, 89
Slovenia 32, 64, 65, 83, 88, 89, 123
Spain 35, 41, 57, 64, 89, 127
Sweden 35, 64, 77, 78, 83, 89, 138

transparency 5, 17, 103, 135, 145–6
tricameralism 64–5

United Kingdom 5, 10, 11, 33, 56, 57, 66, 72, 73, 79, 80, 81, 83, 84, 85, 86, 89, 90, 95, 116, 123, 130, 131, 138, 139

Index of Treaty Provisions

Treaty on European Union (TEU)
Art. 4: 53–4, 62
Art. 5: 7, 8, 33, 41, 69, 71, 73, 76, 86,
  93, 94, 95, 97, 98, 100, 101, 112,
  127, 147
Art. 10: 9, 14, 56, 59
Art. 12: 6, 7–9, 10, 48, 61, 127, 132,
  137, 145
Art. 16: 31
Art. 48: 7, 8, 9, 10, 49, 53, 54, 60
Art. 49: 7

**Treaty on the Functioning of the
  European Union (TFEU)**
Art. 69: 8
Art. 70: 8
Art. 71: 8
Art. 76: 27
Art. 81: 7, 9, 10, 49
Art. 85: 8
Art. 88: 8
Art. 168: 130
Art. 263: 43, 46
Art. 267: 55
Art. 288: 10
Art. 289: 21
Art. 293: 22, 38
Art. 294: 127
Art. 296: 71
Art. 352: 7, 99

Protocol No. 1 TEU/TFEU
Preamble 8, 9, 59
Art. 1: 9, 21
Art. 2: 7
Art. 3: 8
Art. 4: 8, 21, 35, 38, 39, 40, 48
Art. 5: 7
Art. 6: 7
Art. 7: 7
Art. 9: 59
Art. 10: 9

Protocol No. 2 TEU/TFEU
Art. 1: 30
Art. 3: 20
Art. 4: 7, 21
Art. 5: 32, 70, 76, 93, 148
Art. 6: 8, 21, 34–5, 36, 38, 40, 58, 60,
  65, 67, 128
Art. 7: 8, 27, 28, 29, 31, 60, 64, 128
Art. 8: 8, 39, 41, 43–7, 60
Art. 9: 7

Protocol No. 3 TEU/TFEU
Art. 19: 46

**European Convention on Human
  Rights**
Protocol No. 1, Art. 3: 58, 62

Printed in Great Britain
by Amazon